HR for Small Business

An Essential Guide for Managers, Human Resources Professionals, and Small Business Owners

2nd Edition

CHARLES H. FLEISCHER, ATTORNEY AT LAW

SPHINX® PUBLISHING
AN IMPRINT OF SOURCEBOOKS, INC.®
NAPERVILLE, ILLINOIS
www.SphinxLegal.com

Published by Sphinx Publishing, an imprint of Sourcebooks, Inc.
P.O. Box 4410, Naperville, Illinois 60567-4410
(630) 961-3900
Fax: (630) 961-2168
www.sourcebooks.com

Library of Congress Cataloging-in-Publication Data

Fleischer, Charles H.
  HR for small business : an essential guide for managers, human resources professionals, and small business owners / by Charles H. Fleischer. — 2nd ed.
       p. cm.
  Includes index.
(pbk. : alk. paper) 1. Personnel management. 2. Small business—Personnel management. 3. Labor laws and legislation—United States. I. Title.
  HF5549.17.F584 2008
  658.3—dc22
                              2008040037

Printed and bound in the United States of America.
VP 10 9 8 7 6 5 4 3 2 1

Contents

Introduction

Small business owners—BEWARE! Not too many years ago, managing employer-employee relations was relatively simple. Little more was required than meeting payroll and remembering to deposit withholding taxes on time. Since then, life has gotten infinitely more complicated and uncertain. Employment practices that easily passed muster yesterday now expose employers to substantial risk and expense. At the same time, employees have become more knowledgeable about their rights and much less bashful about exercising them.

It is easy to cite examples of practices that may once have been common, but now, depending on the circumstances, could give rise to civil lawsuits and even criminal prosecutions. Do any of these things sound like good ideas?

- *I'll just call my staff independent contractors and avoid the hassles that come with having employees.*
- *Bob worked overtime all day Saturday copying and stapling the proposal, so I'll give him a day off next week.*
- *Nancy quit on me in the middle of her project. There's no way I'm going to pay her for the two weeks' vacation she had coming.*
- *If I hire through a temp agency, I can tell them to send me men for the sales positions and women for the secretaries without having to worry about sexual discrimination.*
- *Becky in Accounting has been dating her assistant. I hear they're having problems, but they're just going to have to work things out.*
- *The next person who gets his salary garnished is out of here!*

If any of these statements strikes a familiar chord, then this book is for you!

Employment is, fundamentally, an economic relationship. The employer seeks an employee who will work competently and dependably in furtherance of the employer's business. The employee seeks regular work at reasonable compensation.

At the same time, the employment relationship is awash in powerful, psychodynamic currents. Employers, having risked their personal capital to keep their businesses afloat, may have unreasonable expectations of loyalty and devotion from their work force. Employees, on the other hand, may feel at sea when subjected to seemingly arbitrary and unexplained decisions by their bosses. Both sides often define themselves and derive their sense of self-worth from the employment relationship—so stormy encounters can be devastating.

Employment is also a highly regulated relationship. Since employers have historically held far greater economic power than individual employees, federal and state governments have felt it necessary to intervene. As a result, employers do not have the freedom to dictate—or even negotiate—many terms and conditions of employment. They must pay minimum wage and time-and-a-half for overtime. They must comply with detailed workplace safety standards. They must conform their employee benefit plans to complicated legal requirements. And they are forbidden from making employment decisions based on a whole host of prohibited criteria.

Employers are also easy targets for the imposition of requirements that otherwise have little to do with the employment relationship. In the income tax area, for example, employers enforce their employees' obligations to the IRS and state taxing authorities by withholding an array of items from employee paychecks. Employers also finance government social policy embodied in workers' compensation and unemployment compensation laws. They must even assist the government in tracking down welfare cheaters and parents who ignore their child support obligations.

This book is aimed at employers who are proving themselves successful at what they do, but who find themselves a bit bewildered by the employment problems that seem to arise with increasing frequency. The first few chapters explore the employment relationship primarily as it is affected by the *common law*—the law we inherited from England and subsequent judicial decisions in this country. Most of the other chapters deal with federal and state statutes that bear directly on the employment relationship or that impose obligations on employers. The goal in each case is to present general principles, highlight the hot issues, and offer specific examples and suggestions to make the employer-employee relationship run more smoothly.

For readability, statutory and case citations have been omitted, no footnotes have been used, and wherever possible, technical legal terms have been avoided. Employment issues are often technical, however, so an extensive glossary has been included at the end of the book.

The employment relationship involves a wide range of complex issues and is also subject to frequent change. Congress, state legislatures, federal and state regulatory agencies, and courts at all levels have a say in the relationship. Any one of these bodies can make illegal tomorrow what was thought to be perfectly legal today. It would be impossible, therefore, to write a fully comprehensive, this-is-all-you-need-to-know treatise.

Reading this book will not make you an employment lawyer or a tax expert. You will not be competent to respond to an Equal Employment Opportunity Commission charge, to set up a pension plan, or to deal with a union-organizing campaign. But you will gain a broad understanding of employer-employee relations, know where most of the dangers lurk, and be alert to situations where professional advice is needed.

While there is no substitute for familiarity with the intricacies of the employment relationship, we dare to offer, at the outset, three rules of conduct for employers. Adopt them now, follow them faithfully, and you will avoid many of the pitfalls discussed here.

1. *Treat your employees reasonably.* They are not indentured servants, nor are they part of your extended family. They usually respond best when treated like reasonable adults, and they may quit—or worse, sue—if they feel unfairly treated.

2. *Focus your personnel policies and decisions directly on accomplishing your business mission.* Leave your biases, prejudices, and social agendas at home.

3. *Keep detailed, current, written records of all personnel actions.* If it is not in writing, it didn't happen.

Chapter

The Employment Relationship

The employment relationship is a mutual, voluntary arrangement between two parties. The employer—which may be a corporation, some other form of entity, or an individual—voluntarily agrees to pay the employee in exchange for the employee's work. The employee—who is always an individual—voluntarily agrees to work for the employer in exchange for pay. The relationship is *voluntary* in the sense that the law will not force anyone to work for a particular employer.

Since the implementation of the Thirteenth Amendment, forced labor through use of physical restraints, threats of physical harm, or threats of legal action is a federal crime. The prohibitions against forced labor also protect persons from compulsory work to pay off a debt—sometimes called *peonage* or *indentured servitude*.

The United Nations International Labour Organization (ILO) has adopted a *Declaration on Fundamental Principles and Rights at Work*, to which the United States subscribes. The Declaration states that all member nations have an obligation to respect four fundamental rights:

1. Freedom of association and the effective recognition of the right to collective bargaining;
2. The elimination of all forms of forced or compulsory labor;
3. The effective abolition of child labor; and,
4. Elimination of discrimination in respect of employment and occupation.

In general, the employment relationship is voluntary from the employer's viewpoint, in that the employer usually has no obligation to employ anyone in particular. In limited circumstances, however, an employer can be forced to hire a particular individual where, for example, the employer rejected the individual's employment application for *discriminatory* or *antiunion reasons*. Additionally, once an employment relationship is established, an employer can be forced to retain or rehire a particular individual as a remedy for violating antidiscrimination or labor laws or if the employee has been in a *protected leave status*, such as military leave or leave under the *Family and Medical Leave Act*.

The employment relationship is often thought of as a *contract* between employer and employee. However, it usually does not take the form of a typical *mutual contract*, where each party makes a promise to the other, such as, "I promise to deliver goods to you next week if you promise to pay me $1,000 in 30 days." Instead, the employment relationship is sometimes described as a *unilateral contract*, where only one party (the employer) makes a promise. "If you come work for me, I will pay you $10 per hour." The employee usually does not promise to work. He or she just shows up, works, and becomes entitled to the promised pay. Circumstances where employer and employee enter into a mutual employment contract are discussed in more detail on the following pages.

Employees, Independent Contractors, and Agents

An employer's work force can be classified as employees, independent contractors, or agents.

Employees

An *employee* is someone whose manner of work the employer has a *right to control*, even if the employer does not actually exercise that control. An entry-level file clerk will likely be subject to close, daily, or even hour-by-hour supervision and is therefore an employee. So, too, is the president of a large corporation, not because he or she is closely supervised, but because the corporation's board of directors has the right to control his or her work. This right to control is illustrated by the legal terms *master* and *servant* traditionally used to describe the employment relationship.

True employees—as distinguished from independent contractors—are sometimes known as *W-2 employees*, referring to the W-2 form issued to them for federal income tax purposes.

Other types of work relationships include *independent contractor* and *agent*. These relationships can overlap somewhat. Although the distinctions may seem technical, they are important because employers have obligations to their employees that they do not have for independent contractors. In addition, employees and agents can impose *legal liabilities* on the employer that independent contractors generally cannot.

Independent Contractors

An *independent contractor*, in contrast to an employee, is someone you engage to perform a certain task, but whose manner of work you do not have a right to control. Good examples are professionals such as doctors, lawyers, or financial consultants, and trade persons such as electricians and plumbers. In each of these examples, the independent contractor's work is governed by professional standards, state and county codes, and the like, with which you are probably not familiar. Your lack of familiarity is precisely why you engage an independent contractor instead of doing the work yourself or having one of your employees do it.

Alert!

Whenever a worker's status as an independent contractor could reasonably be questioned, the safest course is to treat that worker as an employee.

Certainly you can tell your independent contractor what it is you want done, and you remain free to dismiss him or her if you do not like the work. But it is the result you are interested in. The actual manner in which that result is accomplished is up to the independent contractor and is not subject to your control.

Independent contractors are issued *1099 forms* to report income for federal tax purposes, as opposed to *W-2 forms* issued to employees. Unlike employees, independent contractors are not subject to income and payroll tax withholding.

Employers sometimes try to classify their work force as independent contractors, rather than employees, in an effort to avoid being subject to laws and regulations that apply to employees. In response, the various regulatory agencies, such as the *Internal Revenue Service (IRS)*, the *Department of Labor, the Equal Employment Opportunity Commission (EEOC)*, the *Occupational Safety and Health Administration (OSHA)*, state wage-and-hour departments, workers' compensation, and unemployment insurance administrators have adopted complex tests to distinguish employees from independent contractors. These tests tend to be biased in favor of an employer-employee relationship—that is, in favor of finding that the person is covered by the particular law or regulation the agency is charged with enforcing. (Tax issues relating to independent contractors are discussed in Chapter 7.)

QUICK TIP

Some workers are required by law to work under another's supervision. This is true, for example, in various health care professions. Even though the worker may otherwise qualify as an independent contractor, the duty to be supervised may convert the worker into an employee.

Agents

An *agent* is someone you authorize to make contracts for you and to bind you to those contracts. Employees can be agents, but employees do not automatically become agents—it depends on what, if any, additional authority you give them. For example, if you told your employee to take a computer to the shop and make arrangements to have it repaired, you have given your employee authority to act as your agent. When he or she signs a work order in your name, you as the *principal*, not the employee, will have to pay the repair bill.

Similarly, an independent contractor can be, but is not necessarily, an agent. When you engage a landscape architect to prepare a design for the grounds around your new office building, the architect is an independent contractor but not an agent. However, when you then authorize the architect to buy plantings, he or she becomes your agent as well and has the power to obligate you to the nursery.

The consequences of misclassifying an employee or a group of employees as independent contractors can be expensive. For example, the employer might be held liable for income taxes that should have been withheld but were not, for wage-and-hour violations, for retroactive coverage under employee benefit plans, and for back pay, penalties, statutory damages, and interest.

Statutory Employees and Nonemployees

Some laws classify workers as employees or independent contractors regardless of the employer's right of control or lack of control over the manner in which the work is done.

The Internal Revenue Code has four categories of statutory employees:

1. A delivery driver (other than one who delivers milk);
2. A full-time life insurance agent;
3. An individual who works at home on materials or goods supplied by the employer; and,
4. A full-time salesperson who sells merchandise for resale or for use in the buyer's business operation.

The Internal Revenue Code also has two categories of statutory *nonemployees*:

1. Direct sellers of consumer products in the home or a place of business other than a permanent retail establishment; and,
2. Licensed real estate agents.

Workers' compensation statutes, unemployment insurance statutes, and other laws also state who does or does not qualify as an employee for purposes of the statute.

The Employment At-Will Doctrine

Most employment is *at will*. That means there is no fixed period of time that the employment relationship will last and either party is free to terminate the relationship at any time, with or without cause. In other words, the employer may fire, or the employee may quit, for any reason or for no reason at all.

In most states, there is a presumption that any particular employment relationship is at will. The presumption applies unless it is shown that employment for a specific period of time, such as two years, was intended. The fact that the employer and the employee intended the relationship to last a long time or for an indefinite period does not overcome the presumption of at-will employment, since in almost all cases the parties hope—at least at the outset—that the relationship will last a long time or indefinitely. An employer's promise of work *for as long as the job exists and for as long as you want it* is nothing more than indefinite, at-will employment. Even so-called *permanent employment* is still employment at will (although employers should not use the term *permanent* when intending only an at-will relationship).

An important corollary of the at-will doctrine has to do with the *implied covenant of good faith and fair dealing.* In most states, every contract is presumed to contain that implied covenant. Parties to the contract must act reasonably toward each other. However, the covenant is not implied in the normal at-will employment arrangement, since the covenant depends on the existence of an *employment contract with a definite term.* It follows, at least in theory, that an employer may treat at-will employees unreasonably and may fire them without cause. (Of course, it is seldom good practice to do so.)

CASE STUDY: THE AT-WILL EMPLOYMENT RELATIONSHIP

A decision by the U.S. Court of Appeals for the Fourth Circuit involved the question whether an at-will employment relationship is contractual at all. The case was a Section 1981 discrimination action, based on a Reconstruction-era federal statute that extends to all citizens the same right to make and enforce contracts as was previously enjoyed by the white citizens. (See Chapter 14 for more on Section 1981.) The employer argued that since he had no contract with his at-will employee, he could discriminate against the employee without violating Section 1981. The court disagreed, ruling that an at-will employment relationship is contractual, even though it is not a contract for a definite term.

There are four very significant exceptions to the at-will employment doctrine:

1. The contract exception (discussed in the next section);

2. The retaliatory/abusive discharge exception (discussed in Chapter 4);
3. The exception for protected leave (see Chapter 8); and,
4. The discrimination exception (covered in Chapters 14 through 17).

When one of these exceptions applies, discharging an at-will employee may result in a lawsuit, an award of money damages against the employer, or an order that the employer reinstate the employee.

Employment Contracts

An *employment contract* is an agreement between the employer and the employee that the employment relationship will last for a fixed, definite period of time, or that the relationship can be terminated only for cause or under specified conditions. Employment contracts should be in writing, since oral contracts that cannot be performed within one year are generally unenforceable according to the *Statute of Frauds*. Even if an oral contract of employment is enforceable, it can give rise to misunderstandings, and its provisions are difficult to prove. Figure 1.1 lists various topics that a typical contract might include.

In most cases, the employer will want to preserve an at-will employment relationship and avoid being bound by an employment contract or by any implied covenant of good faith and fair dealing. This would be true, for example, in the case of lower-level employees who can be replaced fairly easily. However, in a tight labor market where qualified employees are difficult to find, the employer may want the protection of an employment contract. The employer might also want contract protection for employees in whom costly training is being invested, for employees who have access to closely guarded company secrets, or for employees who have unusual or complicated compensation arrangements.

Note:
Often employment contracts will contain additional provisions for the employer's benefit, such as noncompete and nonsolicitation clauses. (See Chapter 19 for more information on these clauses.)

An employee may want the security of a contract when, for example, the employee is resigning from a stable position to take a job with a start-up company, or making a costly move to the new employer's headquarters. Whether the employer gives a contract in those circumstances depends on the employee's bargaining power and worth to the new employer.

Figure 1.1: **OVERVIEW OF CONTRACT CONTENT**

The contents of any particular employment contract will depend on the circumstances. A typical contract might include provisions dealing with:

- Job description, including employee duties and authority;

- Whether the position is exempt or nonexempt under the Fair Labor Standards Act;

- Beginning date and term of the contract and extensions;

- Compensation arrangements;

- Bonuses and stock options;

- Health and other benefit plans;

- Other fringe benefits—company car, expense account, etc.;

- Exclusivity—no moonlighting, no conflicts-of-interest during term;

- Vacation and sick leave arrangements;

- Grounds for early termination—death, disability, revocation of a required license, etc;

- Confidentiality and trade secrets;

- Ownership of intellectual property—copyrightable and patentable works or inventions;

- Noncompetition and nonsolicitation of customers and fellow employees after termination;

- Liquidated damages for breach by employee;

- Arbitration of disputes; and,

- Indemnification.

Fill-in-the-blank contract forms are available from commercial publishers. Electronic forms can even be purchased or downloaded from the Internet. But if the employment relationship is important enough to justify a contract in the first place, it should be important enough to justify a consultation with employment counsel to be sure the contract fits the particular circumstances and conforms with local law.

Implied Contracts

Although the parties may not have explicitly intended to enter into an employment contract, the employer's actions can inadvertently bind the employer to the same extent as if there were a signed, written agreement. Some courts have found, for example, that the provisions of an employee handbook amount to an employment contract, even though no contract was actually intended. Even the wording of a simple employment letter can create a contract if it implies that a specific time period is contemplated. Consider this letter:

We are pleased to offer you the position of Sales Manager beginning January 1. Your base salary will be $35,000 per year, increasing to $40,000 your second year, and $45,000 your third year. You will also earn an override commission of 2½% on all sales.

We have already made definite plans to expand our market into the southeastern states over the next three years. By the end of the third year, sales should reach $1.5 million, which translates to a commission to you of $37,500. We are counting on you to take the lead in these expansion plans and we have every confidence that, with you at the helm of our sales department, we will reach our goal.

While the letter does not exactly promise a three-year arrangement, it certainly implies that the sales manager should expect to stay that long. Couple that with the sales manager's own testimony that he was indeed promised three years and the employer might find itself bound to such a contract.

Breach of Contract

When employer and employee have agreed that the employment will last a fixed period of time, the courts will generally enforce such an agreement by awarding money damages for its breach. If the *employer* breaches, he or she may be liable not only for the compensation the employee would have earned, but also for fringe benefits such as health insurance, pension plan contributions, stock options, and so on.

If the *employee* breaches, damages are more difficult to measure, since it is difficult to quantify just how a particular employee's performance would have affected future profitability. Absent a *liquidated damages* provision (a provision that specifies in advance the amount of damages to be recovered), the employer's claim might be limited to employment agency fees, employee relocation costs covered by the employer, and any license or similar fees paid by the employer on the employee's behalf. Remember that a court will not order the employee back to work since such an order would violate the Constitution's *involuntary servitude* rule.

Alert!

Even in employment-at-will situations, the employer may be held liable for fraud or deceit if an employee is induced to accept work based on false or incomplete representation as to the conditions of employment. (See Chapter 2 for more on employer misrepresentation during the hiring process.)

Arbitration Agreements

Arbitration of disputes is often viewed as preferable to litigation. Arbitration is generally faster and cheaper; it involves only limited pretrial discovery, the proceedings take place in private, and the results are usually final and unappealable. Since arbitration means no jury trial, an employer who fears a runaway jury and a runaway damage award may view arbitration as a highly desirable alternative to litigation.

Both the *Federal Arbitration Act* (FAA) and its state counterparts say that a contract provision for resolution of future disputes by arbitration is valid and enforceable. The courts have gone so far as to rule that the law favors arbitration and that when a contract contains an arbitration clause, a presumption arises that all disputes relating to the contract must be arbitrated. These principles have been applied to labor disputes under *collective bargaining agreements* and to employment disputes in the securities industry, where arbitration clauses have been common for years.

Alert!

A pre-dispute arbitration agreement—that is, an agreement to arbitrate made at the outset of employment or at some other time before a dispute has arisen—should be distinguished from an agreement to arbitrate made after a dispute has arisen. Courts will almost always enforce a post-dispute arbitration agreement that is entered into knowingly and voluntarily. The enforceability of a pre-dispute arbitration agreement, however, may be open to a variety of objections, such as unfairness, lack of true consent, etc.

For some time, there was a question whether an employee could be forced to submit *federal statutory* claims to arbitration. Suppose an employer routinely requires employees, as a condition of employment, to sign an agreement that subjects all future employment-related disputes to binding arbitration, including discrimination claims based on the various federal antidiscrimination statutes. Under the principle that statutory rights cannot be waived in advance, some federal courts initially ruled that an employee would not be bound by such an agreement, made in advance of any dispute, to arbitrate claims based on federal antidiscrimination statutes.

The Supreme Court, which is the ultimate authority on interpretation of federal law, resolved the question in March 2001. In a decision involving an employee of an electronics store in California, the Court ruled that an agreement to arbitrate discrimination claims was valid and enforceable under the FAA. The Court went on to praise arbitration agreements in the employment context, because of the smaller sums of money normally involved.

The *Equal Employment Opportunity Commission* (EEOC), which opposes binding arbitration of discrimination claims, will not stay its own hand in investigating or attempting to reconcile a discrimination charge just because the parties have entered into an arbitration agreement. In a recent case, an employee of a chain restaurant was fired from his short-order cook job when the restaurant learned he suffered from seizures. In response to the EEOC's suit for violations of the *Americans with Disabilities Act*, the restaurant argued that the employee had signed a pre-dispute arbitration agreement that barred the EEOC's suit. The Supreme Court upheld the EEOC's suit, saying the EEOC has an independent statutory right to pursue whatever remedies it feels appropriate that included not only injunctions against future violations, but also victim-specific relief such as reinstatement and back pay.

QUICK TIP

Arbitration may not always be cheaper than litigation. For example, there are substantial filing fees just to initiate arbitration. And unless the arbitration agreement says otherwise, each party normally pays its own attorney's fees without any right to reimbursement.

Some employers have tried to shift the burden of arbitration costs to the employee, so that the employee ends up paying far more to arbitrate than he or she would to sue in court. Other employers have drafted arbitration agreements that are so one-sided in favor of the employer as to be fundamentally unfair to the employee. Decisions by a number of federal appellate courts have refused to enforce such agreements, ruling that any attempt to burden an employee with excessive costs or to give employers unfair procedural advantages is a denial of the employee's statutory rights. Figure 1.2 lists steps to help ensure the validity of pre-dispute arbitration agreements.

QUICK TIP

For companies that require employees to sign *noncompetition* or *nonsolicitation* clauses, an arbitration agreement should have an exception allowing the employer to go to court for an injunction to bar an employee's or former employee's violation of the clause.

Arbitration provisions should not be placed in the employee handbook, since the employee handbook is not intended to be a contract of employment. (The fact that an employer has an arbitration-of-disputes policy may be mentioned in the handbook.) For those employees with whom the employer has a formal contract of employment, the arbitration provision would be included there. For at-will employees, the employer should use a separate written document, dated and signed by the employee, that contains both the desired arbitration provision and a disclaimer to the effect that the arbitration provision is not a contract of employment, and does not change the at-will status of the employee.

Figure 1.2: PRE-DISPUTE ARBITRATION AGREEMENT

Despite the Supreme Court's blessing, legal issues involved in pre-dispute arbitration agreements continue to arise, particularly in the area of fairness and cost-shifting. To help ensure their validity, arbitration agreements should:

• Contain a *clear and unmistakable waiver* of the employee's right to go to court and should specify that arbitration is *final and binding*;

• Specifically identify the *types of potential claims* that the employer intends to submit to arbitration—claims under Title VII, the ADA, the ADEA, state human rights and fair employment practices acts, county and local nondiscrimination laws, claims for abusive discharge, pay disputes, etc.;

• Provide for a *neutral* arbitrator;

- Allow at least minimal *discovery*;

- Not burden the employee with *costs* in excess of those he or she would incur in court;

- Be *balanced, fair to both sides,* and not attempt to give the employer any procedural advantages;

- Be *binding on the employer* as well as the employee; it should not obligate the employee to arbitrate while giving the employer the option of arbitrating or not;

- Not attempt to take away any of the *employee's substantive statutory rights* or limit an employee's statutory remedies; and,

- Require the arbitrator to issue a written award.

Business Owners' Employment Status

Business can be conducted in a variety of forms, from the sole proprietorship to the publicly-held, multinational corporation. In between are general partnerships; small or close corporations that have elected S status for federal income tax purposes (S corps); limited liability partnerships (LLPs); limited liability companies (LLCs); and professional corporations (PCs).

The right choice of business entity goes beyond the scope of this book. This section is concerned with the status of business owners who also work for the entity they own. Are they considered employees of the entity? And what liability do they have for entity obligations or the negligence of other employees? The answers depend on the specific type of entity involved and on certain tax elections available to those entities.

Sole Proprietorships

A *sole proprietorship* is a business owned by a single individual in his or her individual name. While a sole proprietor can have employees, he or she is considered *self-employed* and can never be an employee of the business. Sole proprietors report their business income and expenses on Schedule C of Form 1040 for federal income tax purposes.

Sole proprietors are personally liable for their own negligence and, as employers, they are *vicariously liable* for the work-related negligence of their employees. They are also *personally* liable for the business's obligations, such as wages, lease payments, business loans, and vendor invoices. For liability reasons, a sole proprietorship is usually not a recommended form for doing business.

General Partnerships

A *general partnership* is a group of individuals who share profits and losses of the partnership's business. Partnerships are treated as separate entities for some purposes and as *pass-through* entities for other purposes. For example, a partnership can have employees (other than the partners themselves) and file its own income tax returns. However, partnerships generally do not pay any income tax. Instead, any net income or loss shown on the partnership return is allocated to the partners according to the partnership agreement. The partners pay tax on their allocated share (as shown on Form K-1 that the partnership issues to them) whether or not net income has actually been distributed to them in cash. The partners themselves are considered to be self-employed.

Partners are personally liable for partnership obligations, just like sole proprietors. Also, each partner is considered the *agent* of each other partner and is personally liable for the negligence and contractual obligations of each partner. (Think of a partner as a sole proprietor with multiple personalities.) This is the main reason for the popularity of S corps and, more recently, LLPs and LLCs.

S Corporations

An *S corp* is just like any other corporation formed under state law, but it has elected S status for federal income tax purposes. (The S refers to the Internal Revenue Code subchapter that permits the election.) As a result, it is treated much like a partnership for federal income tax purposes, yet it retains the limited liability features of a corporation. An owner of an S corp is considered self-employed and gets a K-1, just like a partner in a partnership. However, there is no personal liability for corporate obligations or for the negligence of other employees or co-owners. Because they have characteristics of both corporations and partnerships, S corps (along with LLPs and LLCs) are sometimes called *hybrids*.

S corp status is available only to small business corporations with one class of stock and fewer than 100 shareholders. Only individuals, decedent's estates, and some types of trusts can be shareholders. Partnerships and other corporations cannot own stock in an S corp.

Limited Liability Partnerships and Limited Liability Companies

Owners of LLPs (who are called partners) and owners of LLCs (who are called members) are the equivalent of partners in a general partnership for tax purposes. Therefore, they are normally considered self-employed and they get year-end K-1 forms showing their taxable shares of LLP or LLC profits. However, LLPs and LLCs (or any other entity treated as a partnership under state law) may take advantage of the IRS's check-the-box rule and elect to be taxed as corporations. Worker-owners would then be treated as employees, just as with any other corporation.

Regardless of an LLP's or LLC's status for tax purposes, its partners or members have no personal liability for obligations of the LLP or LLC, or for the negligence of other partners, members, or employees.

QUICK TIP

Small businesses with only a few owners may find it advantageous to organize as LLCs, and then elect to be taxed as S corps. This arrangement enjoys simplicity of organization, pass-through tax status, and protection of owners from personal liability. In addition, it allows an income tax deduction for the employer's portion of FICA due with respect to compensation paid to owner-employees. Had the LLC not elected corporate taxation status, all compensation to owner-employees would have been subject to self-employment tax for which no deduction is available.

Professional Corporations

Traditionally, professionals like doctors, lawyers, accountants, and so on were only permitted to practice as sole proprietors or as partnerships. The fear was that if they practiced in corporate form their professional judgment would be compromised by being subjected to the wishes of a corporate board of directors. At the same time, however, federal income tax law (particularly regarding pension plans) strongly favored corporations over partnerships. So professionals brought pressure on state legislators and licensing boards to allow them to incorporate. The result was the *professional corporation* (PC).

QUICK TIP

Depending on a variety of factors, owners of a professional corporation may or may not be counted as employees for federal antidiscrimination law purposes. In a case known as *Clackamas Gastroenterology Associates*, the Supreme Court applied the common-law test of whether the employer controls the means and manner of the worker's work performance, in determining whether the physician-shareholders in a medical practice should be counted as employees.

PCs are in every respect true corporations under state law. An owner who works for the PC is usually classified as an employee and receives a W-2 at year-end, just like employees of other corporations. (PCs can elect S corp status, in which case owners are treated as self-employed for federal tax purposes.) However, only licensed members of the particular profession for which the PC was organized can be shareholders, directors, and officers.

Professionals who work for a PC are *personally liable* to their clients for *professional negligence*, regardless of their status as employees for other purposes. But the good news is that they are not personally liable for the negligence of their fellow professionals—a liability they would have if they had organized in partnership form.

C Corporations

Large businesses have little choice in their type of entity. To participate effectively in capital markets they must organize in corporate form. They also cannot qualify as S corps under the Internal

Revenue Code because they have a broad shareholder base, and perhaps several classes of stock. C *corp* shareholders may work for the corporation but they have no special status as shareholder-employees. Both the president who owns ten thousand shares and the janitor who owns ten shares get W-2 forms, and neither is liable for *corporate obligations* or the negligence of fellow employees.

Note:

Although sole proprietors and partners are considered self-employed, many workers' compensation statutes allow them to opt-in and obtain coverage. Conversely, while members of LLCs and corporate officers are covered by workers' comp statutes, they are often permitted to opt-out of coverage. (Workers' compensation insurance is discussed in Chapter 11.)

Chapter 2

The Hiring Process

Employers and employees have numerous interactions during the employment relationship. While any of these interactions can give rise to liability, the following stand out as particularly critical:

- Hiring;
- Evaluating (discussed in Chapter 3); and,
- Terminating (see Chapter 4).

Steps in the Hiring Process

The hiring process has one purpose—to exchange enough information so that the parties can make an informed decision about whether to enter into an employment relationship. Good hiring practice involves the collection of appropriate information untainted by information that should not be the basis for a hiring decision. The hiring procedure usually involves the following steps.

Job Description

In order to focus on job qualifications, the employer should first prepare a clear, written description of the job being offered. The description should include at least the following:

- *Essential functions* of the job (the critical functions that go to the heart of the job and that the person holding the job must, unquestionably, be able to do);
- *Less critical functions* that the employee may be called upon to perform from time to time or that could be done by others if necessary;
- *Special skills required*, such as ability to operate complex equipment;
- *Special education, licenses,* or *certificates* required;
- *Title* or *position* of the person to whom the employee reports;
- *Number and classification of persons who report* to the employee;
- Whether the employee is *exempt* or *nonexempt* under the *Fair Labor Standards Act*; and,
- *Date the description was prepared* or most recently revised.

The job description should be prepared before the job is advertised and before any candidates are considered.

Advertising the Opening

Any want ads you run or notices you post should describe the job being offered, not the person you think you are looking for. Expressions such as *recent graduate* or even *energetic person* could provide evidence of age discrimination if the position is filled by a younger candidate after an older candidate has been turned down. Expressions that indicate a gender preference such as *gal Friday* or *waitress*, for example, should also be avoided. (Discrimination is discussed in detail in Chapters 14, 15, 16, and 17.)

Alert!

Use of only a single method for recruiting unduly restricts the candidate pool and discourages workplace diversity. Word-of-mouth recruiting, for example, has been attacked by the EEOC as potentially being discriminatory.

Internet Recruiting

Advertising job openings via the Internet is a convenient, relatively inexpensive way to attract résumés—and that is the problem. An employer can be overwhelmed with the number of responses and lack sufficient staff time to screen them effectively. Screening software, while effective, may inadvertently discriminate if the wrong key words are used to do the screening. Employers who limit their recruitment to this medium should also be alert to possible disability discrimination claims if their website lacks accessibility features.

Application

A written application form should be developed for initial screening purposes. The application form should obviously not ask for information that the employer is prohibited from considering as part of the hiring process. Some seemingly innocuous inquiries can also cause trouble. For example, the applicant should not be asked to attach a photograph. Age or birthdate questions should be saved until after the applicant has been hired (although for child labor purposes, the employer should ask whether the applicant is at least 18). Similarly, immigration status questions should be saved for later and the application should be limited to the question, "Are you legally eligible to work in the United States?" Even a question about whom to contact in an emergency should be avoided in the initial application, since it could reveal marital status or family information.

Interview

Interviews should be conducted by experienced personnel using a standard written interview form. The interview form should be limited to questions or topics directly relevant to job performance and the interviewer should stick to the form, noting the applicant's responses on the form itself. By having and following a standard written form, the employer can more easily show that no inquires about prohibited matters were made, and that no particular applicant was singled out for special questioning.

It is difficult to get a feel for an applicant's personality and communications skills if all that is asked are yes-or-no questions, so interviewers naturally like to ask open-ended questions, such as "Why do you want to work here?" or "Tell me what you like and don't like about your current job." There are risks to open-ended questions, however, particularly when they are not strictly job-related, because they may elicit personal information that can later form the basis of a discrimination claim.

Another common pitfall in the hiring process is family status. Suppose an interviewer asks, "Do you have any family responsibilities that could keep you from getting to the office?" The applicant responds, "I'm a single parent and my son has special needs, but I have day care arrangements that work pretty well." Later, when checking with the applicant's previous employer, the interviewer learns of serious attendance and tardiness problems. If the applicant is rejected, the employer is open to charges of violating the *Americans with Disabilities Act* or other antidiscrimination laws.

An employer may not ask, "Are you disabled?" or, "Do you have any medical conditions that could interfere with your performance?"

However, an employer may say, "Can you do this job?"—provided the question is asked of every applicant and not just those who may appear to have disabilities.

Pre-employment Testing

Title VII makes it unlawful for an employer, when selecting candidates for employment, to adjust the scores of, use different cutoff scores for, or otherwise alter the results of employment-related tests on the basis of race, color, religion, sex, or national origin. Even short of such blatant discrimination as using different cutoff scores, tests that have the unintended effect of excluding certain groups could result in *disparate impact discrimination*. For enforcement purposes, the EEOC has adopted a *four-fifths rule*—if a particular test (or any other selection procedure, for that matter) excludes any race, gender, or ethnic group at a rate that is less than four-fifths that of the highest rate, the exclusion rate will be considered evidence of discrimination.

Tests also need to be *validated*—that is, shown by statistical or other evidence to be good predictors of job performance. The EEOC has adopted detailed regulations on validation requirements, which go beyond the scope of this book. The regulations also require employers to keep records on the impact of their testing procedures, classified by gender, race, and ethnic group. (See Chapter 17 for a discussion of restrictions on medical testing under the Americans with Disabilities Act.)

Background Checks

Once you have a short list of candidates, or have tentatively chosen a single candidate, it is time for background checking. This could include, as appropriate, calls to references and prior employers, ordering a consumer report, ordering a criminal convictions check, and obtaining a copy of the candidate's driving record. It may even include a drug test. Background checking will *not* include a lie detector test, and until you have actually made a conditional offer to the candidate, it will not include a medical exam.

QUICK TIP

Special notice and disclosure requirements apply to credit reports and background checks. (See Chapter 18 for more details.)

Internet Searches

Faced with concerns about the accuracy of résumés, the reliability of reference information, and the risk of negligent employment claims, employers are more and more turning to the Internet to investigate prospective employees. There they can often find a wealth of information. For example, a job candidate may be listed on the website of a club or organization in which he or she is a member. Or the candidate may maintain a blog on a topic of special interest. Some candidates, perhaps out of youthful exuberance (and indiscretion), may even brag electronically about alcohol consumption, drug use, or sexual exploits, providing photos or videos of the conduct being described.

An employer's collection and use of online information raises a number of legal questions. For example, postings can reveal information—such as ancestry, family status, religious affiliation, political belief, even sexual orientation—that is otherwise unavailable to the employer and that should not be considered in the hiring process. Once an employer has obtained such information, it is open to a charge of using the information in the decision-making process.

In addition, some states prohibit employers from considering after-hours activities in making employment decisions, so long as the activity is otherwise lawful and doesn't interfere with job performance. Even in the absence of such laws, the obtaining of such information may amount to a common-law invasion of privacy. And if the employer obtained the information by circumventing a security device, such as by guessing a password or by misrepresenting the employer's identity, the employer may have violated federal law, such as the Electronic Communications Privacy Act.

Employers who decide to include Internet searches as part of the application process might consider using a non-decision-maker to screen purely personal or otherwise irrelevant information, so that the ultimate decision-maker has only job-related data on which to base his or her decision.

Offer

When you have finally identified a single candidate and background checks have been completed and are satisfactory, the next step is to make an offer. A *written* offer is recommended to avoid any misunderstandings and reduce the possibility of disputes down the road. For *at-will* employees, the offer will usually be in the form of a simple letter. Figure 2.1 is an example of a written offer.

New Employee Procedures

The following steps should be taken when the employee actually starts work:

- Obtain evidence of the employee's eligibility to work in the U.S. and complete Form I-9 (discussed in Chapter 21);
- Administer a medical exam if desired (requirements for medical exams are covered in Chapter 17);
- Have the employee complete IRS Form W-4 and the appropriate state counterpart (see Chapter 7);
- Obtain any additional personal information not given on the application, such as birthdate, emergency contact, and so on;
- Collect information as to the employee's race, sex, and national origin if required to file Form EEO-1 (see Chapter 14);
- Deliver copies of the employee handbook and other applicable work rules, policies, etc., and obtain a signed receipt;
- Deliver a copy of the employee's job description and obtain a signed receipt;
- Have the employee sign an arbitration agreement if appropriate (see Chapter 1);
- Have the employee sign confidentiality, noncompete, and nonsolicitation agreements if appropriate (discussed in Chapter 19);
- Obtain a HIPAA certificate of creditable coverage from the employee or his or her previous employer if you offer group health insurance;
- Have the employee enroll in any benefit plans for which he or she is then eligible; and,
- Within twenty days after the employee begins employment, notify the appropriate state agency of the new hire.

Figure 2.1: **WRITTEN OFFER LETTER**

We are pleased to offer you the position of Senior Programmer at a starting salary of $62,000 per year, beginning September 1, 2008. This offer is subject to your furnishing sufficient evidence that you are eligible to work in the United States and to a satisfactory medical exam at the company's expense [if required].

Vacation and sick leave policies, benefit plans, and other Company rules and policies are explained in our Employee Handbook, a copy of which will be given to you on your start date. You are expected to read and be familiar with the Employee Handbook.

This letter is not intended to be a contract of employment. You will be an at-will employee of the Company, meaning that either you or the Company can terminate the employment relationship at any time for any reason, with or without cause.

If you accept this offer, please sign and return the enclosed copy of this letter no later than August 15, 2008.

You should report to John Smith at 8:30 a.m. on your first day of work to complete the hiring process.

Very truly yours,

ABC COMPANY

By _____Jane Jones_____

President

I accept this offer of employment:

Signature: _____

Date: _____

Directory of New Hires Database

Federal law requires each state to establish a *Directory of New Hires database* that is then shared with other states to track persons who have child-support obligations. (See Chapter 6 for more detailed information.) The information is also used to detect fraud or abuse in welfare and unemployment programs. The states, in turn, have passed laws to establish the *Directory* and to require in-state employers to report new hires within twenty days after hiring. The one-page form can be mailed or faxed. Forms can be obtained, and in some cases completed, online.

Multistate employers (employers with employees in more than one state) have two reporting options: they may report each newly hired employee to the state where the employee is working, following the new hire reporting regulations of that particular state; or they may select one state where they have employees working and report all new hires to that state electronically. Employers must choose between the two options; they cannot use both. Employers who choose the second option must register with the U.S. Department of Health and Human Services as a multistate employer.

Note:
More information on new hire reporting is available from the Office of Child Support Enforcement of the U.S. Department of Health and Human Services at: http://151.196.108.21/ocse.

Employee Résumé Fraud

Prospective employees sometimes lie on their job applications. When the position being applied for involves risk to the public, the employer should take reasonable steps to verify the information. Even when no obvious risk is involved, the employer may wish to verify education or past experience that bears on the applicant's qualifications for the job.

While ferreting out these lies is becoming increasingly burdensome, there are a number of steps an employer can take to assure that they get an accurate picture of the candidate:

• Check all references;
• Ask each reference to furnish the name of another person who knows the candidate and check with that person as well;

- Require the candidate to complete a standard written employment application and check the application against the résumé for inconsistencies;
- If the candidate claims knowledge or experience in a particular technical field, have one of your technicians participate in interviewing the candidate;
- Require candidates to present original documentation in support of résumé claims (degrees, certifications, drivers' licenses, etc.);
- Obtain official transcripts directly from schools the candidate attended;
- Obtain driving records from state motor vehicle authorities;
- Search the Internet for publicly-available information (but see the discussion earlier in this chapter about Internet searches);
- Contract with companies to obtain background investigations, criminal convictions checks, and credit checks (but be sure to comply with the *Fair Credit Reporting Act* requirements, discussed in Chapter 18); and,
- Hire candidates provided by employment agencies that pre-screen their referrals.

But suppose a falsified résumé slips past the employer and is not discovered until months or years down the road. What rights and remedies does the employer then have?

At-will employees may, of course, be discharged for any reason (except a prohibited reason) or for no reason. As for those employees with employment contracts, if the résumé contains a false statement about some material matter (that is, about a matter that a reasonable person would find significant) and the employer actually relied on the statement in offering employment, then the employment contract is the product of the employee's *fraud*. The employer may treat the contract as void and discharge the employee so long as the employer acts promptly after discovering the fraud. However, if the false statement is an obvious typographical error (say, inversion of two digits in the date for previous employment), it is trivial, or it is so inherently improbable that the employer could not reasonably have relied on it, then the contract of employment remains enforceable.

QUICK TIP

For both contract and at-will positions, it is a good idea to include in the employment application a certification by the applicant that the application is truthful and that all supporting items such as transcripts, reference letters, etc., are genuine.

After-acquired evidence—even evidence of a serious nature that would have been grounds for firing had it been discovered earlier—is not a complete defense to a discrimination claim. But it does limit the remedies that are available to the aggrieved employee. As the Supreme Court said in such a case, it makes no sense to compel an employer who fired an employee for discriminatory reasons to re-hire the employee, and then turn around and fire the employee again based on résumé fraud. But it does make sense to award back pay for the period between the wrongful firing and the time the résumé fraud was discovered.

Misrepresentation by the Employer during the Hiring Process

Suppose an employer makes an offer of at-will employment and, in the process, makes certain statements to the prospective employee about the nature of the job, working conditions, etc. The applicant relies on those statements, accepts the job, turns down other offers, and begins work. Then, for the first time, the employee learns that the employer's pre-hiring statements were untrue and that actual job conditions are much less favorable than as represented. It could be argued that the employee has no basis to complain about the employer's false pre-hiring statements, since in an at-will relationship, the employer has the absolute right to change working conditions at any time and to fire an employee whenever the employer feels like doing so. However, several court decisions have ruled that an at-will employee who, in reliance on an employer's false statements, resigns from another job can sue the employer for fraud, deceit, and negligent misrepresentation.

CASE STUDY: EMPLOYER LIABLE FOR MISREPRESENTATION

When an applicant for a physical therapist position at a hospital was interviewed, the hospital's CEO represented that the hospital's contract with an outside therapy provider would be ending and that the hospital would be bringing physical therapy services in-house. However, the CEO lacked authority to make those changes on his own. He also lacked authority to hire without approval by certain other officials. Nevertheless, the CEO made a firm offer to the therapist.

The therapist accepted the offer and turned down another opportunity. Only then did he learn that the offer had not been authorized and that, in fact, the offered position was not available. In the therapist's suit against the hospital for negligent misrepresentation, the hospital argued that since the offer was only for at-will employment, the hospital could have gone through with the hiring, then fired the therapist the next day. The court answered that argument by saying that while the at-will nature of the offer would affect the amount of damages that could be awarded, that factor had no bearing on whether the therapist could bring suit for negligent misrepresentation in the first place.

Note:

An employer can protect itself from negligent misrepresentation suits brought by disappointed applicants by being careful about what is said.

In the application process, the employer should:

• Describe the job accurately by furnishing a written job description that is complete and up-to-date;
• Give accurate estimates of job features that are likely to be of interest or concern to an employee, such as overtime requirements, travel, etc.;

- Allow the applicant an opportunity to review the employee handbook and other important policy statements with which the applicant will be expected to comply if hired;
- Furnish copies of all agreements the applicant will be required to sign upon hiring, such as agreements dealing with noncompetition, nonsolicitation, work-for-hire, arbitration, and so on;
- Describe the hiring process, including who makes the decision to offer a job and what further approvals, if any, are necessary;
- State clearly and explicitly that the offer is conditioned on approval by the company's board of directors or by some other official, if that is the case;
- Disclose such facts as the company is about to move its facilities, is considering a possible bankruptcy, or is facing the loss of an important contract or some other event that could significantly affect the applicant's job;
- Give the applicant a firm date by which the company will make a decision and, if the company has not made a decision by that deadline, contact the applicant, inform him or her that the decision is still pending, and ask if the applicant wishes to continue being considered;
- Inform the applicant promptly once a decision is made; and,
- If the applicant is being rejected, send a note confirming the rejection and thanking the applicant for his or her interest; do not encourage the applicant to think he or she is still under consideration if that is not the case.

Employee Handbooks

While there is no obligation for an employer to have a written employee handbook, many employers find them to be a valuable management tool.

Advantages

Handbooks promote uniformity in treatment of employees, particularly for larger employers with several layers of management. That in turn improves morale and frees the employer from a stream of requests for special treatment.

Handbooks are also a convenient source of information for job applicants and new hires, as well as existing employees. They promote efficiency and they help to establish an institutional culture. They set out rules of workplace behavior which, if willfully violated and result in termination, provide the employer with a defense to an unemployment insurance claim or an abusive discharge suit. Finally, they provide evidence of employer compliance with law in areas such as workers' compensation, equal employment, and sexual harassment.

Employers who choose to have an employee handbook should not overlook the requirement that if the handbook describes leave policies and the employer is covered by the *Family and Medical Leave Act*, the handbook must include a description of extended leave benefits under FMLA. (See Chapter 8 for more details.) And since an employer *must* have a written sexual harassment policy to be able to defend against sexual harassment charges, the handbook is the obvious place to set out that policy. (See Chapter 15 for specifics.)

When distributing employee handbooks to employees, have each employee sign an *acknowledgment* that he or she has received the handbook and will read it. Such acknowledgments are helpful in meeting an employee's claim that he or she was unaware of a particular policy or procedure contained in the handbook.

Disadvantages

The downside is that an employee handbook or similar statement of policy might be considered a *unilateral contract*—that is, a one-sided *offer* by the employer to abide by the provisions of the handbook that the employee *accepts* simply by working for the employer. In other words, courts may treat a poorly worded handbook as converting an at-will employment relationship to a contractual relationship that limits an employer's right to fire.

An employer who wishes to adopt an employee handbook but who does not want to be contractually bound by its provisions can take the following steps to reduce, if not eliminate, the risk of contractual liability:

● Include prominent disclaimers that the handbook is not a contract of employment and is not intended to change the at-will status of any employee;

- State that the handbook is intended only as a convenient source of information about the company and its current practices and procedures, which are subject to change at any time without prior notice;
- State that employees are free to resign at any time and that the company is free to discharge an employee at any time, with or without cause;
- State that the company is not bound to follow any particular disciplinary procedures and that the company need not be consistent in imposing discipline;
- Avoid statements such as the company *promises* or *guarantees* or *will take* specified action in certain circumstances; and,
- Avoid any requirement that employees sign an agreement to comply with or be bound by the handbook.

In addition to an employee handbook, some companies have a *managers-only manual*, distributed only to managers, setting out required procedures for them to follow for discrimination complaints, discipline, termination, and so on, involving their subordinates. Placing procedural requirements in a managers-only manual, rather than the employee handbook, makes it more difficult for rank-and-file employees to claim that the company is contractually obligated to follow the procedures.

Dress Codes

An employer may generally impose a dress code or grooming code on employees, so long as doing so has a legitimate business reason and so long as the code is not discriminatory on the basis of gender, race, religion, or other protected criteria. (Dress codes as a form of sex discrimination are discussed in Chapter 15. Also see Chapter 14 regarding dress codes and religious discrimination.)

QUICK TIP

Relaxing dress code standards may be a reasonable accommodation required of an employer for an employee suffering from a medical condition covered by the *Americans with Disabilities Act*.

Dress codes are nothing new. For example, safety considerations may warrant banning long sleeves or flowing skirts. Companies often require their delivery personnel to wear identifying uniforms sporting the corporate colors. Physicians wear white lab coats. Lawyers wear conservative suits and carry briefcases. In office settings, suit jackets, ties, and appropriate slacks for men and suits, skirts, and blouses for women have long been the unofficial uniforms. The only exceptions might be casual, summertime Fridays, or special allowances for persons with medical conditions or temporary injuries.

Casual, summertime Fridays are giving way to casual everyday all year. *Casual* can mean anything from a comfortable old sports jacket with leather elbow patches to a beer-stained T-shirt and torn jeans; from a blouse and slacks to a bare midriff.

If you decide to go casual, keep the following points in mind.

- Your dress policy should be in writing (the employee handbook is a good place) and well publicized.
- The policy should contain a clear definition of *business casual.* For example: *Dress and grooming should be neat and consistent with a professional office atmosphere. Clothing should be clean and without rips or excessive wear. Women may wear dresses, blouses, sweaters, slacks, skirts, blazers, and dress sandals; men may wear shirts with collars, polo shirts, sweaters, chino slacks, jackets, and dress sandals.*
- The policy should also contain a clear statement of what is *not permitted.* For example: *The following are examples of items that do not qualify as "business casual" and are not permitted at any time: T-shirts; tank tops; halters; jeans; shorts; sweats or similar athletic clothing; see-through clothing; clothing that exposes areas normally covered by business attire; clothing that exposes underwear; work boots; beach sandals; and sneakers.*
- Managers should have the authority to determine that casual dress for their immediate staff is inappropriate on particular days, such as when customers or visitors are expected.
- Since not everyone is comfortable wearing casual clothes to work, those who would prefer to dress more formally should feel free to do so.

- The consequences of inappropriate dress should be spelled out. For example: *Employees who report to work unacceptably dressed may be required to return home to change and will be charged with leave during their absence.*
- The policy should be consistently and even-handedly enforced.

Personnel Files

The employment relationship generates a vast array of documents. Some of them are required by law and must be retained for specified time periods. Good examples are Form I-9 and wage-and-hour records. Other documents, though perhaps not legally required to be retained, provide evidence of legal compliance. A copy of the *New Hire Report* form submitted to the State Directory of New Hires falls in this category. Finally, there are documents that management needs, like job descriptions, evaluations, and disciplinary actions to make sound employment decisions.

Employers should maintain a separate *personnel file* for each employee. The file should not be a waste basket containing everything related to the employee. Instead, management should determine in advance what documents are, and are not, to be kept in the file. In addition, the file should be organized into sections so that particular items can be located easily. A checklist placed on top of each section avoids misfiling and enables management to see, at a glance, whether it is complete and current. Files should be reviewed periodically to assure compliance with established requirements and procedures.

The contents of a typical personnel file might include:

- Employment application, along with supporting materials such as résumé, transcripts, and interview notes;
- Recommendation letters and reference checks;
- Copies of restrictive covenants with the employee's prior employers;
- Offer letter and any contractual documents, such as restrictive covenants, arbitration agreements, and so on;
- Form I-9;
- Copy of New Hire Report form;
- Tax withholding forms (W-4, W-5, and state equivalents);

- Job description, including a statement whether position is exempt or nonexempt;
- Copies of any required licenses or certificates required for the position;
- Receipt for employee handbook;
- Testing materials, if the employee was required to take any tests as part of the application process;
- Training records relating to job competency, safety, sexual harassment policies, etc.;
- Evaluations;
- Commendations and disciplinary actions;
- Personal information—home address, home telephone, name of spouse, etc.—and emergency contact (but see Chapter 18 about employee privacy);
- Benefit plan participation records (application, beneficiary designation, etc.);
- Exit interview notes; and,
- Recommendation letters and notes of references given to prospective employers.

Employers should also establish a *records retention policy*. When particular documents are required by law, the law usually specifies how long they need to be retained. In the absence of a specific requirement, the applicable *statute of limitations* should be the guide. (A statute of limitations says that a claim may be barred unless suit on the claim is filed within a specified time period, such as three years.) Convenience also plays a role. For example, if the employer commonly receives reference inquiries up to two years after an employee leaves, then the employer may want to retain relevant records at least that long in order to respond.

Employers also need to establish rules for who has access to personnel files and who may add, remove, or change file contents. Access restrictions also need to be in place for files that are maintained electronically. Also, backup information needs to be kept off-site to protect against disasters and sabotage.

Alert!

A variety of federal laws and regulations, including the *ADA* and *HIPAA*, require that medical records and information be kept separate from general personnel files. Access should be further restricted to a need-to-know basis and all persons with access should be trained in handling such records.

Litigation Hold

With the explosion of employment-related lawsuits, just about every organization can expect to get sued, sooner or later, by a disgruntled employee. Once a suit is pending, a process known as discovery begins, during which the employee's attorney can require the employer to answer written questions under oath, to furnish personnel files and a variety of other documents, and to attend depositions at which the attorney takes testimony for use at trial.

It goes without saying that when an employer receives a formal request for documents from opposing counsel, the employer cannot simply destroy the documents and then claim they do not exist. (Whether or not the employer actually has to produce all the requested documents is another issue, but destruction is not an option.)

However, the duty to preserve evidence, known as a *litigation hold*, begins long before receipt of a formal request. The courts have generally taken the view that a party has a duty to preserve evidence when the party is on notice that the evidence is relevant to pending litigation or an administrative charge, or when the party *should have known* that the evidence may become relevant to *future* proceedings. Destruction of evidence in these circumstances, known as *spoliation*, can expose the party to significant court-ordered sanctions.

The litigation hold applies not only to paper documents, but to email and other electronic data as well. Therefore, when litigation has begun or appears likely, the employer should suspend existing policies for automatic deletion of electronic data and should preserve electronic media such as backup tapes.

Employee Access

A number of states have statutes affording an employee the right to see his or her personnel file, copy it, and rebut any negative evaluations or comments contained in the file. However, absent a statute affording such rights or a contract or collective bargaining agreement in which the employer has agreed to grant access, the employer does not have to allow an employee access to the file.

Even in the absence of a statute or agreement, it is probably a good idea to allow employees access to their personnel files. One approach is to allow an employee to inspect the file generally, but to only get copies of documents he or she has signed. So if an employee wants a copy of a disciplinary notice, for example, he or she first has to sign it, which places the employer in the desirable position of having a receipted copy of the notice.

Another advantage of a policy allowing an employee access to his or her other personnel files is that it promotes open communication and a healthier, less secretive work environment. Yet another advantage is that if an employee has access but fails to dispute unfavorable information, he or she is in a poor position to complain about subsequent personnel actions or references that are based on the information. Perhaps most important, under an open access policy managers and supervisors are likely to be more disciplined in how they keep personnel files and what they put in them.

Chapter  **3**

Evaluating Performance

▶ **Reasons for Evaluating**
▶ **Legal Considerations**
▶ **Disciplinary Actions**

Evaluating an employee is a whole lot easier if there is a history of open communication and regular feedback. In short, the process should not be full of surprises.

Some employers have their employees fill out a self-evaluation form that the evaluator then reviews and comments on. While that approach may ease the manager's burden, it seems less direct. The employee may end up feeling not only that his or her work habits need improvement, but also that his or her character, honesty, and self-insight are under attack as well.

> **Note:**
> Since evaluations themselves are not usually considered adverse actions, a bad evaluation will normally not justify a claim of discrimination or retaliation. However, imposing discipline or terminating an employee based on a discriminatory evaluation can give rise to a claim.

Some organizations use what are known as *360-degree evaluations* (also called *360-degree assessments* or *multirater feedback systems*). These involve evaluations not only by an employee's supervisor, but also by peers, direct reports, and in some cases, internal or outside customers and clients. 360-degree evaluation programs need to be planned with particular care, and the procedures and objectives need to be clearly understood and communicated to employees. Follow-up is also critical; otherwise, substantial time will have been wasted collecting useless or unused data.

Reasons for Evaluating

Regardless of the type, there are some good reasons to do evaluations if they are done properly. They provide a rational basis on which to promote, discipline, and terminate. They provide powerful evidence to meet a claim that adverse action was taken for discriminatory or other improper reasons. Employees—particularly newer employees who may be uncertain of their performance—like them. If not done properly, however, they do more harm than good.

Legal Considerations

Below are a few suggestions for evaluating employees. Figure 3.1 gives an evaluation disclaimer that should also be considered.

- If you have an evaluation policy, follow it. Nothing looks more suspicious than a negative evaluation done just before taking adverse action, especially where the employer's past evaluation procedures have been haphazard and intermittent.
- Use a written form containing a standard set of objective criteria.
- Avoid vague, subjective comments like *unprofessional, bad attitude,* or *poor work habits.* Such comments offer little guidance.
- Avoid comments that could be construed as discriminatory, such as *Your approach to the job is stale* (age discrimination), *You need a softer, less aggressive demeanor with clients* (sex discrimination when directed to a female employee), or *I know your wife's health has been a distraction for you* (disability discrimination).
- Keep job descriptions up-to-date. Employees will feel unfairly treated if they are criticized on aspects of their jobs for which they did not know they were responsible.
- Tie comments on job performance—whether positive or negative—to the job description.
- Tie comments on behavioral problems to the employee handbook or other written policy statement.
- Give specific examples to support all comments—*Jane's report last May on production problems in the York, PA, plant was prompt, thorough, and contained many good suggestions. This is typical of the high quality of her work.*
- If you evaluate annually, be sure the evaluation considers the entire past year and not just the last few months.
- Discuss your evaluation with the employee and offer him or her an opportunity to comment in a private, confidential setting. Reduce the employee's comments to writing and include them in the employee's personnel file.
- Follow up on any specific deficiencies noted in the evaluation, and make a record of your follow-up in the employee's personnel file.
- Provide regular feedback—particularly, positive feedback—between evaluations.

Disciplinary Actions

Assuming you have made the decision to issue an *employee handbook*, to what extent should you spell out in the handbook the substantive reasons that will trigger discipline? If your handbook says that employment will only be terminated for cause, or for specified reasons, then regardless of the number and prominence of disclaimers in the handbook, you will have converted at-will relationships into employment contracts that can only be terminated for cause. Similarly, if your handbook describes procedures for discipline or termination— for example, *employees will be counseled on their shortcomings before more severe discipline is imposed*—failure to follow those procedures will subject you to a lawsuit that you will lose.

Figure 3.1: EVALUATION DISCLAIMER

An evaluation that is misleadingly favorable might convince an employee that he or she has long-term prospects with the company, when in fact that is not true. Therefore, any evaluation that is shared with the affected employee should contain the following disclaimer:

This evaluation is solely for the Company's benefit. Nothing in this evaluation is intended to change or affect in any way the at-will employment relationship between the Company and the employee or to limit or affect the Company's or the employee's right to terminate the employment relationship at any time for any reason.

Larger organizations may find it helpful to develop internal guidelines distributed only to management (a managers-only manual) covering termination and disciplinary matters. Guidelines might specify who has authority to fire or discipline; what types of discipline may be imposed; how notices of adverse actions are to be communicated to employees; and what opportunity (if any) employees will be given to contest adverse actions. However, those guidelines should not be published in a general distribution employee handbook. In short, employers should act reasonably, but, unless they intend to create employment contracts, they should not make commitments to their employees as to the specifics of how discipline will be imposed.

Progressive Discipline

Most authorities recommend *progressive discipline*. For less serious offenses, the steps typically include:

- oral warning, done in private;
- written warning;
- suspension without pay;
- demotion; and then,
- termination.

Each of these steps should be accompanied by a current, written, signed, and dated entry in the employee's personnel file describing the offense and the action taken.

Alert!

In suspending without pay, the employee must be paid for all past work. Loss of pay can only occur for the period the employee is suspended.

Offenses meriting a multi-step approach might include tardiness, excessive absenteeism, minor neglect of work, violation of company parking regulations, violation of smoking regulations, or frequent personal phone calls. More serious offenses justifying immediate suspension, demotion, or termination might include insubordination; theft or unauthorized use of company property or property of fellow employees; use or possession of illegal substances or weapons; other illegal activity such as gambling on company premises or use of company facilities to transmit obscene material; violence or threats of violence against supervisors; racial or sexual harassment; other forms of intentional discrimination; falsifying records or reports; and willful disregard of important company policies such as workplace safety procedures.

Even when conduct would otherwise justify immediate termination, it is often better to suspend the employee first. This allows tempers to cool and provides an opportunity for a more objective assessment of the situation.

This list of offenses is not, of course, complete. Discipline needs to be tailored to each employer's circumstances. A restaurant, for example, will be far more concerned about the failure of its kitchen staff to report communicable diseases than will a computer software company whose programmers work at home.

QUICK TIP

Currently, illegal drug use is not protected by the *Americans with Disabilities Act* (ADA). However, drug addiction and alcoholism are disabilities that can trigger company obligations under the ADA.

Last Chance Contracts

Depending on the seriousness of the offense, some employers use a *last chance contract* in which the employee agrees, in writing, that he or she is being given one final opportunity to correct the problem and will be terminated if it is not corrected. Then, if the problem later recurs, the employer is on solid ground in following through with termination.

Chapter

4

Termination

Adverse action against an employee, whether some form of discipline short of termination or termination itself, should bear a reasonable relationship to the employer's legitimate business needs. An employee may, for example, have an offbeat lifestyle or hold views on social issues that are personally offensive to the employer. If the employment relationship is at will, it may be terminated for these very reasons. But if the employee's lifestyle or social views do not interfere with his or her work and are not otherwise disruptive to the workplace, a termination may be unwise.

Consider the effect on morale of a termination where the reason bears no relation to the company's business. Consider also the risk of a lawsuit. While a suit in these circumstances would probably be unfounded, it is always possible that the court will find a violation of some previously unrecognized public policy. Even a successful defense costs money and time and it creates turmoil in the workplace. (If you have never had to answer written interrogatories propounded by your former employee's attorney, produce box loads of personnel records, or suffer through depositions of half your work force, you are in for an unpleasant surprise.) Consider, finally, the effect of such a termination on your unemployment insurance rate.

Exit Interviews

When an employee quits or is terminated, the employee should normally be interviewed by a senior member of management just prior to departure. If the termination is not completely voluntary (for example, the employee was fired or the employee quit after being offered the opportunity to do so in lieu of being fired), two members of management should conduct the interview together.

If the termination is voluntary, the employee may be asked about the reasons for quitting. Often the employer can gain valuable insight at this juncture into morale or other problems such as a hostile sexual or racial environment. However, the employee should not be pushed to respond if reluctant. If the termination is involuntary, the reasons for termination have probably already been stated to the employee. If not, they may be simply (and truthfully) stated at this point, but an extended discussion serves no purpose and it could rile tempers unnecessarily and compromise the employer's legal position.

Alert!

Giving a false or ambiguous reason for termination may seem less painful, but it can make defending an unemployment insurance claim or a suit for abusive discharge or discrimination more difficult. For example, telling an employee that he or she *is not a good fit* means little and may lead the employee to believe that the termination is for an illegal reason, such as discrimination.

Exit interviews should be conducted in private and in a closed office. If the employee has been fired or is leaving under unfavorable circumstances, the departure should be accomplished with as little commotion and embarrassment as possible. Security guard escorts and other forms of intimidation should be avoided unless absolutely necessary. Failure to observe these rules risks a claim of defamation. (Defamation liability is discussed later in this chapter.)

Points of Discussion

The following matters, as applicable, should be accomplished during the exit interview:

- collect keys, security passcards, ID badges, and other property belonging to the employer;
- confirm the employee's current address and phone number;
- instruct the employee to remove all personal belongings;
- inform the employee as to when a final paycheck will be available and determine the employee's wishes as to whether the check should be mailed or held for pickup;
- inform the employee of *COBRA* or other continuation benefits under any medical expense insurance plan maintained by the employer;
- inform the employee of any conversion privileges available under any health, life, disability, or other insurance plans maintained by the employer;
- inform the employee of any rights or obligations regarding retirement plan participation and benefits;

- remind the employee of any continuing confidentiality, non-compete, and nonsolicitation obligations;
- remind the employee of the employer's policy on references;
- depending on the circumstances of the termination, inform the employee that he or she is prohibited from returning to the employer's premises and will be considered a trespasser if he or she returns; and,
- depending on the circumstances of the termination, obtain a signed release of liability from the employee in exchange for a severance package or other consideration.

QUICK TIP

A release will be unenforceable if the employee gets no additional benefit beyond what he or she is already entitled to. To validate a release, offer the employee a severance payment as consideration. (See Chapter 19 for more detailed information.)

Alert!

Depending how they are structured, severance payments could be deemed *nonqualified deferred compensation*, triggering unintended tax consequences for the departing employee and a claim of misrepresentation or breach of contract against the employer. (Nonqualified deferred compensation plans are discussed in Chapter 9.)

The employee should be asked to sign a written acknowledgment that all the above points have been discussed. If the employee refuses to sign, the points should be covered in a letter to the employee and a copy should be placed in the employee's personnel file.

Upon Completion of Exit Interview

Immediately after the exit interview, the interviewers should prepare a file memo summarizing the interview, including any reasons given by the employee for a voluntary quit. If not previously accomplished, the employee's access to the company's computer network should be terminated. This is also a good time to change other employees' passwords, since employees often know each other's passwords.

Alert!

Releases of claims under the *Age Discrimination in Employment Act* must comply with detailed statutory requirements to be effective. (See more specific information in Chapter 16.)

Promptly after the interview, the employer should (as applicable):

- Notify human resources and payroll of the employee's status change and request a final paycheck;
- Arrange for issuance of a final W-2 at year's end (or within 30 days if the employee requests it sooner);
- Arrange for issuance of a certificate of creditable coverage per the *Health Insurance Portability and Accountability Act*;
- Terminate any signature authority the employee has over employer bank accounts or other financial accounts;
- Notify insurers and retirement plan managers of the employee's status change;
- Notify affected employees of the termination (without discussing the reason);
- Notify others of the termination, such as security personnel, customers, vendors, financial institutions, etc., with whom the employee had contact (again, without discussing the reason); and,
- Notify persons receiving garnishment or withholding order payments from the employee's wages of the employee's status change.

Final Pay

A departing employee is entitled to be paid at the agreed rate for all work actually performed up to the time of termination. The employer cannot withhold wages on the ground that the employee failed to give two weeks' or some other specified notice before quitting. Nor can the employer dock the wages of a fired employee on the theory that the employee's work quality was unacceptable.

State law also specifies *when* a departing employee must be paid. In some states, the final paycheck need not be issued until the next regular payday. In others, the departing employee must be paid immediately or within a few days of termination, depending on the circumstances of termination.

The employer may deduct from the employee's paycheck any claims the employer has against the employee, so long as the employee has agreed to the deduction. Suppose, for example, that the employee borrowed money from the company, to be repaid out of future paychecks. Or suppose the employer advanced unearned leave on the understanding that, in the event of an early termination, the employee would make reimbursement out of the final wages. In these examples, an appropriate setoff against the employee's paycheck is permitted. However, the employer should not deduct the amount of a disputed claim or any other amount not agreed to by the employee, since doing so may violate wage-and-hour laws.

Termination for Cause

Sometimes an employer is willing to give up the right to terminate an employee at will and offer job security in the form of an employment contract. For example, the labor market may be tight and the employer may be having trouble attracting qualified candidates, a particular position may just be difficult to fill, or a highly desirable candidate may be of interest to the competition.

One way to promise job security is to offer employment for a specified period of time as long as the employee's performance remains satisfactory or to agree that employment can be terminated only for *cause* or *good cause*. (See Figure 4.1 for a definition of *cause*.) When an employer makes such an offer to a prospective employee, and the employee accepts the offer and begins work, the employer is bound by the arrangement. The employee is no longer at will, and he or she cannot be dismissed except as stated in the contract.

Alert!

An employer may unintentionally be limited to terminating only for cause as a result of statements inadvertently made in the employee handbook. (See Chapter 2 for tips on drafting employee handbooks to reduce this risk.)

What does *cause* or *good cause* mean in this context? The parties to a contractual arrangement are free to spell out in their contract exactly what they mean by the term. For example, if the employee needs a particular license in order to work (such as a plumbing license), suspension or revocation of the license might be listed as a cause for termination. Convictions for certain types of crimes, insubordination, drunkenness, and physical assaults on customers or fellow employees might also be on the list. There may also be explicit dos and don'ts set out in a employee handbook or job description.

The employment relationship itself implies certain duties on the part of the employee, including a duty to show up for work in reasonably fit condition, a duty to have and exercise reasonable skill in performing the job, a duty of loyalty and honesty, and a duty to refrain from insubordinate and threatening behavior. A substantial breach of any of these implied duties is cause for termination.

Figure 4.1: **DEFINITION OF CAUSE**

In the absence of a definition or clear indication of the meaning of cause in a contract of employment or an employee handbook, the courts have defined the term along the following lines:

fair and honest reasons, regulated by good faith on the part of the employer, that are not trivial, arbitrary, or capricious, unrelated to business needs, goals, or pretextual. A reasoned conclusion, in short, supported by substantial evidence gathered through an adequate investigation that includes notice of the claimed misconduct and a chance for the employee to respond.

In a recent Wyoming case, the court adopted a definition similar to the above. The court went on to say that, in determining whether an employer had cause for termination, the question is not, "Did the employee in fact commit the act leading to termination?" Rather, the question is, "Was the factual basis on which the employer concluded a dischargeable act had been committed reached honestly, after an appropriate investigation and for reasons that are not arbitrary or pretextual?" In other words, the courts are not going to second-guess an employer's *business judgment* so long as the decision to terminate is reached honestly and fairly.

Constructive Discharge

When the law looks behind the form of a transaction to discover its true substance, it uses the strange term constructive. In a *constructive discharge*, it may appear on the surface that the employee quit, but because of the underlying circumstances the law concludes that he or she was fired.

Take, for example, the employee who is told that unless he quits he will be fired. It is easy to see why the law would view that as an involuntary termination. An employer's request for a resignation will be treated the same way.

But the concept of constructive discharge goes beyond the *quit-or-be-fired scenario*. When an employer permits working conditions to become so intolerable that a reasonable person would quit, an employee who actually does quit rather than suffer the conditions will be deemed to have been fired. Suppose, for example, that serious safety hazards exist at the workplace that the employer knows about but refuses to fix. Or suppose that a minority employee is subjected to regular and pervasive racial harassment by supervisors and fellow employees.

Alert!

Employer liability for harassment is not dependent on the employee actually quitting. Merely subjecting an employee to severe and pervasive harassment can constitute illegal discrimination. (Review Chapter 15 for more information.)

Under certain circumstances, a change in title or duties could amount to a constructive discharge. For example, the president of a company, whose contract specifies that he is the chief executive officer, might be able to claim constructive discharge upon being required to report to the newly appointed chairmen, even though the president's salary remains the same.

The point of a constructive discharge is that an employer will be held liable to precisely the same extent as if it had directly fired the employee. If there was a contract of employment and insufficient grounds for termination, the employer will be answerable for breach of that contract. And in the racial harassment example given above, the employer can be charged with illegal racial discrimination.

Retaliation

Most federal and state laws that grant statutory rights to employees go on to prohibit employers from *retaliating* against their employees for exercising those rights. Examples include:

- federal and state antidiscrimination laws;
- federal and state wage-and-hour laws;
- federal labor laws;
- federal and state workplace safety laws;
- state workers' compensation laws;
- whistleblower laws, such as the *False Claims Act*, that encourage employees to report government fraud; and,
- federal corporate ethics laws, such as the *Sarbanes-Oxley Act* (discussed later in this chapter).

These statutes effectively modify the at-will employment relationship by prohibiting an employer from terminating or otherwise retaliating against an employee, despite the employee's at-will status.

Ironically, retaliation claims sometimes become the tail wagging the dog. In the discrimination arena, for example, an employee may have a weak or improbable claim of race or sex discrimination. When the employee complains, however, the employer responds by firing the employee. In effect, the employer has converted a weak discrimination claim, which the employee would probably have lost, into a strong claim of retaliation that the employee will likely win.

While the acts constituting retaliation must be sufficiently adverse to dissuade a reasonable employee from pursuing a claim of discrimination, they need not be employment-related. For example, the acts need not involve a firing, demotion, undesirable transfer, or similar job-related punishment, so long as they would likely discourage the ordinary employee from exercising his legal rights.

CASE STUDY: RETALIATION

In a recent federal appeals court case, a father and son were both employed by the same organization. When the father complained of discrimination, the employer retaliated by firing the son. The court said that form of retaliation is also illegal under federal antidiscrimination laws. As the court pointed out, to retaliate against a man by hurting a member of his family is an ancient method of revenge and is not unknown in the field of labor relations.

Whistleblower Regulations

Persons who go public with violations of law by their employers, particularly violations involving fraud against the government, are known as *whistleblowers*. In the absence of specific statutory protections, whistleblowers may find themselves out of a job with little right to complain. A number of jurisdictions have decided, however, that whistleblowers should receive some limited protection.

A pre-Civil War federal statute known as the *False Claims Act* permits anyone who learns about fraud against the U.S. Government to file a lawsuit in the name of the Government. For example, suppose a computer company that has a contract to provide programming services to the Treasury Department overbills for time spent in writing a software program. If a disgruntled company employee learns of the overbilling and files suit against the company under the False Claims Act, a provision of the Act prohibits the company from firing or otherwise retaliating against the employee. The Act provides the employee with an incentive to sue by allowing him or her to collect a percentage of any recovery from the suit.

Some states have enacted their own whistleblower laws protecting employees who disclose government fraud at the state level.

Abusive Discharge

An important variation on the retaliation theme can arise when there is no statute expressly prohibiting retaliation, but when some significant, well-established *public policy* is involved. When a firing tends to undercut such a policy, courts may characterize the discharge as *abusive* or *wrongful* and allow the employee to recover damages against the employer despite an at-will employment relationship.

To illustrate, suppose an employee is instructed to make a delivery using the company truck. The employee points out that the truck's safety inspection sticker has expired and that it is illegal to drive a truck with an expired sticker. In addition, brake repairs are needed for the truck to pass re-inspection. The employer's supervisor insists that the delivery be made anyway, and when the employee refuses, he is fired. Many states would view that as an abusive discharge, because it undercuts an important state highway safety policy.

There are no clear answers as to what public policies will override the at-will employment doctrine. The doctrine of abusive discharge has been developed (and is still developing) on a case-by-case basis as suits come before the courts. In addition, judges' views of what is and what is not important and well-established public policy differ from state to state and over time.

One consistent theme has emerged from the cases—firing an employee for *refusing to commit an illegal act* or for *fulfilling a duty required by law* is abusive and will provide grounds for a wrongful discharge suit. Another theme involves an employee's exercise of rights granted or protected by law. For example, employees covered by workers' compensation statutes have a right to file claims for work-related injuries and cannot be fired (or otherwise disciplined) for doing so. Refusal to take a lie detector test is also not grounds for firing, since in most circumstances administering the test would be illegal.

Things become less clear when the employee is engaged in conduct that is permitted by law or seen as socially desirable but is not necessarily protected by law.

CASE STUDY: RIGHT TO CONSULT WITH COUNSEL

Suppose a dispute arises between employer and employee, and when the employee threatens to contact a lawyer for advice regarding the dispute, he or she is fired. Is the right to consult with counsel so fundamental that termination for exercising that right violates public policy?

A 1994 federal case applying Iowa law concluded that termination under those circumstances did violate Iowa public policy. That same year an Ohio court reached the same conclusion. But a decision by Maryland's highest court in 2003 ruled otherwise, saying that while access to counsel may be favored, there is no violation of any clear mandate of Maryland public policy in firing an employee for involving counsel in an employment dispute.

Knowing how to proceed in the face of uncertain and changing rules can be difficult for an employer. At the least, a prudent employer should hesitate to fire an at-will employee for engaging in an activity that is protected or encouraged by the law or that is usually considered of value to society, or for refusing to engage in illegal conduct or conduct that is usually considered immoral or otherwise improper.

Off-Duty Conduct

In a number of states it is illegal to fire or discipline an employee for his or her lawful, off-duty conduct. For example, in the District of Columbia, an employer cannot discriminate against an employee who smokes (although the employer has no obligation to allow smoke breaks during working hours).

Defamation Liability

It may be surprising to learn that one of the more significant liabilities an employer faces is defamation. In fact many, if not most, abusive discharge cases include claims of defamation.

To defame someone is to make a false statement of fact that injures the person's reputation. A *written* defamatory statement is *libelous*; a *spoken* defamatory statement is known as *slander*. In order for a person to have a good claim of defamation, the false statement must be *published*—communicated either in writing or orally to some third person. Generally, to be defamatory the statement must be one of fact, such as, "John stole office supplies for his personal use." Mere statements of opinion, such as, "John does not use office supplies efficiently," are not usually defamatory.

Conduct can also amount to defamation. Suppose that after being informed of a termination, an employee is escorted off the employer's premises by senior management. Even though the employee may feel embarrassed, that conduct alone does not constitute a defamatory publication. But suppose that instead of being escorted by management, the company uses its security guards who, in the process, search the employee and question him or her at length about suspected stealing, all in front of his or her coworkers. That conduct could give rise to a good defamation claim.

Privileged Statements

A statement that might otherwise be defamatory can sometimes be *privileged* or protected by law from a claim of defamation. Privileges come in two types: *absolute* and *conditional* (sometimes called *qualified*). When a member of Congress makes a speech on the House floor, for example, the statements are absolutely privileged, meaning that he or she can never be sued for defamation, no matter how offensive the words might be. In contrast, employers who give references for former employees, who issue warnings and termination letters, and who offer candid employee evaluations, are entitled only to a *conditional* privilege.

The employer's privilege is *conditional* because it can be lost if the communication is:

- made without any *legitimate business purpose*;
- made with knowledge of its *falsity* or with a *reckless disregard* for its truth or falsity;
- made with *malice*, *spite*, or *ill will* toward the employee; or,
- disseminated *beyond* those who have a business need to know.

To illustrate, suppose an employee is terminated, finds a new position, and *after* starting work at the new job the old employer contacts the new employer and, without being asked, relates derogatory information about the new employee. This *blacklisting* of a former employee will be compelling evidence of malice and will also void any privilege defense.

Unfortunately for the employer, issues of legitimate business purpose, malice, spite, ill will, and excessive dissemination usually turn on the specific facts of each case. As a result, even weak defamation claims may result in protracted and expensive court proceedings.

Job References

Job references present a special problem. On the one hand, if the employer provides highly detailed information about a former employee, including factual statements and opinions that go beyond what the prospective new employer specifically asked, the employer runs a substantial risk of a defamation or invasion of privacy claim. On the other hand, if the employer undertakes to provide a reference but then provides a skimpy or inaccurate one, or leaves out favorable information, a defamation claim may loom as well.

Alert!

Giving a bad reference for a former employee in retaliation for the employee's filing a discrimination claim is itself illegal discrimination under Title VII. (See Chapter 14 for more details.)

Rather than run these risks, some employers have adopted a *neutral reference* or *no comment* policy under which they do no more than confirm dates of employment and perhaps title and salary. While such a policy may be the safest for individual employers, it has a social cost in restricting the amount of pertinent information available to prospective employers. Less qualified workers may get jobs that more qualified applicants would have received had full information been available. Worse, persons who would otherwise be rejected because of the danger they pose to the public may not be weeded out in the application process.

A middle ground is to adopt a *no comment* policy but to make an exception where the employee or former employee approves in writing the content of a proposed reference letter, authorizes its issuance, and releases the employer from liability for issuing the letter.

Whatever policy you adopt, be sure it is communicated to all employees and that it is faithfully followed. The policy should also identify those persons within the company who are authorized to give out reference information and it should prohibit everyone else within the company from doing so.

Some states offer a measure of protection for employers who provide information to prospective employers about an employee's or former employee's job performance or reason for termination. In these states, mere negligence in providing an erroneous reference is not sufficient to support a defamation suit. Instead, the unhappy employee must show that the employer acted maliciously or intentionally in disclosing false reference information.

Compelled Self-Publication

A bizarre twist on the law of defamation deserves mention. Suppose an employer terminates an unsatisfactory employee and tells the employee the reason for the termination. Further, suppose the employer tells no one else about the reason and, consistent with the employer's *no comment* policy, confirms only the dates of employment, job title, and salary to a prospective new employer. No defamation claim could possibly be brought, right?

Unfortunately, no. Some courts have adopted a doctrine known as *compelled self-publication*, which holds that since the employee must honestly tell a prospective employer about the reason given for the termination, the employee has no choice but to defame him- or herself and may therefore sue the former employer. Fortunately, the doctrine of compelled self-publication is not widely recognized.

Giving an inaccurate reference may expose an employer to third-party liability. For example, if a former employer is asked for a reference by a subsequent employer but fails to mention the employee's dangerous propensities, and the employee later causes injury or damage, the former employer may be liable.

Intentional Infliction of Emotional Distress

Another ground on which an employer can be held liable is intentional infliction of emotional distress. In general, if an employer (or anyone else, for that matter) acts in an extreme or outrageous way and either intentionally or recklessly causes someone else to suffer severe emotional distress, the victim of such conduct can recover damages in court. Claims for intentional infliction of emotional distress are sometimes coupled with charges of harassment based on sex, race, etc.

CASE STUDY: EMPLOYER POTENTIALLY LIABLE FOR INTENTIONAL INFLICTION

In a strange case involving Georgetown University in Washington, D.C., an employee of the University claimed that her supervisor placed two electrically-operated noisemakers outside the supervisor's door aimed at the employee's workplace. According to the employee, the devices emitted an unbearably loud, static-sounding, piercing, humming, and droning noise every hour of the workday for some nine months, causing the employee extreme emotional distress. Despite her complaints, the University did nothing. The District of Columbia Court of Appeals ruled that the employee stated a good claim for intentional infliction of emotional distress and that the case should not have been dismissed by the trial judge.

Corporate Ethics and the Sarbanes-Oxley Act

The rash of corporate scandals by publicly-traded companies prompted Congress to pass tough new legislation. Although the *Sarbanes-Oxley Act of 2002* focuses primarily on accounting oversight and corporate governance, the Act contains a number of provisions that directly affect high-level, and in some cases lower-echelon, employees of publicly-traded companies. Highlights of the Act include the following.

- *Certification of financial statements.* The Act requires the Securities and Exchange Commission (SEC) to issue rules requiring a company's principal executive and financial officers to certify the company's financial statements as true and complete. In the event of any failure to comply with reporting requirements such that financial statements have to be restated, those same officers must forfeit their bonuses and incentive compensation for a twelve-month period.
- *Blackouts.* Whenever a company imposes a blackout by prohibiting pension plan participants from trading in company stock, company directors and executive officers are also prohibited from selling any stock they may have acquired through their employment with the company. Plan administrators must give advance notice of the blackout to plan participants and beneficiaries, including a statement of the reason for the blackout.
- *Loans.* Subject to certain narrow exceptions, companies are now prohibited from making personal loans or extending credit to their directors and executive officers.
- *Code of Ethics.* Companies must report to the SEC whether they have adopted a code of ethics for their senior financial officers and, if they have not, why they have not. Figure 4.2 suggests some prohibited activities that could be addressed in your company's Code of Ethics.
- *Document retention.* The Act requires the SEC to adopt rules governing companies' retention of documents relating to financial audits and reviews. Knowing and willful violation of the rules is a criminal offense.
- *Fitness to serve.* The SEC is authorized by the Act to prohibit persons who are deemed unfit from serving as officers or directors if they have violated rules governing deception or fraud.

• *Whistleblowing.* It is also now criminal for a company to retaliate against an employee who assists in any investigation by
federal regulators, Congress, or company supervisors, or who
provides information to federal law enforcement officers. Any
person who suffers unlawful retaliation may also initiate a civil
proceeding for reinstatement, back pay, and other damages.

For more on Sarbanes-Oxley, go to: http://sec.gov/spotlight/
sarbanes-oxley.htm.

Figure 4.2: **CODE OF ETHICS**

Even if your company is not publicly traded and subject to the
Sarbanes-Oxley Act, it is a good idea to have a corporate code
of ethics for employees covering the president on down. Prohibited activities, many of which are illegal as well as unethical,
might include:

• hiring relatives;

• carrying phantom employees;

• borrowing money from subordinate employees, vendors, or
customers;

• accepting bribes, kickbacks, expensive gifts, or lavish entertainment from vendors or customers;

• accepting discounts on purchases from vendors or customers that
are not offered to the general public;

• falsifying business records, tax returns, or reports to government
agencies;

• carrying off-the-books accounts or funds;

• performing paid services for customers on a personal basis outside
normal company channels;

- blacklisting employees, customers, or vendors;

- fixing bids or sharing pricing or cost information with competitors; and,

- requiring customers to buy unwanted products in order to get products they do want.

Employee Due Process

We so often hear terms like *due process, freedom of speech, freedom of the press, freedom of information, etc.,* that we may be tempted to think these rights apply in all our relationships. Not so. The constitutional right of due process limits the ways in which the *government* can deal with us. Our free speech right only prevents government censorship. Federal and state *Freedom of Information Acts* and sunshine laws only guarantee us access to certain government information and proceedings.

Except for government employees, the employment relationship generally does not include employee due process rights. An at-will employee can be arbitrarily disciplined or fired without any right to a hearing, without any opportunity to explain or justify the supposedly offending conduct, and without any opportunity to confront the person who supposedly reported the offending conduct. Of course, arbitrariness is seldom the best way to manage employees.

There are a few limited exceptions to an employer's ability to act out of sheer arbitrariness. An employer cannot, for example, discriminate on the basis of race, ethnicity, gender, or other irrelevant characteristics; an employer cannot discharge an employee in violation of public policy; and an employer cannot act contrary to its contractual obligations.

When an employee does have an employment contract, or when an employee is a member of a union that has a collective bargaining agreement, an employer's right to discipline or discharge the employee is typically limited by the contract to *for cause* terminations. The contract may also provide a grievance procedure, leading to binding arbitration, should an employee dispute the employer's personnel action. Even absent an employment contract, statements in an employee handbook dealing with disciplinary procedures may rise to the level of a contractual obligation.

The Fifth Amendment

The Fifth Amendment to the U.S. Constitution protects a variety of personal rights. Among them is that no person *shall be compelled in any criminal case to be a witness against himself.* In other words, no one may be compelled, under threat of being held in contempt of court, to answer questions under oath when it is reasonable to assume that the answers could help convict the person of a crime. Although the Amendment is limited to compelled testimony in criminal cases, the Supreme Court has held that the protection applies in a range of situations in which testimony is coerced, including civil cases, grand jury proceedings, depositions, and appearances before Congress.

The privilege is limited to testimony and does not extend to compelled production of physical evidence such as handwriting exemplars, blood specimens, and so on. Nor does the privilege protect documents from compelled disclosure, unless by the very act of producing the document the person is admitting the existence or possession of the document and thereby incriminating himself.

Corporations and other organizations have no Fifth Amendment privilege. So if a corporation is served with a subpoena for records, it has no basis, at least under the Fifth Amendment, to resist the subpoena and refuse to produce the records. While corporate officials can claim the privilege in order to protect *themselves* from incrimination, they cannot claim privilege to protect their corporate employer.

If employees are invited or required to testify, an employer *cannot* in any way encourage employees to claim the privilege, threaten them should they fail to do so, or promise rewards for doing so. This type of conduct could amount to an *obstruction of justice*—a serious crime that will likely get the prosecutor's attention. Employers also need to avoid indirect encouragement. This can arise, for example, when the employer urges employees to be represented by the same attorney who represents the company, and the attorney, in turn, advises the employees to claim the privilege.

Employers are generally free, however, to require their employees to testify, and to discipline them if they refuse and claim the privilege. Remember that the Fifth Amendment is designed to protect against government coercion, not private coercion.

Alert!

In jurisdictions where the abusive discharge exception to the at-will employment doctrine is unsettled, employers should be cautious in firing an employee for claiming the privilege. It is conceivable that a court will find a public policy protecting an employee's Fifth Amendment rights.

Downsizing and Mass Layoffs

Terminating an employee is among the most difficult tasks facing any employer. When a decision is made to lay off a significant portion of the work force, the difficulty and the legal risks are multiplied. Particularly in tough economic times, laid-off employees will have a more difficult time finding new employment, so their incentive to sue is even greater.

QUICK TIP

When an exit incentive program is made available to a class or group of employees, coupled with a severance agreement and release, the *Older Workers Benefit Protection Act* requirements may be triggered. (Review Chapter 16 for more details.)

While the legal risks associated with a mass layoff can never be entirely eliminated, employers can take steps to reduce their exposure by:

- Considering other cost-saving alternatives to a layoff, such as offering wage rate or hour reductions to employees;
- Developing and documenting the business reasons for the layoff;
- Focusing on *positions*, not *people*, to be eliminated;

- hiring an outside expert to help decide what positions to eliminate;
- making sure that layoff decisions are not influenced in any way by discriminatory factors, such as race, gender, or age;
- using an outside expert to review the unintended impact along race, gender, and age lines once tentative layoff decisions have been made;
- offering severance packages, early retirement packages, or other exit incentives in exchange for a release of all claims; and,
- following customary exit interviews and procedures for each individual being laid off.

Worker Adjustment and Retraining Notification

The federal *Worker Adjustment and Retraining Notification (WARN) Act* requires an employer with one hundred or more employees to provide notification sixty days in advance of a planned plant closing or mass layoff. In determining whether an employer meets the one-hundred-employee floor only full-time employees are counted, unless part-time employees in the aggregate work at least four thousand hours per week, in which case part-time employees are counted as well.

A *mass layoff* for *WARN* purposes is a layoff of at least fifty employees at a single site, which amounts to at least 33% of the employees at that site. So if an employer has one thousand employees at a given site and lays off one hundred, that would not be a mass layoff.

The sixty-day notice must be given to the affected employees, to the state dislocated worker unit, and to the chief elected official of the local government where the plant closing or layoff is to occur.

The *WARN Act* recognizes that in some circumstances it may not be possible for employers to give the requisite notice. The Act's so-called *unforeseeable business circumstances exception* is applicable when a similarly situated employer exercising commercially reasonable business judgment would not have foreseen the closing. So long as an employer is exercising reasonable business judgment, the employer will not be held liable under WARN for failing to predict economic conditions that may affect demand for the organization's products or services.

Chapter 5

Wage-and-Hour Requirements

Wage-and-hour requirements are a mix of federal and state law. The principal federal law is the *Fair Labor Standards Act* (FLSA) enacted in 1938.

In general, and subject to the exemptions discussed later in this chapter, the FLSA applies to all employees of an enterprise engaged in interstate commerce or in the production of goods for interstate commerce if the enterprise is of the following type and/or meets the following minimum annual sales volume:

- Retail and service establishments—$250,000;
- Construction companies—no minimum;
- Laundries, cleaners, and tailors—no minimum;
- Hospitals, nursing homes, schools, and other institutions—no minimum; and,
- All other enterprises—$250,000.

Minimum Wages

The FLSA requires every covered employer to pay each employee the minimum wage—$6.55 as of July 2008 and $7.25 beginning July 2009. The minimum rate for newly hired employees who are under twenty years of age is currently $4.25 per hour, but that rate is applicable only during the first ninety days of employment. Although an employee need not receive the minimum wage for every hour worked, the employee must average the minimum wage over a forty-hour week.

There is a long list of occupations that are exempt from minimum wage requirements. The exceptions are narrowly drawn, however, and in some cases apply only in very limited circumstances. Employers should assume that they owe the minimum wage to each of their employees unless they have obtained competent advice to the contrary.

Volunteer Employees

Among the potential pitfalls for an employer is the *volunteer employee*. Although the FLSA and Department of Labor regulations permit the use of volunteers by government agencies and they permit student workers to participate in college-sponsored programs, they generally do not allow use of volunteers in private business.

EXAMPLE: Suppose an architectural firm receives an inquiry for summer employment from a third-year architecture major at the state university. She says that job opportunities are extremely tight and, in order to gain experience, she is willing to work for free. Since the proposed arrangement would likely be of direct benefit to the employer and the student would, most likely, be performing for free work that the employer normally has to pay for, the FLSA's minimum wage requirement probably applies.

Tips

Special rules apply to employees who receive tips. Tips may be counted against the minimum wage, but only up to $3.72 per hour at this writing. In other words, the employer must pay at least $2.13 in cash wages and, if actual tips combined with cash wages do not equal the minimum wage, the employer must make up the difference. (Some state minimum wage laws do not count tips or count tips only up to a lesser dollar amount.)

Note:

Tips are subject to withholding and other tax requirements just like regular compensation. (See Chapter 7 for more specific information regarding tax requirements.)

State and Local Laws

The states are free to adopt higher minimum wages and some have done so. Some state and local governments have decided to get involved in minimum wage issues by adopting so-called living wage laws that require government contractors doing business with those jurisdictions to pay their employees a minimum wage substantially in excess of the federal and state floor. Instead of living wages, some states have laws that require government contractors to pay their employees at *prevailing wage* rates.

Pay differentials based on gender or on any other prohibited consideration such as race, national origin, etc., are illegal under antidiscrimination laws. (See Chapter 15 for more information.)

Penalties

In general, the FLSA and state wage-and-hour requirements cannot be waived by the employee, and any private agreement that purports to modify those requirements is void. Penalties for violating the FLSA and state laws are substantial, including liquidated damages, attorneys' fees payable to the employee involved, criminal fines, and even prison sentences.

Overtime

Overtime requirements give rise to issues of how much to pay and when to pay. The basic rules for nonexempt, private sector employees are:

- The maximum number of hours an employee may work in any workweek without receiving overtime compensation is forty;
- Overtime compensation is 1½ times the employee's regular rate of pay per hour; and,
- Overtime compensation must be paid on the regular payday for the period in which the overtime workweek ends (or as soon thereafter as practical if the amount due cannot be computed by that payday).

Calculating Work Time

The workweek is a period of 168 hours (7 x 24). It is up to the employer to establish when the workweek begins and ends, and it need not coincide with pay periods. Where the two do not coincide (for example, where the employer's pay period is semimonthly—twenty-four paydays per year), each paycheck includes regular pay for thirteen, fourteen, fifteen, or sixteen days and includes overtime pay for one, two, or three workweeks, depending on how many workweeks end during the particular pay period involved. The workweek cannot be repeatedly changed in order to manipulate overtime obligations.

Overtime must be paid at 1½ times the employee's *regular hourly rate*. In general, the regular hourly rate is the hourly rate actually paid the employee for the normal, non-overtime workweek for which the employee is employed. Employers are not required to compensate their employees on an hourly rate basis. They may, for example, compensate on piece-rate, salary, commission, or other basis, but in such cases a regular hourly rate must be computed to determine what the overtime rate should be. In computing the regular hourly rate, all remuneration for employment must be included, such as commissions and production bonuses. (Check Figure 5.1 for possible pitfalls in calculating work time.) However, the FLSA specifies that the following items are *not* included in computing the regular hourly rate:

- Gifts, so long as they are not measured by or dependent on hours worked, production, or efficiency;
- Payments made while the employee is on leave;
- Expense reimbursements;
- Bonuses paid in the sole discretion of the employer and not pursuant to any prior contract or promise;
- Profit-sharing payments;
- Employer contributions to employee benefit plans; and,
- Premium payments for work on weekends and holidays, so long as the premium rate is at least 1½ times the rate for regular work.

EXAMPLE: Suppose a company's normal workday is 9:00 a.m. to 5:30 p.m. with an hour for lunch. That equates to 37½ hours of work per workweek. If an hourly employee works 39½ hours in a particular week, at what rate should he be paid for the extra two hours? The company is free to adopt a policy of paying overtime at 1½ times the normal rate after 37½ hours, but it is not required to do so. The company is in full compliance with wage-and-hour laws if it pays only straight time for the two hours, since overtime obligations only kick in after forty hours.

Employers should not overlook the effect of holidays, vacations, and other time off on their overtime obligations. In order for time to be counted toward overtime, the employee must actually be at work. Even though an employee may be on paid leave, if he or she is not actually working, the time is not included in computing overtime. For that reason, overtime is usually not a problem during periods such as the Christmas week, when many employees take time off.

Figure 5.1: **PITFALLS**

Wage-and-hour violations can occur unintentionally. Employers should be alert to the following pitfalls.

- *Would you mind running an errand for me on your lunch hour? I'd appreciate it if you'd take the late mail to the post office when you leave today. Could you drop off this package on your way in tomorrow?* If these favors take more than a few minutes of an employee's time, they need to be counted for overtime computation purposes.

- *Company policy prohibits overtime unless explicitly approved by your supervisor.* If the time actually required to complete the assigned job is more than the standard workday, an official policy limiting overtime will not excuse the employer from paying time and a half.

- *I need you to carry a beeper. In your job, you're on call 24 hours a day. You can't drink on your off hours, since I may need you in on short notice. I want you at home where I can reach you.* Restrictions on off hours can trigger overtime obligations if they substantially limit the employee's freedom. The *you're on call 24 hours a day* dictate, without more, is probably not a substantial restriction, nor is the alcohol prohibition. But the beeper requirement could be, if the beeper's range is very limited. The stay at home requirement definitely would need to be counted as work time.

- *For next week's project I'm going to consider you an executive.* Even if the employee does perform executive-level duties, a week is not sufficient to convert him or her from nonexempt to exempt. Exempt functions must account for more than 50% of the employee's total job requirements, and they must be part of his or her regular duties, not just part of a temporary assignment.

- *The company encourages you to get involved in civic and charitable activities in the community.* Truly volunteer activities, performed after working hours, are not compensable. However, activities performed during normal working hours with the approval of the employer are compensable and need to be counted for overtime purposes. Even after-hours activities can be compensable if they are done at the employer's specific request or direction, or if the employer *coerces or pressures* the employee into volunteering.

Portal-to-Portal Act

Another area of risk involves activities immediately prior to and immediately after regular work periods. The *Portal-to-Portal Act* (an amendment to the FLSA) makes clear that an employee's *commuting time*—time walking, riding, or traveling to and from the actual place of performance of the principal activity or activities that such employee is employed to perform—is not compensable for minimum wage or overtime purposes. Similarly, activities that are *preliminary* or *postliminary* to principal activities are not compensable.

On the other hand, an activity is compensable if it is primarily for the employer's benefit; if there is an express written or oral contract that the employer will pay for the activity; or if it is compensable by custom or practice. Examples of activities which may or may not be compensable, depending on the circumstances, include: changing into or out of a work uniform; punching a time clock; waiting in line to punch a time clock; settling up a cash register drawer at the end of a shift; cleaning or repairing tools; showering after working with hazardous or toxic materials; and inspecting a motor vehicle prior to driving a delivery route.

Alternatives to Overtime

Overtime obligations significantly increase an employer's payroll costs. In addition to time and a half, other costs such as payroll taxes, workers' compensation premiums, and retirement plan contributions may increase as well. So it is usually in an employer's interest to avoid overtime when possible. The following alternatives to overtime may be available, depending on the employer's specific circumstances.

Comp Time

If an employee who normally works an eight-hour day happens to work nine or ten hours on a particular day, he or she may be offered the opportunity (or may even be required) to work fewer hours on another day, so long as it is in the same *168-hour workweek*. However, with few exceptions overtime may not be taken as *compensatory time (comp time)* in another workweek. If overtime is not offset by time off within the same 168-hour workweek, wages at the overtime rate must be paid. This rule applies regardless of the pay periods established by the employer. For example, even though the pay period may be every two weeks, forty-five hours of work in week #1 cannot be offset by thirty-five hours in week #2.

The rule also applies even if the employee is perfectly willing to waive overtime pay and take comp time the following week. Suppose, for example, that an employee wants to take an extended vacation later in the year and offers to build up comp time so that regular paychecks will continue during the vacation. The request cannot be honored, since neither the employer nor the employee can agree to an arrangement different from the overtime requirements of federal and state law.

On a number of occasions, Congress has considered amending the FLSA to permit comp time in the private sector. (Comp time has long been allowed for federal government employees.) Organized labor has generally been opposed to any such change, however, and the proposed amendments have all died without passage.

Time Off Plan

There is one exception to the rule that comp time in workweek #2 does not satisfy the employer's obligation for overtime in workweek

#1—the so-called *time off plan*. Suppose an employer pays every other week. If a nonexempt salaried employee works overtime in workweek #1, the employer can give the employee time off in workweek #2 at the rate of one and one-half hours for each hour of overtime worked in workweek #1. By paying the employee the regular salary for both workweeks, the employer fully satisfies the overtime obligation.

EXAMPLE: Suppose an employee normally works forty hours per workweek and is paid a biweekly salary of $800 ($400 per week). If the employee works fifty hours in workweek #1, the employee can take (or be ordered to take) 15 hours off in workweek #2, since 1.5 times the 10 hours of overtime worked in workweek #1 equals 15. In this example, the employee has worked a total of seventy-five hours over both workweeks, but will be paid his or her regular biweekly salary of $800. In effect, the employer satisfies its overtime obligation by paying *comp time* at a premium rate instead of paying a cash premium.

A time off plan only works if the employer's pay period is longer than one workweek and if overtime occurs in the first workweek. In the above example, if the overtime occurred in workweek #2, the employer would have to pay the overtime premium in cash.

Belo Plan

Belo plans (from a Supreme Court case of that name) are available only for employees whose duties necessitate irregular hours because of the nature of the work. Examples might include on-call service workers and emergency repair crews. Under a Belo plan, the employer enters into a contract with the employee that guarantees the employee a fixed salary regardless of the number of hours worked. The contract specifies a regular hourly rate for the normal forty hours and one and one-half times that regular hourly rate for guaranteed overtime (so long as total time covered by the plan is no more than sixty hours per workweek).

EXAMPLE: A power company employee's job is to restore electrical service following outages caused by storms, traffic accidents, construction mishaps, and so on. The amount of work needed is unpredictable, typically varying anywhere from thirty to fifty hours per workweek, so the employer enters into a contract guaranteeing the employee a fixed weekly salary of $550, representing forty hours at $10 per hour and ten hours at a $15 overtime rate. In other words, the contract guarantees the employee ten hours of overtime each week. Then, regardless of the number of hours worked (up to the agreed total of fifty hours in this example), the employer has no additional overtime obligation. Of course, if the employee works fewer than fifty hours, he or she still gets paid $550.

In the above example, any time worked in excess of fifty hours would have to be compensated at $15 per hour. While the parties could have agreed to guarantee more than ten hours of overtime, their agreement could not go beyond twenty hours of overtime under a Belo plan.

Half-time Plan

Belo plans are only available when the inherent nature of the work necessitates irregular hours and when the number of hours per workweek varies both above and below a normal forty-hour workweek. In contrast, under a *half-time plan* (sometimes called a *fluctuating workweek plan*), the fluctuation can be subject to the employer's control and hours worked can routinely exceed forty.

Under a fluctuating workweek plan, the employer and employee agree that the employee will be paid a fixed salary covering all time worked in the workweek. This should be a written agreement by which the employee clearly acknowledges that the fixed salary covers the straight-time component of all hours worked even if they exceed forty. For any given workweek, the employee's regular hourly rate is computed by dividing the fixed salary by the number of hours actually worked in that workweek. If the number of hours worked exceeds forty, the employer pays the employee one-half (not one and one-half) of his or her regular hourly rate for the hours exceeding forty. The reason the employer pays only half-time for the overtime is that the straight-time component is already covered by the fixed salary.

EXAMPLE: Employer and employee agree to a fixed salary of $400 per week. If, in a particular workweek, the employee works 50 hours, then the employee's regular hourly rate for that workweek is $8 ($400 ÷ 50). Therefore, the employer's overtime obligation for that workweek is $40 (½ of $8 x 10 hours) and total compensation due the employee for that workweek is $440. Now suppose the employee works 55 hours. His regular hourly rate would then be approximately $7.27 ($400 ÷ 55) and the total compensation due would be $454.53 ($400 + ½ of $7.27 x 15 hours).

As this example shows, as overtime increases, both the regular hourly rate and the overtime rate decrease. If the employee worked 80 hours in a particular workweek, his or her regular hourly rate would then drop to $5.00 per hour, which is below the minimum wage and which would therefore violate federal law. The fixed salary under a half-time plan must be high enough to guarantee at least the minimum wage.

Exemptions from Overtime Requirements

Overtime requirements are subject to a long list of exemptions. An employee (or position) covered by one of these exemptions is referred to as *exempt* and is not entitled to time and a half for overtime. In contrast, an employee (or position) not covered by any exemption is referred to as *nonexempt* and is entitled to overtime.

White Collar Exemptions

Probably the most significant exemptions for most businesses are for salaried employees employed in a bona fide *executive, administrative,* or *professional capacity.* These exemptions, together with the exemption for *outside salespersons,* are sometimes called the *white collar* exemptions. For an employee to qualify as exempt in one of these categories, his or her position must meet one of the *duties tests* specified in Department of Labor regulations and described below. In most cases, a *salary test* applies as well, requiring that the employee be paid on a salary basis of at least $455 per week.

An *executive* is an employee whose primary duty is management of the enterprise in which he or she is employed (or of a customarily

recognized department or subdivision thereof). An executive customarily and regularly directs the work of two or more other employees and has the authority to hire or fire other employees (or
whose suggestions and recommendations as to the hiring, firing,
advancement, promotion, or any other change of status of other
employees are given particular weight).

A *business owner* falls under the executive exemption if he or
she owns at least a 20% bona fide equity interest in the enterprise
in which he or she is employed and qualifies as an executive for
overtime exemption purposes, even if he or she does not satisfy the
salary test of $455 per week.

An *administrator* is an employee whose primary duty is the
performance of office or nonmanual work directly related to
the management or general business operations of the employer or
the employer's customers. His or her primary duty must include the
exercise of discretion and independent judgment with respect to
matters of significance.

QUICK TIP

Even though an employee may be exempt from minimum wage and
overtime requirements, the employer must still comply with the FLSA's
equal pay provisions, which prohibit gender-based wage discrimination. (See Chapter 14 for more information.)

A *professional* is an employee whose primary duty is the performance of work either:

• Requiring knowledge of an advanced type in a field of science
  or learning customarily acquired by a prolonged course of specialized intellectual instruction, such as an accountant, nurse,
  medical technologist, dental hygienist, or chef (a *learned professional*); or,
• Requiring invention, imagination, originality, or talent in a
  recognized field of artistic or creative endeavor (a *creative
  professional*).

Employees who are licensed to practice *law* or *medicine* qualify as exempt professionals whether or not they meet the $455 per week salary requirements. (For these purposes, medical practitioners include not only physicians but also osteopaths, podiatrists, dentists, optometrists, and veterinarians.) Teachers also qualify as exempt professionals whether or not they meet the $455 per week salary requirement.

Computer programmers and others with highly specialized knowledge of computers qualify as professionals so long as they are paid either on a salary basis of at least $455 per week or on an hourly basis of at least $27.63 per hour.

Highly compensated employees—employees who earn at least $100,000 per year—are exempt so long as at least *some* of their duties (but not necessarily their primary duties) are executive, administrative, or professional. In addition to the $100,000 per year requirement, they must also be compensated on a salary basis of at least $455 per week.

Executives, administrators, and professionals will not lose their exemption by being temporarily assigned to nonexempt work, even for assignments lasting several weeks, so long as their primary duties fall within the definitions of executive, administrator, or professional.

More information about the white collar exemptions is available at: www.dol.gov/esa/regs/compliance/whd/fairpay/fs17a_overview. htm.

Salary Basis

As previously stated, for an executive, administrator, or professional to be exempt, he or she must generally be paid on a salary basis of at least $455 per week. DOL regulations provide that an employee will be considered as paid on a salary basis if he or she *regularly receives each pay period on a weekly, or less frequent basis, a predetermined amount constituting all, or part, of his or her compensation, which amount is not subject to reduction because of variations in the quality or quantity of the work performed.*

Under this definition, an employee must generally be paid a full week's compensation for any week in which he or she performs any work, without regard to the number of days or hours worked. In other words, so long as the employee is ready, willing, and able to work a full week, the employer cannot reduce the compensation for the week just because the employer does not have any work available.

An employee will not qualify as salaried under DOL regulations if the employer docks wages for jury duty, temporary military leave, or attendance as a witness in court lasting less than a week. However, the employer may *reduce* an employee's salary by the amount the employee is paid as a juror or witness or for military service.

If an employee fails to report to work for a day or more for *personal reasons* (other than sickness or accident), the employer may dock his or her salary for each full day (but not for a partial day) the employee is absent without affecting the employee's exempt status. (Deductions for absences of a day or more relating to sickness or accident are also permitted if the employer has a plan, policy, or practice of providing alternative compensation under those circumstances.) But if the employee is absent for *less than a day*, no deduction is allowed. In short, if an employer treats exempt employees as if they were hourly instead of salaried, they will cease being exempt.

Alert!

Many employers mistakenly think that all salaried employees are automatically exempt. To the contrary, while being salaried is one of the requirements for exemption, the employee must also qualify as an executive, administrator, or professional as defined in DOL regulations.

Department of Labor regulations do allow certain deductions from the pay of an exempt employee without affecting the employee's exempt status: for penalties imposed for infractions of safety rules of major significance, such as rules prohibiting smoking in explosive plants; and for disciplinary suspensions of one or more full days for infractions of workplace conduct rules pursuant to generally applicable written policies, such as policies prohibiting sexual harassment or workplace violence.

QUICK TIP

Federal law protects the jobs of employees on military leave. Many states offer similar job protection to employees called to jury duty or to testify as a witness in a court case. (See Chapter 8 for more details regarding employee job protection.)

The Department of Labor's definition of *salary basis* says that *all or part* of an employee's compensation must be pre-determined. This means that an employee will be considered salaried even if some portion of his or her compensation is paid in the form of commissions or bonuses that vary depending on productivity or other factors. However, the pre-determined amount must satisfy the minimum salary requirements—$455 per week for most white collar exemptions.

Improper Deductions

Improper deductions from an otherwise exempt employee's salary will convert that employee, and other employees in the same job classification who work under the manager who made the improper deduction, to nonexempt status. Any overtime worked while the improper deductions were being made will then have to be paid at time and a half.

Under the so-called *window of correction* rule, isolated or inadvertent deductions will not cause loss of exemption. However, the employer must have a policy in place that prohibits improper pay deductions and includes a mechanism for employees to complain about a deduction. (See Figure 5.2 for an example of such a policy.) Once an improper deduction is brought to the employer's attention, the employer must reimburse the employee and must make a commitment to comply in the future.

Figure 5.2: WINDOW-OF-CORRECTION POLICY

The following policy will help assure that inadvertent deductions from a salaried exempt employee do not convert the employee to nonexempt.

The Company prohibits deductions from the compensation of exempt employees that could result in loss of exempt status. Any exempt employee who believes an improper deduction has been made from his or her compensation is encouraged to submit a complaint, preferably in writing, to the Company's payroll officer. The Company will promptly investigate the complaint. If the Company determines that the deduction was improper, the Company will promptly refund the deduction to the employee. The Company commits itself to compliance with applicable wage-and-hour laws, including those governing exemptions from overtime pay.

Other Exemptions

Other exemptions may be significant for some employers. Unlike executives, administrators, and professionals, there are a few exemptions that do not require payment of a fixed salary. These include *outside salespersons* who are customarily and regularly employed in making sales away from the employer's place of business; and *drivers, drivers' helpers, loaders,* and *mechanics* for motor carriers whose duties affect safe operation of commercial motor vehicles in interstate commerce and who are subject to regulation by the U.S. Department of Transportation.

Even if an employer is not subject to federal overtime requirements under the FLSA, it may be subject to state overtime requirements. State law is similar to the FLSA, but states often have different exemptions from overtime. Different exemptions also apply to work performed under government contracts. (See Chapter 22 for more on government contractors.)

Settling FLSA Wage Disputes

When an employer underpays an employee in violation of the FLSA, the employee may recover not only the balance of wages owed, but also additional liquidated damages equal to the unpaid amount, and the attorneys' fees incurred in pursuing the claim. In cases of underpayment, the employer and employee generally cannot enter a binding settlement agreement in which the employer agrees to pay something less than the full amount due.

In a 1945 decision, the Supreme Court invalidated a settlement agreement between an employer and an employee which did not include a provision for payment of liquidated damages to the employee. The Court reasoned that the FLSA affords statutory rights that simply cannot be waived. A year later the Court ruled that even where there was a bona fide dispute between the parties as to the employer's overtime obligation, a settlement agreement would not be enforceable. However, in that case the dispute involved a *legal issue* of whether the employer was engaged in interstate commerce and, therefore, whether the FLSA applied. The Court left open the question whether a bona fide dispute over a *factual issue*, such as how many hours of overtime the employee actually worked, might support a settlement agreement in which an employee agrees to compromise his or her FLSA claim.

The question left open by the Court in 1946 remains unanswered today. So, to resolve disputes where an employer does not want to roll over and pay whatever the employee claims due nor fight it out in court, the employer should request the Department of Labor to participate in and supervise a settlement. Prudent employers will want to involve the Department of Labor in just this way, particularly if substantial amounts are in dispute or a whole class of employees claims to have been underpaid.

Other Wage Regulations

The states regulate many other aspects of wage-and-hour requirements. Typical requirements are that employers:

- Establish regular pay periods;
- Pay hourly workers at least twice a month and pay salaried employees at least monthly;
- Pay in U.S. currency; and,
- Pay terminated employees within a specified time period after termination.

If bonuses and commissions are part of an employee's regular compensation package, they must be paid just like other wages.

Note:
Although direct deposit of employee paychecks is a great convenience to employer and employee alike, employers may be barred under state wage regulations from insisting that employees participate in a direct deposit program.

All employers are *required* to deduct taxes and related items from employee paychecks and amounts subject to garnishment. (Chapters 6 and 7 give more details regarding deductions from an employee's paycheck.) Employers may deduct other amounts agreed to by the employee, such as voluntary contributions to a retirement plan, the employee's contributory portion of health insurance premiums, and so on. Employers are generally *prohibited* from deducting amounts on account of workers' compensation benefits, unemployment insurance, or other amounts claimed due from the employee, like reimbursement for breakage or for mistakes on customer accounts.

Federal and state laws also impose certain record-keeping requirements. In general, employers must keep records for at least three years showing the name, address, Social Security number, and occupation of each employee; the employee's rate of pay; the amount actually paid each pay period; and the hours worked each day and each workweek. The records are subject to onsite inspection by wage-and-hour officials.

Child Labor

Both federal and state laws regulate child labor. On the federal side, the Fair Labor Standards Act (FLSA) prohibits *oppressive child labor*, which is defined as employment of any child who is under the age of 16, regardless of the occupation; and employment of a child who is between the ages of 16 and 18 in mining, manufacturing, or any other industry the Secretary of Labor finds particularly hazardous.

Excluded from the definition is:

• Employment in a family business, so long as the employment is not in mining, manufacturing, or other particularly hazardous industry;

- Agricultural employment (with parental consent if the child is under 14 and only when school is not in session if the child is under 16);
- Employment as an actor or performer in movies, the theater, and radio and television productions;
- Delivering newspapers to consumers; and,
- Making wreaths at home and harvesting forest products to be used in wreath-making.

QUICK TIP

Specific work, such as serving alcoholic beverages or driving commercial vehicles, may be subject to additional age restrictions under state law.

Separate federal legislation prohibits the employment of children in the production of child pornography for distribution in interstate commerce.

State regulation of child labor differs from jurisdiction to jurisdiction. The definition of *minor* may vary, for example. Each state also has its own list of exclusions reflective of prominent local industries or regional customs.

Minors need a *work permit*, typically issued through the school system, before being able to work. Employers must keep permits on file and available for inspection. Even when a minor is properly permitted to work, additional restrictions may apply, such as when and how many hours a minor may work. These time restrictions vary depending on whether school is or is not in session.

The illegal employment of minors exposes the employer to substantial criminal and civil penalties.

Priority of Wages and Benefits in Bankruptcy

At any given time, an employer usually owes wages to employees. Depending on the frequency of pay periods and the lag between the end of a pay period and the date checks are issued, nonexempt employees could be owed as little as a few days' pay or as much as a few weeks' pay. Exempt employees and employees who are due commissions may be owed substantially more. Similarly, at any particular time employers with pension or other benefit plans usually have an unfunded obligation to those plans.

When an employer's assets are being administered in bankruptcy court, the U.S. Bankruptcy Code specifies an order of priority for payment of claims against the employer. High on the priority list are amounts due to employees and to employee benefit plans. Under the Bankruptcy Code, the items that come before claims of the employer's other unsecured creditors include wages, salaries, and commissions (including vacation, severance, and sick leave pay) earned during the ninety-day period prior to the filing of the bankruptcy petition, capped at $10,000 per employee as of this writing; and contributions due to employee benefit plans arising from services rendered during the 180-day period prior to the filing of the bankruptcy petition, also capped at $10,000 per employee as of this writing.

Antitrust Considerations

Federal antitrust laws generally prohibit contracts, combinations, and conspiracies in restraint of trade. It would be illegal, for example, for a group of service station operators in a particular region to fix prices by reaching an agreement among themselves that none of them will sell gasoline below $3.40 a gallon.

Likewise, employers may not engage in *wage-fixing* agreements. Suppose a particular industry faces a labor shortage so that employers in that industry are unable to attract all the employees they need. Rather than engage in a bidding war (that the employers perceive as just running up everyone's labor costs without solving the problem), they decide to impose a cap on wages by mutual agreement. *This is illegal.*

It is perfectly legal for *employees*, whether unionized or not, to conspire among themselves in an effort to better their wages, benefits, and working conditions. However, they lose this ability when they conspire with employers outside the scope of legitimate employee objectives. The Supreme Court ruled, for example, that an agreement between a coal miner's union and one set of mine owners, that the union would insist on specified wage standards in its negotiations with other mine owners, violated the antitrust laws. (Chapter 24 covers unions and labor relations in more detail.)

Predatory Hiring

One other issue deserves mention—*predatory hiring*. Wholly apart from contracts, combinations, and conspiracies, an employer might well have liability under the antitrust laws if, without regard to its own business needs, it targets a competitor's employees in order to harm the competitor's business. The risks here can be reduced if the new employer can demonstrate a genuine business need for the employees, and if it can show that a particular competitor was not targeted, but that qualified employees were sought from a range of sources.

Chapter

Wage Attachments and Assignments

- ▶ Garnishments
- ▶ Withholding Orders
- ▶ Tax Levies
- ▶ Debtors in Bankruptcy
- ▶ Department of Education Garnishments
- ▶ Wage Assignments

The obligations an employer owes its employees under wage-and-hour laws (discussed in Chapter 5) are trumped by a variety of court-ordered garnishments and wage attachments. When an employee's wages are garnished or attached, the employer satisfies its wage-payment obligations by paying a portion of the employee's wages to a third party to whom the employee is indebted.

Garnishments

When an employee's creditor sues your employee on an unpaid debt and obtains a court judgment, the creditor is authorized to execute on the judgment, meaning that the creditor can try to collect the judgment out of assets belonging to the employee. One of those assets is the stream of wage payments the employee becomes entitled to as he or she works for you. Collecting a judgment out of an employee's wages is known as a *garnishment*. The cast of characters in that arrangement is the judgment *debtor* (your employee), the judgment *creditor* or *garnisher*, and you, the *garnishee*.

An employer usually first finds out about a garnishment when served with a court *writ* (or *order*). (When the garnishment relates to family support obligations in a domestic relations case, it is called a *withholding order*.) The employer must respond by filing an answer in court within the time limit specified in the writ, stating whether the judgment debtor is in fact an employee and, if so, what his or her wages are. The employer may assert defenses to the garnishment, including any defenses the employee could assert. If the employer states that the judgment debtor is not an employee, that usually ends the matter, unless the judgment creditor requests a hearing to explore the issue further.

Alert!

Some employers may be tempted to help their employees evade garnishments and withholding orders by falsifying information about compensation or paying employees off-the-books. Doing so exposes the employer to criminal prosecution as well as civil liability.

Attachable Wages

Assuming the judgment debtor is an employee, the employer will then be required to withhold the *attachable wages* of the employee and remit them periodically to the *garnisher* (the judgment creditor) until the judgment is paid or the employment ends. The garnishment applies to any wages that are unpaid at the time of the attachment, as well as wages that become due in the future. The *attachable wages* are limited by the federal *Consumer Credit Protection Act* to the *lesser* of (a) 25% of the employee's disposable earnings (after deducting tax and similar withholdings and after deducting the employee's portion of any medical insurance premiums) or (b) the amount by which the weekly disposable earnings exceed thirty times the federal minimum hourly wage. The writ of attachment will say exactly how to compute the amount to be withheld.

Note:

Even though an employer is making payments to a garnisher, the employer must treat the payments as part of the employee's compensation for purposes of computing income tax withholding, FICA, etc. (See Chapter 7 for more details.)

Penalties

Penalties for ignoring a garnishment can be substantial. In some circumstances, the employer might be held in contempt or might be required to cover the costs and attorneys' fees incurred by the garnisher to enforce the garnishment. The employer might even have to pay double wages—once to the employee and again to the garnisher. In other words, it's a good idea to take garnishments seriously.

If the employee quits or is fired while the garnishment is in effect, the employer's obligation to remit attachable wages ends. (In some states, rehiring an employee within a short time period automatically revives the garnishment.) If several garnishments for the same employee are received, the employer must honor the garnishments in the order they are served, paying off the first one completely before starting payments on the next one.

Federal law prohibits an employer from firing an employee because the employee's wages are subjected to attachment for any one indebtedness within a calendar year. Many states have similar laws protecting the jobs of garnished employees. One federal district court ruled that an employer was not free to fire a employee for a second garnishment, since the employer was obligated to satisfy only one garnishment at a time.

Wages Subject to Garnishment

State law defines what constitutes *wages* for garnishment purposes. The definition generally covers bonuses and commissions, as well as regular compensation. In some states, employee tips may also have to be included.

Contributions to a pension plan that is subject to the *Employee Retirement Income Security Act* (ERISA) are exempt from garnishment, even where state law seems to provide otherwise. ERISA requires plan documents to contain a provision protecting benefits from an employee's creditors and ERISA preempts (supersedes) state law relating to pension plans. (ERISA is covered in Chapter 9.)

Withholding Orders

A withholding order is a special kind of wage attachment issued in a domestic relations case in connection with spousal or child support.

Alimony and child support used to be the exclusive concerns of state courts. With enactment of the *Child Support Enforcement Act* in 1975, the federal government got involved in a big way. Under the Act, each state must establish a formal program, which is subject to approval by the Secretary of Health and Human Services, for locating noncustodial parents and obtaining child support and support for the spouse (or former spouse) with whom the noncustodial parent's child is living. *Child support* must include health care coverage whenever it is available to the noncustodial parent at a reasonable cost, without regard to enrollment or open season restrictions.

Note:

Each state has a Directory of New Hires (discussed in Chapter 2) along with support guidelines and collection procedures, in accordance with the Act.

When an *existing* employee who is obligated to make support payments becomes more than thirty days delinquent, the delinquency will usually result in issuance of a withholding order directing the employer to withhold the support payments from the employee's wages. Within twenty days after an employer hires a new employee, the employer must submit the employee's name, Social Security number, and other identifying information for inclusion in the state's Directory of New Hires. If that information matches with an outstanding withholding order, then the state sends a notice directing the employer to withhold the required amount from the employee's wages.

As with garnishments, the federal *Consumer Credit Protection Act* also sets limits on the amount of wages that may be withheld pursuant to a withholding order. However, the limit may be as high as 65% of disposable earnings if the employee is in arrears in support payments and has no new spouse or dependent children to support.

Pursuant to the *Child Support Enforcement Act*, withholding orders will direct the employer to remit withheld payments not to the employee's child or to the parent who has custody of the child, but instead to the state agency or court that monitors enforcement of such orders.

Employers are prohibited from retaliating in any way, such as by firing or disciplining an employee who is the subject of a withholding order. States may, however, permit employers to charge a fee for processing withholding orders.

(Also related to family support obligations are *Qualified Medical Child Support Orders* (QMCSOs) discussed in Chapter 10.)

Tax Levies

When your employee fails to pay his or her federal income taxes, the IRS can collect the unpaid taxes from you, the employer, by serving you with a levy. Levies, like garnishments, require the employer to pay to a third party (in this case, the U.S. Treasury) some portion of the wages otherwise due the employee in order to extinguish the employee's debt to that party. Corporate officials who are responsible for payroll matters can have personal liability for disregarding a tax levy.

State law also provides means for collecting delinquent taxes through garnishment of salary or wages. The procedures and exemptions differ from state to state.

If your employee disputes the validity of the levy and sues you for unpaid wages, you are discharged from any obligation or liability to the employee because you made payments in accordance with an IRS levy.

Debtors in Bankruptcy

Chapter 13 of the federal *Bankruptcy Act* is entitled *Adjustment of Debts of an Individual with a Regular Income*. Under Chapter 13, a debtor with a regular income may ask a bankruptcy court to prohibit creditors from suing him or her or otherwise attempting to collect debts. In exchange, the debtor must propose a plan to pay down the debts out of ongoing disposable income (generally defined as income not reasonably necessary for the support of the debtor). The plan can last no more than three years and it must be designed so that the creditors receive at least as much under the plan as they would have received had the debtor simply brought all assets into court in a Chapter 7 liquidation.

Alert!

Federal law prohibits discrimination against persons who have filed for bankruptcy.

If the bankruptcy court approves (confirms) the plan, then the court will issue an order directing the debtor's employer to pay specified amounts to a Chapter 13 trustee. The trustee, in turn, makes periodic payments to the creditors. Bankruptcy orders are exempt from the limitations imposed by the *Consumer Credit Protection Act*.

Department of Education Garnishments

Under the federal *Higher Education Act*, the U.S. Department of Education may garnish the *disposable pay* of individuals who are delinquent in repaying *student loans* made, insured, or guaranteed by the federal government. Under the garnishment procedure, the Department issues a withholding order to the employer. If the employer fails to withhold in accordance with the order, the employer can be sued not only for the amount that was not withheld but also for attorneys' fees and punitive damages. The term *disposable pay* is defined as compensation remaining after deduction of any amounts required by law to be withheld.

Employers may not retaliate by discharging or disciplining an employee whose pay is subject to a Department of Education withholding order. Employers are also prohibited from refusing to hire a prospective employee because he or she is the subject of a Department of Education withholding order.

Wage Assignments

An *assignment* of wages is different from a garnishment. Garnishments are government orders with which the employer must comply. Assignments, on the other hand, are private agreements between an employee and a third person—usually a creditor to whom the employee owes money—that may or may not be valid, depending on whether they comply with state law.

State law often restricts the ability of an employee to make a voluntary assignment of wages. It may also impose specific requirements and procedures in order to make a valid assignment. The safest practice is for an employer to adopt a uniform policy and distribute it to all employees, such as through the employee handbook, stating that the employer will not honor any wage assignments and—except as otherwise required by law—will pay all wages directly to the employee (or will direct-deposit them in the employee's account) without regard to any assignment.

Chapter 7

Tax Considerations

Tax considerations drive, or at least help shape, any number of transactions in the business world. The same is true for the employer-employee relationship. With combined federal and state income tax rates at or above 40%, the deductibility of employer expenditures becomes a critical factor in a business's survival. At the same time, employees look to limit or defer tax on their employment-related benefits. The result is a complex web of employer opportunities and requirements.

Deductibility of Wages and Benefits

Wages and benefits paid to employees are deductible from the employer's gross income for purposes of computing the employer's federal and state income tax, so long as the amounts are reasonable, ordinary, and necessary. This means, for example, that for a corporate employer who is in the 39% marginal federal tax bracket and the 7% state tax bracket, forty-six cents of each additional dollar in wages and benefits is effectively paid by federal and state governments in the form of reduced tax liabilities.

QUICK TIP

As an alternative to taking a *deduction* for wages, an employer may claim a *work opportunity tax credit* against its income tax for wages paid to targeted groups of hard-to-employ individuals, such as welfare recipients and certain veterans and ex-felons. The credit is generally limited to 40% of the first $6,000 ($2,400) in first-year wages for each such employee.

As a general rule, whenever the employer takes a deduction for a wage or benefit payment, the employee who receives the payment must include it in his or her own gross income for federal and state tax purposes. The IRS keeps track of these shifting tax burdens by requiring employers to report employee payments on Form W-2 and payments to independent contractors on Form 1099.

QUICK TIP

When employer-sponsored group health insurance covers an employee's *domestic partner*, the premium is taxable income to the employee. (See Chapter 10 for more information.)

There are, however, important exceptions to the general rule. One exception is for items of *deferred compensation*—compensation that the employee cannot immediately enjoy, such as qualified retirement plan contributions. It may make little difference to an employer whether compensation to employees is in the form of wages, or partly in wages and partly in the form of a qualified retirement plan contribution, since both are fully deductible if they are within the limits imposed by law. But it can make a big difference to the employee because of the time value of money.

Take, for example, an employee whose marginal tax bracket for federal and state tax purposes is 46%. For each additional dollar received in wages, forty-six cents is paid to the government and only fifty-four cents is left to invest. (The employee's portion of FICA and Medicare reduce this even more.) Worse, any income earned on that fifty-four cents is also subject to current taxation.

In contrast, a dollar of deferred compensation is not subject to immediate tax, so the full dollar can be invested without reduction for taxes. In addition, earnings on that dollar—called *inside build-up*—are not subject to immediate tax either. In the end, the employee should have a much greater nest egg than if he or she had received and invested taxable wages. Of course, that nest egg is subject to income tax as it is withdrawn during retirement, but in most cases, the employee is still better off, particularly since the tax bracket in retirement is probably lower than when actively working.

There are other important exceptions to the general rule that whatever the employer deducts, the employee must report. For example, employer contributions to group health insurance, health savings accounts, and group term life insurance up to $50,000 in coverage (all discussed in Chapter 10) are generally deductible by the employer but not includible in the employee's income.

Some noncash *fringe benefits* may be deductible for the employer but (subject to specified limits and conditions) not includible in the employee's gross income. These include:

- *No-additional-cost service*—a service to an employee that the employer normally provides to its customers, so long as doing so is without substantial additional cost to the employer;
- *Employee discounts* on goods (so long as the discount does not exceed the employer's profit margin) and on services (so long as the discount does not exceed 20% of the retail price);
- *Working condition benefits*, such as upscale office appointments and use of a company car for business purposes;
- *De minimis benefits*, such as use of the copying machine or office supplies for personal purposes, and such as eating facilities at or near the employer's premises (so long as the facility is operated on at least a break-even basis and so long as the employer does not discriminate in favor of highly compensated employees); and,
- *Transportation benefits*, including a transit pass, parking, or cash reimbursements for those items.

Federal tax law allows companies to deduct all *ordinary and necessary expenses* of carrying on a trade or business. This includes reimbursements to employees who have incurred expenses on behalf of their employers. But special rules apply to transportation and travel expenses. For example, while companies can reimburse their employees for, and then deduct, *actual expenses* incurred in operating an automobile for business, IRS regulations have long allowed use of *standard mileage rates* in lieu of providing substantiation for actual expenses. (At this writing, the standard rate for business use of an automobile is 58.5 cents per mile.)

The IRS takes a similar approach to *per diem* business travel expenses (meals, lodging, and incidental expenses), allowing standard reimbursement/deduction rates instead of requiring substantiation of actual expenses. Employers may use one of two methods to reimburse employees, either of which will satisfy the substantiation requirement: the high-low method, available only for travel within the continental U.S., which allows a deduction of $237 per day for specified high-cost areas, and $152 for all other areas within the continental U.S.; or the federal per diem rates method, based on location-specific rates established by the federal government for cities within the continental U.S. (the CONUS rates) and outside the continental U.S. (the OCONUS rates). A complete listing of those rates is available at: www.gsa.gov/perdiem.

> **Note:**
> A full listing of high-cost areas is contained in IRS Publication 1542, available at: www.irs.gov.

The deduction for food, beverages, and entertainment (but not lodging) is limited to 50% of the otherwise deductible amount, subject to a number of exceptions. Amounts paid to employees in excess of deductible amounts constitute income to the employees and are subject to withholding requirements and payroll taxes.

Limitations on Deductibility

Most business corporations are classified as C *corporations* for federal income tax purposes. C corps are separate taxable entities whose taxable income is determined by starting with the corporation's gross revenue and deducting the cost of goods sold, salaries, rent, and other expenses. After paying tax on the resulting net income, the corporation may choose to distribute some or all of what is left to its shareholders in the form of a dividend. Dividends represent taxable income to the shareholders.

Because a C corp is a taxable entity, income is taxed twice on its way through the corporation to its shareholders. One tax is paid at the corporate level and a second tax is paid at the individual shareholder level. Particularly in the case of small, closely-held corporations, where the shareholder-owners are also the directors, officers, and employees, this double taxation burden is problematic.

One way to avoid double taxation is to accumulate income inside the corporation and not pay dividends. But depending on the amounts involved, the corporation may end up owing an *accumulated earnings tax* that is designed to stop that very practice.

Another way to avoid double taxation is to elect *S corporation* status. (This is discussed more completely in Chapter 1.) Although S corps are generally not subject to tax as separate entities, there are restrictions on who may elect S status. There may also be undesirable tax consequences to S corp owners.

Yet another way is to pay year-end bonuses to owner-employees. Through careful calculation, the bonuses can be set so that the corporation has virtually zero taxable income and it pays almost no tax. (It is usually not possible to reach *exactly* zero, since some cash expenditures during the year, such as equipment purchases, may not be deductible, but they reduce the amount of cash available to pay bonuses.) The owner-employees, of course, will owe tax on the bonuses along with whatever other compensation they receive, but that is still just one tax, not two.

The taxpayer corporation has the burden of proving that its compensation payments are reasonable under Internal Revenue Code Section 162. And particularly where the taxpayer corporation is controlled by the employees receiving the compensation, the payments are subject to careful scrutiny by the IRS to be sure that they truly represent (deductible) compensation for services rendered, rather than disguised (nondeductible) dividends. In determining whether compensation is reasonable, the courts look at a number of factors, including the following:

- The employee's qualifications;
- The nature, extent, and scope of the employee's work;
- The size and complexity of the employer's business;
- A comparison of salaries paid with the employer's income;
- Prevailing rates of compensation for comparable positions in comparable companies;
- The amount of compensation paid to the employee in prior years; and,
- Whether the employer offers pension and profit-sharing plans to its employees.

These factors are applied on an individual employee basis, rather than in the aggregate to a group of employees. In other words, it does not matter that the company's overall deduction for compensation is reasonable. Each individual employee's compensation must be reasonable as well.

QUICK TIP

Payments to partners in a partnership and to members of a limited liability company are generally treated as nondeductible distributions rather than deductible wages and salaries. This occurs even when the partner or member works for the partnership or limited liability company.

Public Companies

Under I.R.C. Sec. 162(m), publicly-held corporations also face limits on the amount they can deduct. In general, the Code places a $1 million per year cap on deductions for remuneration paid to *covered employees*—defined as the chief executive officer and the four highest paid officers other than the CEO—unless the board of directors takes special steps to authorize higher compensation.

The Securities and Exchange Commission (SEC) has adopted disclosure rules requiring each publicly-held company to disclose in its annual proxy statement the amount of compensation paid to its *high level executives*—its chief executive officer, chief financial officer, and its three other most highly compensated executive officers. The company also must disclose the criteria used in reaching executive compensation decisions and the relationship between the company's executive compensation practices and corporate performance.

Independent Contractors

Recent news articles illustrate the hazard of misclassifying employees as independent contractors. Microsoft, for example, agreed to pay almost $100 million to a group of so-called *temporary* workers who should have been, but were not, classified as regular employees entitled to participate in Microsoft's benefit plans. Time-Warner faced similar problems, although the amount at stake was only a few million dollars. At this writing, FedEx faces a possible IRS fine of $319 million for treating its delivery drivers as independent contractors.

In addition to benefit plan participation, employees (but not independent contractors) are subject to federal and state income tax withholding. They are entitled to have employer FICA contributions made on their behalf. Also, they are covered by workers' compensation and unemployment insurance for which the employer must pay premiums. So if an employer wrongly treats a group of employees as independent contractors over a period of years, the total cost of remedying the error can be substantial.

Traditionally, the question whether a worker is an employee or an independent contractor turns on whether the employer has a right to control the manner in which the worker does his or her job. (See Chapter 1 for more details.) This is sometimes known as the *common-law test*. In order to determine whether there is or is not a right of control, a number of subsidiary factors are considered, such as who sets the worker's hours, whether the worker works for one or several employers, whether the worker or the employer provides necessary tools and workspace, whether the worker has specialized knowledge or requires a license or a professional degree to do the job, and so on. The problem with the common-law test is its lack of certainty. If the employer guesses wrong, disaster can strike.

In an effort to resolve this uncertainty, Congress enacted legislation to provide a *safe harbor* for employers. Under these safe harbor provisions, an employer's treatment of a worker as an independent contractor is relatively safe from IRS challenge if:

- The employer has never treated the worker as an employee;
- The employer filed all required tax reports and returns relating to the worker on a timely and consistent basis; and,
- The employer had a reasonable basis for treating the worker as an independent contractor.

The employer will be considered to have a reasonable basis for treating the worker as an independent contractor if the employer relied on a court decision involving facts similar to the employer's own or if the employer relied on rulings or technical advice from the IRS. The employer can also demonstrate a reasonable basis if a *significant segment of the industry* in which the worker is engaged has a *long-standing recognized practice* of treating such workers as independent contractors. A *significant segment* of the industry is 25%. However, the employer will not have a reasonable basis for treating a particular worker as an independent contractor if the employer has other workers doing similar jobs who are treated as employees.

While the IRS can still challenge a safe harbor classification, the burden of proving that the classification is wrong falls on the IRS. In order to ensure that the safe harbor provisions are fully effective, the IRS must provide the employer with a written notice of the provisions when it audits an employer in connection with a worker classification issue. The IRS is also prohibited from issuing regulations or rulings dealing with the safe harbor provisions.

CASE STUDY: SAFE HARBOR PROVISIONS SATISFIED

A company licensed as a residential service agency wants to provide nonskilled, home health aides for the elderly in the Washington, D.C., area. Before opening for business, the company conducts a survey of some twenty to thirty local competitors. It finds that approximately 80% of the agencies surveyed treat their aides as independent contractors, while only 10% treat them as employees. (The other 10% did not respond.) Upon opening additional offices in Baltimore and Richmond, the company conducts similar surveys in those areas and obtains similar results. Based on these surveys, the company classified its workers as independent contractors. The company's reliance on its surveys is reasonable and the company's classification of its aides is accepted by the court.

Another approach to resolving the employee/independent contractor issue for federal tax and withholding purposes is to ask the IRS to decide. Upon filing Form SS-8 (either by the employer or by the worker whose status is in doubt), the IRS will determine whether the worker is an employee or an independent contractor. The determination can then be relied on for safe harbor purposes. It is probably fair to assume that the IRS resolves close questions by concluding that the worker is an employee, not an independent contractor. So as a practical matter, the SS-8 route may not be very helpful to employers.

Suppose an employer incorrectly classifies a worker as an independent contractor when, in reality, the worker should have been treated as an employee. As an independent contractor, the worker pays a self-employment tax equal to 100% of the FICA tax ($12,648 at this writing, assuming earnings of at least $102,000). Had the worker been properly classified as an employee, however, the employer would have paid only half the FICA amount, or $6,324, and the employer would have paid the other half. So the question arises whether, as a result of misclassification, the worker has a claim against the employer for the $6,324 that the employer should have matched but did not.

In a recent case, the Eleventh Circuit Court of Appeals ruled that FICA is a tax statute that only the federal government can enforce and that it does not create a private right of action. In other words, so far as FICA is concerned, an employer may be liable to the government for misclassification, but the employer is not liable to the misclassified employee.

Federal Withholding Requirements

We are all used to seeing a long list of deductions and withholdings on our pay stubs. Some of them are voluntary, like the employee portions of retirement plan contributions and health insurance premiums. Others are required by law.

How does the employer know how much to withhold? And what is done with the money? The first step in the process is for the employer to obtain an *Employer Identification Number* (EIN). The number has nine digits, as do Social Security numbers, but instead of being in the format 123-45-6789, an EIN is formatted 12-3456789. EINs are obtained by filing Form SS-4 with the IRS and may also be obtained by phone or facsimile or by completing an online application at: www.irs.gov/businesses/small.

The next step is for the employee to submit IRS Form W-4 and the applicable state equivalent to the employer. This must be done at hiring time and whenever the employee's tax withholdings need to be changed. Form W-4 calls for basic information—the employee's name, address, Social Security number, marital status, etc. It also contains a worksheet for figuring the number of exemptions to be claimed on the employee's tax return and various other factors that affect the employee's tax liability. These factors, known as *allowances*, are then totaled and entered on the form. Finally, Form W-4 permits the employee to claim a complete exemption from federal income tax withholding under certain conditions.

Alert!

When a Form W-4 claims more than ten withholding allowances, or when it claims an exemption from withholding and the employee's wages are normally more than $200 per week, the W-4 must be submitted to the IRS. The IRS may then direct the employer to withhold on some different basis.

The employer has four basic federal tax obligations relating to employees. These are:

- Federal income tax;
- Social Security tax (FICA);
- Medicare tax; and,
- Unemployment insurance contributions.

The first three are discussed below. Unemployment insurance is covered in Chapter 12.

Federal Income Tax

With Form W-4 in hand, the employer turns to a set of tables issued by the IRS in Circular E, *Employer's Tax Guide* (also known as Publication 15), to determine how much to withhold from each paycheck. The tables are based on four variables:

- The frequency of paydays (weekly, biweekly, etc.);
- The employee's marital status as shown on Form W-4;
- The amount of the wage payment; and,
- The number of allowances claimed by the employee.

Circular E is really the employer's Bible when it comes to federal employment tax matters. It can be downloaded from the IRS's website by searching for Publication 15 at: www.irs.gov.

Social Security (FICA) Tax

At this writing, the tax rate for the employee is 6.2% on a maximum wage base of $102,000, which translates to a maximum withholding of $6,324. The employer must match whatever amount is withheld from the employee. So for an employee whose annual salary is at least $102,000, the total payment on account of Social Security is $12,648, half of which is withheld from the employee and half of which is the employer's own *matching contribution*. The amount to be withheld from each paycheck is simply 6.2% of the gross payment until the maximum amount ($6,234) has been withheld. These rates and the wage base are subject to periodic change.

Medicare Tax

The Medicare tax rate is 1.45% of all wages for the employee and a matching amount of 1.45% for the employer. There is no wage base cap—the Medicare tax applies to all wages. The amount to be withheld from each paycheck is 1.45% of the gross payment.

Exceptions

In general, all employees who are U.S. citizens or resident aliens are subject to withholding for federal income tax, FICA, and Medicare.

QUICK TIP

Many dealings with the Social Security Administration can be accomplished online. For more information, see the *Business Services Online Handbook* at: www.ssa.gov/employer/bsohbnew.htm.

Circular E contains a list of situations where special rules apply, including:

- Nonresident aliens;
- Household employees;
- Clergy; and,
- Disabled and deceased workers.

Independent contractors are also exempt from withholding requirements. However, a few, limited types of workers called *statutory employees* are required by law to be treated as employees, even though they would otherwise qualify as independent contractors. (See Chapter 1 for more information.)

Irregular Pay

Questions sometimes arise regarding withholding on back wages paid to an employee for some earlier year. Suppose, for example, that the employer and employee are in dispute over the exact amount due, and the dispute gets resolved in court years after the employee did the work. Or suppose back pay is awarded in connection with a discrimination suit or an unfair labor practice complaint. Should the employer treat the wages as paid when they were *originally due* or as paid in the year they were *actually paid*? (The question can make a big difference if the tax rate or FICA ceiling has changed.) The IRS has long taken the position that the wages should be treated as paid currently. The Supreme Court recently affirmed that position.

Other taxable benefits subject to withholding include bonuses, commissions, expense reimbursements (unless the reimbursement is pursuant to an arrangement that requires the employee to verify expenses), payments in kind, meals, and lodging (unless provided for the employer's convenience on the employer's premises).

Tips

In addition to withholding for wages, the employer must withhold on account of *tips*. Employees are required to report tips to their employer no later than the 10th of the month after the tips are received, unless tips for the month are less than $20. The report should include not only cash tips the employee receives directly from customers, but also tips received in a sharing arrangement with other employees and tips paid by the employer on credit card charge slips. Employees may use Form 4070 (contained in IRS Publication 1244) or a similar statement to report tips to their employers.

The employer then must figure tax withholdings, payroll taxes, and garnishments just as if the tips were wages paid by the employer. However, the employer is not liable to taxing authorities or garnishers for more money than actually comes into the employer's hands. Employers who operate *large food and beverage establishments* (defined as employing more than ten people, who work more than eighty hours per week in the aggregate) must file Form 8027 annually with the IRS showing total tips.

It should be no surprise that employees who receive cash tips do not always make full reports to their employers. The IRS has addressed the problem in a number of ways.

8 Percent Rule

The *8 percent rule* is applicable to food and beverage establishments that have more than ten employees on a typical business day. Under the rule, if total reported tips are less than 8% of gross receipts, then the employer must assume that tips have been under-reported to the extent of the difference and allocate that difference among those employees who customarily receive tip income. However, if the IRS can be convinced that average tips for the particular business are less than 8% of gross receipts, then the percentage will be reduced, but not below 2%.

Aggregate Estimation Method

For payroll tax purposes (FICA, FUTA, and Medicare), the IRS sometimes uses an *aggregate estimation method* to determine an employer's liability—a method recently approved by the Supreme Court. To illustrate, suppose a restaurant's employees report tips totaling $100,000 in a particular year, which in turn are reported to the IRS by the restaurant. Suppose further that during a compliance audit the IRS discovers that the $100,000 represents only tips shown on charge slips and does not include tips by cash-paying customers. The IRS may assume that cash customers tip at the same rate as charge customers, use that assumption to determine total tips, and allocate total tips among the restaurant's service employees. In other words, the IRS may use a *top down methodology*. It does not have to estimate on an employee-by-employee basis.

QUICK TIP

Tips may be counted against the employer's federal minimum wage requirement, but only up to $3.72 per hour at this writing, regardless of the actual amount of tips received and reported. (See Chapter 5 for more details.)

Tip Rate Determination Agreement

The IRS has developed a form agreement (known as a *TRDA*) pursuant to which the IRS and the employer determine and agree in advance on the rate of tips to be reported by employees. TRDAs require that at least 75% of the affected employees join in the agreement.

Tip Reporting Alternative Commitment

The IRS has developed another form agreement (known as a *TRAC*) for food and beverage industry employers under which the employer promises to establish an education program for its employees and to establish procedures designed to assure accurate tip reporting. In return, the IRS promises to assess payroll taxes based solely on reported tips.

Attributed Tip Income Program

The IRS has developed yet another program for food and beverage industry employers to report tip income. Known as ATIP, the new program is a voluntary, three-year pilot which began January 1, 2007. Under ATIP there is no one-on-one meeting with the IRS to determine eligibility and there is no individual agreement between the employer and the IRS. Instead, the establishment simply elects to participate by checking the ATIP box on Form 8027. To be eligible, at least 20% of the establishment's gross receipts from food and beverage sales must be by charge card. The ratio of charged tips to total charges is the establishment's *charged tip rate* and the charged tip rate, less two percentage points, is the establishment's *formula tip rate*. The formula tip rate then determines the gross amount of tips to be reported and allocated among tipped employees. At least 75% of tipped employees must agree to participate in the program.

The IRS promises that it will not initiate a tip examination for any period an establishment participates in ATIP. For more information, see Rev. Proc. 2006-30, available at: www.irs.gov.

Restaurants do not like to act as tax police over their employees. They argue that the IRS has used the *aggregate estimation method* to coerce restaurants into participating in tip reporting programs. Congress has been sympathetic to restaurants' complaints. For one thing, Congress included in the *Internal Revenue Service Restructuring and Reform Act of 1998* a prohibition against IRS threats to audit a restaurant in an attempt to coerce it into a tip reporting program. Second, federal tax law allows restaurants a dollar-for-dollar credit against their own income tax for any FICA tax they pay on employee tips. Finally, penalties and interest do not begin to run for FICA tax on unreported tips until the IRS actually assesses the amount it claims is due.

Other Taxable Payments

Suppose an employee is laid off under circumstances that could give rise to a claim of abusive discharge. Fearing a claim, the employer obtains a written release of claims from the employee and, as consideration for the release, makes a lump sum payment to the employee. Or suppose the employee refuses to sign a release and instead files a lawsuit that results in a money judgment against the employer. Are those payments deductible by the employer and taxable to the employee? Are they subject to withholding requirements? Are they subject to W-2 or 1099 reporting requirements?

It has long been the rule that the proceeds of a personal injury action (a suit claiming injury to the body or person of the plaintiff) are *excluded* from taxation and from any withholding or reporting requirements. In the past, the parties to an employment dispute often characterized payments in settlement of the dispute as damages for emotional distress, injury to reputation, and so on, to avoid tax obligations.

QUICK TIP

The settlement of an employment dispute should be in writing and include a provision by which the employee, former employee, or applicant for employment clearly releases all employment-related claims against the employer. If the release is intended to cover an actual or potential age discrimination claim, the release must conform to special rules contained in the *Age Discrimination in Employment Act*. (See Chapter 16 for specifics on age discrimination.)

In 1996, the Internal Revenue Code was amended to narrow the exclusion. The Code now states that gross income does not include damages received on account of personal *physical* injuries or *physical* sickness. A private letter ruling by the IRS defines personal physical injuries as *direct unwanted or uninvited physical contacts resulting in observable bodily harms such as bruises, cuts, swelling, and bleeding.*

QUICK TIP

Workers' compensation benefits are exempt from income tax. (Review Chapter 11 for details.)

As a result of the 1996 amendment, most payments in employment dispute situations will be includible in the recipient's gross income for federal income tax purposes. At the same time, the payments will be deductible by the employer. In addition, since damages in an employment dispute usually are based on lost wages, the payments are generally viewed as the equivalent of employee compensation and therefore subject to wage withholding and FICA requirements.

When an employer and employee settle an employment dispute, they may agree to treat only a portion of the settlement payment as wages and allocate the remainder to *emotional distress*. The IRS will respect such an allocation *for wage withholding and FICA purposes*, so long as the allocation is reasonable, but the IRS will nevertheless view the entire payment as taxable income to the employee. Therefore, the employer should report the portion allocated to wages as W-2 income and the portion allocated to emotional distress as 1099 income not subject to withholding.

Sometimes the employer will agree to pay the employee's attorney's fees as part of a settlement. Prior to the *American Jobs Creation Act of 2004*, most courts took the view that the attorney's fee portion of the settlement was taxable income to the employee, even when the attorney's fee portion was paid directly to the employee's lawyer. The American Jobs Creation Act now provides that, in most employment dispute situations, the attorney's fee portion is *not* taxable income to the employee, although it is taxable, of course, to the lawyer.

When negotiating a settlement agreement, a prudent employer should insist that the agreement explicitly state how all payments are being allocated and how they will be reported for tax purposes. If the agreement attempts to characterize any portion of the payment as nontaxable (a risky arrangement), the agreement should at least contain a provision requiring the recipient to indemnify the employer should the IRS later recharacterize the payment as taxable.

Garnishments

When an employer satisfies a garnishment by paying a portion of the employee's salary to the employee's creditor, the employer is discharging a debt the employee owes. Economically, it is as if the employer paid wages to the employee and the employee, in turn, paid down the debt. So for tax withholding and reporting purposes, a garnishment payment is treated just like a wage payment to the employee.

State Withholding Requirements

Most states impose their own taxes on income and require employers to withhold against that tax. State withholding requirements can get confusing, particularly when there are employees who commute to work from out of state. For each employee, the first step is to determine the state or states in which the employee may have to file a state income tax return. If the employee both lives and works in the same state, then only that state's withholding requirements apply. If the employee lives in one state but commutes to work in another state, then both states' withholding requirements need to be considered, since the employee potentially has tax filing obligations in both states. (Those few states that do not have any income tax at all can be ignored.)

Even though an employee may have a tax filing obligation in a particular state, the employer might not be required to withhold under that state's law. This could occur if the employer itself is not subject to the jurisdiction of that particular state, because the employer has no office in that state and does not do business in that state. Take, for example, a Maryland company whose employees all work in Maryland, but some of whom live in Virginia. Virginia might like the company to withhold for the company's Virginia employees, but if the company is not subject to Virginia's jurisdiction, Virginia has no power to compel the company to withhold. At the same time, Maryland, where the company is subject to jurisdiction, has no interest in enforcing Virginia's tax laws.

The company could withhold Maryland income tax from all its employees. But this would mean that its Virginia employees would face a big Virginia tax bill not covered by withholdings, plus they would need to deal with Maryland to get some or all of their Maryland withholdings back. To resolve this situation, Maryland and Virginia have entered into *reciprocal agreements* with each other. Under these agreements, the Maryland company in the example above withholds Maryland tax from its Maryland employees and Virginia tax from its Virginia employees.

Many other states that have common borders have entered into reciprocal agreements similar to those between Maryland and Virginia. Contact your state employment tax office for details.

Earned Income Credit

The *Earned Income Credit* (EIC) is a tax credit available to low-income employees. The amount of the credit ranges from a few hundred dollars for an employee with no dependent children to more than $4,000 for an employee with two or more dependent children. The credit is *refundable*, meaning that if the credit reduces the employee's tax liability below zero, not only does the employee owe no tax, but the government pays the amount of the negative tax to the employee. The employee claims the credit when his or her federal tax return is filed.

The EIC is normally a matter just between the employee and the IRS. However, when an employee expects to be in a negative tax situation at the end of the year, he or she may notify the employer of that fact using *Form W-5*. The employer is then obligated to advance the negative tax to the employee (up to a maximum of $1,597) with his or her paychecks. Only employees with one or more dependent children are eligible for advances. The IRS's Circular E contains tables for determining the amount to be included in each paycheck. The employer is reimbursed for the advances by claiming them as a credit on its withholding tax deposits for other employees.

Deposit and Reporting Requirements

The timing and method of depositing withheld taxes and the employer's portion of FICA and Medicare taxes depend on the amount of taxes involved. In general, if the annual amount is less than $50,000, the deposits are made monthly to an authorized financial institution such as a national bank. (An employer owing less than $2,500 in employment taxes per quarter may remit those taxes with its quarterly return, rather than depositing the taxes separately.)

If the amount is $50,000 or more, deposits are made semiweekly. However, if an employer accumulates a tax liability of $100,000 or more on any day during a deposit period, the deposit must be made by the next banking day.

Note:

An employer's deposit reporting requirements are spelled out in IRS Publication Circular E, which can be found at: www.irs.gov.

FUTA (federal unemployment tax) is generally deposited quarterly, although if the amount due in any one quarter is $100 or less, it may be carried forward and added to next quarter's liability.

Trust Fund Penalty

Taxes withheld from employees are considered to be held by the employer in trust. Rather than just owing the money to the IRS, the employer is treated as having a *fiduciary duty* to assure that deposits get made as required by law. If the employer fails to do so, the IRS may impose a trust fund penalty equal to the amount of the undeposited tax *in addition* to collecting the tax itself. Further, the corporate shield offers no protection when it comes to withholding taxes. So even an employer who has incorporated will be *personally liable*.

The trust fund penalty may be imposed on any person responsible for collecting, accounting for, and depositing the tax. *Responsible persons* can include corporate officers, employees, directors, anyone who signs checks or has authority for spending business funds, and even volunteers of nonprofit organizations. (Volunteers of tax-exempt organizations are relieved of personal liability if they are serving in an honorary capacity; if they do not participate in the day-to-day or financial operations of the organization; and if they had no actual knowledge of the failure to withhold or make the required deposit—so long as there are at least some remaining responsible persons left to pay the taxes.) Liability for withholding taxes and for trust fund penalties is *not* dischargeable in bankruptcy.

CASE STUDY: BUSINESS OWNER PERSONALLY LIABLE

A recent decision by the U.S. Court of Appeals for the Sixth Circuit (headquartered in Cincinnati) ruled that the sole owner of a limited liability company was personally liable for both the employees' and the employer's portion of FICA taxes, even though the employees involved worked for the LLC itself, not for its owner. The court reasoned that under IRS regulations, a single-member LLC is treated as a sole proprietorship for federal tax purposes and therefore the LLC's owner should be treated as the employer. At this writing the IRS has issued proposed regulations to treat single-member LLCs as separate entities for employment tax purposes, but it remains to be seen whether those regulations will be adopted.

W-2s

No later than January 31 of each year, employers must issue a W-2 form to each employee reporting the employee's compensation for the prior calendar year. Copies of those W-2 forms are then transmitted to the Social Security Administration using Form W-3. If an employee quits or is terminated during the year, the employer must, if so requested by the employee, issue a W-2 within thirty days. W-2s may also be filed electronically. For more information, go to: www.ssa.gov/bso/bsowelcome.htm.

Alert!

Firing the employee or taking other adverse action against him or her solely on the basis of a name and SSN mismatch could be discriminatory.

The employee's name and Social Security number (SSN) shown on the W-2 must match the Social Security Administration's (SSA's) records. When they do not, SSA issues a *no-match* letter. Receipt of a no-match letter does not necessarily mean that the employee is an illegal alien or that he or she has falsified the W-4 form submitted when hired. The mismatch could be the result of an employer error in recording the employee's SSN on the W-2, an employee name change through marriage or divorce, or an error on the employee's W-4. Of course, it could also be the result of the employee's using someone else's number or just making one up.

QUICK TIP

SSA has a number of procedures available for verifying Social Security numbers beforehand. The procedures are explained at: www.ssa.gov/employer/ssnv.htm.

The U.S. Immigration and Customs Enforcement (ICE) of the Department of Homeland Security has recently issued new regulations regarding an employer's response to a no-match letter. Although ICE says these regulations provide a *safe harbor* for employers, many have argued that they actually impose new obligations on the employer. In any event, the regulations say that on receipt of a no-match letter the employer should, within thirty days after receipt of the letter, verify that the mismatch was not the result of a record-keeping error on the employer's part and request the employee to confirm the accuracy of employment records. If these don't resolve the matter, the employer must, within ninety days after receipt of the no-match letter, ask the employee to resolve the issue with SSA.

If any of these steps leads to resolution of the problem, the employer must follow instructions on the no-match letter itself to correct information with SSA and retain a record of the verification with SSA. If none of these steps resolves the problem, the employer must, within three additional days, complete a new I-9 form without using the questionable Social Security number and instead use documentation presented by the employee that conforms with the I-9 document identity requirements and includes a photograph and other biographic data. If the employee is unable to produce appropriate alternative I-9 documentation, then presumably he or she must be fired.

Alert!

At this writing ICE has been temporarily enjoined from enforcing the new regulations and is working on revisions.

QUICK TIP

Independent contractors who have been paid more than $600 during the prior calendar year are issued Form 1099-MISC by January 31. Partners in general partnerships, members of limited liability companies that have not elected to be taxed as corporations, and shareholders of corporations that have elected S corp status are issued K-1 forms at the time the partnership, LLC, or S corp files its own tax return. (See Chapter 1 for more information.)

Payroll Services

For very modest charges, a commercial payroll service will:

- Calculate each employee's deductions and withholdings;
- Issue net checks to employees using the employer's preprinted check stock (or make deposits directly to the employees' bank accounts);
- Provide a check stub to each employee showing current and year-to-date earnings, deductions, and withholdings;
- Make all required federal and state tax deposits;
- Prepare all federal and state reports; and,
- Prepare W-2 forms and appropriate transmittal forms.

Particularly for smaller employers, this service is difficult to beat. Be cautioned, however, that the employer will be held responsible if the payroll service fails to make required tax deposits. For that reason, it is a good idea to check with the IRS periodically to be sure no deficiencies exist. The address on file with the IRS for mailing deficiency notices should be the employer's address, not that of the payroll service.

Chapter

8

Leave Policies

With a few exceptions discussed later in this chapter, there is no obligation for an employer to offer any leave at all. Of course, most employers do so because it is customary, it is humane, and not doing so would place the employer at a competitive disadvantage in the marketplace.

Vacation and Sick Leave

A typical vacation formula for regular, full-time employees might give ten days (two weeks) per year for the first two or three years of employment and fifteen days (three weeks) per year after the third or fourth year. Limitations are commonly placed on the amount of vacation that can be carried forward—a *use-it or lose-it policy*. This encourages employees to take regular vacations, which in turn improves morale. It also avoids the disruption of extra-long absences.

QUICK TIP

For employers covered by Title VII of the federal Civil Rights Act or equivalent state law, a temporary disability caused by pregnancy or childbirth must be treated the same under the employer's sick leave policy as a temporary disability caused by other medical conditions. (See Chapter 15 for more detailed information.)

Sick leave is often ten days per year. Employers need to specify in their employee handbooks what is covered by sick leave and what is not. For example, must the actual employee be sick or does a sick child or spouse also qualify? How about routine, nonemergency medical and dental visits for the employee or for the employee's child? And believe it or not, the policy needs to address sick pets as well.

Alert!

A number of jurisdictions are considering legislation requiring employers to provide at least some paid leave. San Francisco and the District of Columbia already have such laws.

When time off for an injury or illness extends more than a few days, employers may want to require written verification from the employee's health care practitioner. After a serious illness or injury, *certification of fitness for duty* may be required on the employee's return. These policies, too, should be spelled out in the employee handbook and applied uniformly to avoid claims of favoritism or discrimination.

Alert!

An employer policy that requires a health care provider's certification to state a diagnosis of the condition that gave rise to the absence may violate the Americans with Disabilities Act. A federal appellate court recently ruled that since a diagnosis might reveal an underlying disability, the requirement runs afoul of the ADA's prohibition on inquiring about disabilities.

To eliminate any implication that employees are hired for a year period, it is good practice to express vacation and sick leave as the number of hours accrued per pay period rather than the number of days accrued per year. For example, for an employer that pays semimonthly (twenty-four times a year), ten days of vacation per year translates to 3.33 hours per pay period. For the same reason, *vacation* or *paid leave* is preferred over *annual leave*.

In general, a terminated employee must be paid wages accrued up to the time of termination. If the employer's announced policy is to cash out accrued leave at termination, then the employee has earned the contract right to be cashed out, just as the right to wages has been earned. On the other hand, in most states, the employer is free to adopt a policy of not paying for unused leave at termination or limiting the amount of leave which will be paid.

Some employers have a policy that if an employee quits without giving the normal two-weeks' notice, or is fired for cause, any accrued but unused vacation leave is forfeited. Such a policy is enforceable in most states so long as it is explained to employees *beforehand*. But the law differs on this point. Some courts have held that unused leave *must* be cashed out on termination, regardless of the employer's policy to the contrary.

Alert!

Vacation and sick leave benefits that an employer provides out of its general assets are exempt from *Employee Retirement Income Security Act* requirements. However, if the employer establishes a dedicated fund to cover those benefits, ERISA may apply. (ERISA is discussed in Chapter 9.)

FMLA Coverage and Eligibility

Some employers consider the *Family and Medical Leave Act* (FMLA), the *Americans with Disabilities Act* (ADA), and workers' compensation laws to be a three-legged stool upon which employees rest while milking their employer. It is true that prior to those laws, an employer could fire an employee for taking extended leave, no matter how good the reason, and had no obligation to offer a returning employee his or her old job or any job at all. It is also true that under certain circumstances, an employee could now be entitled to the protections of all three laws at the same time. The real problem for employers, however, is not so much that these laws give employees too many rights, but that the laws are complex and compliance can be tricky.

When leave qualifies under FMLA, a covered employer must:

- Grant an eligible employee up to twelve weeks of unpaid leave, including intermittent leave as needed, within a twelve-month period;
- Restore the employee to his or her former job upon return to work, or to an *equivalent job* (a job that is virtually identical to the former job in terms of pay, benefits, and other employment terms and conditions); and,
- Maintain group health insurance coverage for the employee, including family coverage, on the same basis as if the employee had continued to work.

Employers are covered under the FMLA if they have fifty or more employees for at least twenty weeks during the current or preceding calendar year. (From time to time Congress considers lowering this fifty-employee threshold, but it has not done so as of this writing.) An employee is potentially eligible for FMLA leave if each one of the following conditions is met:

- The employee works for a covered employer;
- The employee has been on the job for a year or more;
- The employee has worked at least 1250 hours during the previous year; and,
- There are at least fifty employees who work at the location where the employee works or within seventy-five miles of that location.

The only exception to the duty to grant FMLA leave is for *key employees* whose absence would cause substantial and grievous economic injury to the operations of the employer—a tough standard to say the least. If the employer intends to deny leave on this basis, the employer must first notify the affected employee and give the employee an opportunity to change his or her mind about taking FMLA leave.

An eligible employee is entitled to FMLA leave when the employee:

- Has a serious health condition;
- Needs to care for a spouse, child, or parent with a serious health condition;
- Needs to care for a newborn child; or,
- Adopts a son or daughter, or has a child placed with the employee for foster care.

Serious health condition is defined as an illness, injury, impairment, physical, or mental condition that involves:

- Treatment as an in-patient in a hospital, hospice, or residential medical care facility;

- A period of incapacity requiring absence of more than three days from work, school, or other regular activity and that involves continuing treatment by a health-care provider;
- Any period of incapacity due to pregnancy or prenatal care;
- Any period of incapacity due to a chronic, serious health condition;
- A period of incapacity that is permanent or long-term, even if there is no effective treatment; or,
- Absences to receive multiple treatments where the underlying condition, if left untreated, would likely result in incapacity of more than three consecutive days.

U.S. Department of Labor (DOL) regulations expand on the statutory definition. DOL regulations say that a condition qualifies as *serious* if the employee is incapacitated for more than *three consecutive calendar days* and the condition requires treatment *two or more times* by a health care practitioner. Even the flu can satisfy this test, according to a decision by the Fourth Circuit Court of Appeals in Richmond, Virginia.

A recent amendment to FMLA allows a spouse, child, parent, or next of kin of a member of the Armed Forces to take up to 26 weeks of leave to care for the service member when he or she is undergoing medical treatment, recuperation, or therapy, or is temporarily disabled with a serious illness or injury. A further amendment allows up to 12 weeks of leave because of a *qualified exigency* arising when a spouse, child, or parent of the employee has been called to active duty. This further amendment will not become effective until the U.S. Department of Labor issues regulations defining the term *qualified exigency*.

QUICK TIP

For employers covered by the *Family and Medical Leave Act*, unexplained or undocumented leave should never result in automatic discipline. The employer should first make an effort to determine whether the leave qualifies as FMLA leave and, if so, whether the employee wishes to take FMLA leave.

The *Family and Medical Leave Act* requires employers to respond promptly to employee requests for leave under FMLA. Employers may require a *medical certification* of the serious health condition from a *health care provider*. The employer must allow the employee fifteen days to obtain the certification. The employer may, at its own expense, obtain a second opinion from another health care provider of the employer's own choosing, so long as the health care provider is not under contract with, or regularly used by, the employer. If the two opinions differ, the employer and employee together choose a third health care provider, whose opinion is final and binding. Optional Form WH-380, developed by the Employment Standards Administration of the U.S. Department of Labor, may be used for these medical certifications. The form is available at: www.dol.gov/esa/whd.

The list of health care providers whose medical certifications can trigger FMLA leave is long and somewhat surprising. As might be expected, it includes doctors of medicine and osteopathy, but they need to be licensed only in the state in which they practice, not necessarily in the state where the employer or employee is located. The list also includes: podiatrists; dentists; clinical psychologists; optometrists; chiropractors; nurse practitioners; nurse midwives; clinical social workers (so long as they are practicing within the scope of their licenses); Christian Science practitioners; and any health care provider recognized by the employer's health care benefits manager. Foreign as well as U.S.-licensed health care providers are included.

Alert!

For disabilities covered by the *ADA*, the employer may be required to offer leave as a reasonable accommodation, so long as doing so does not cause an undue hardship. A requirement to offer ADA leave is separate from FMLA leave requirements and may even extend beyond the twelve-week FMLA obligation.

FMLA Benefits

An employee on FMLA leave is entitled to no more than twelve weeks' leave within a twelve-month period. The employer has some options in determining when the twelve-month period begins and ends. For example, a calendar year may be used, the employer's fiscal year may be used, an *employment year* based on the employee's start date may be used, or a rolling twelve-month period that looks back from when the employee requests FMLA leave may be used. Under a rolling twelve-month period, the employer may deny a new FMLA leave request if, during the immediately preceding twelve-month period, the employee has taken the full twelve-week entitlement. Whatever option the employer chooses must be applied consistently to all employees.

An employer must continue group health insurance coverage during FMLA leave on the same basis as if the employer had continued to work. This means that if the plan was noncontributory (where the employer pays 100% of the premium), the employer must continue to do so for employees under FMLA leave. On the other hand, if the plan is *contributory* (that is, if the employees pay some portion of their premiums), the employer may require an employee on FMLA leave to continue contributing on the same basis. The employer has a right to recover the employer's portion of the premiums if the employee does not return to work when FMLA leave ends. If the employer has no group health plan, the employer does not have to provide health insurance during FMLA leave.

The employer may, but is not required to, continue other benefits for employees on FMLA leave. Seniority, for example, need not accrue. The employer may also insist that the employee use vacation, sick leave, or other paid leave before going on unpaid FMLA leave.

QUICK TIP

When a husband and wife are employed by the same employer, they are entitled only to a combined total of twelve weeks' FMLA leave if the leave is based on the birth of a child or the placement with them of a child for adoption or foster care.

When FMLA leave ends, the employer is required to restore the returning employee to the same or an equivalent position. Department of Labor regulations define *equivalent position* as one that is virtually identical to the employee's former position in terms of pay, benefits, and working conditions—including privileges, prerequisites, and status. Assignment of an employee to a different shift on return from FMLA leave violates the equivalent position requirement.

Employers who are covered by FMLA should follow these guidelines.

- Post the FMLA notice (WH Publication 1420) required by the U.S. Department of Labor.
- Adopt a FMLA policy and publicize it to your employees (See Fact Sheet No. 28 of the DOL's Employment Standards Administration).
- If the employer has an employee handbook or a collective bargaining agreement, set out the policy in those documents.
- Be alert to leave that may qualify under FMLA, and make inquiry to determine whether FMLA might apply whenever an employee requests any type of leave.
- Never discipline an employee for unauthorized absence without first determining whether FMLA might apply.
- When an employee requests FMLA leave, notify the employee promptly (within one or two business days) whether the leave will qualify under FMLA, whether you require a medical certification or other documentation in support of the leave, and what the employee's rights and responsibilities are while on FMLA leave (DOL Form WH-381 satisfies the employer's notice requirements).
- Maintain group health insurance for the employee during FMLA leave on the same basis as if the employee has continued to work (the cost of which may be recovered from the employee if the employee does not return to work after FMLA leave expires).
- Upon termination of FMLA leave, restore the employee to the same or an equivalent position.

Note:

The Department of Labor documents mentioned in this section are available at: www.dol.gov/esa/regs/compliance/whd/1421.htm.

FMLA leave may be terminated for an employee who states, unequivocally, that he or she does not intend to return to work or who fails to comply with their employer's requirement to furnish periodic reports justifying continued leave.

A Department of Labor regulation requires employers to notify their employees when leave is being treated as FMLA leave. The regulation goes on to say that if an employer fails to do so, the leave taken does not count against an employee's FMLA entitlement. The validity of the regulation was recently tested before the Supreme Court. The Court upheld the regulation's notice requirement, but it struck down—as contrary to the FMLA—the *penalty* for failing to give notice. In other words, employers are required to notify employees when leave is being treated as FMLA leave, but failure to do so does not necessarily result in disqualification of the leave as FMLA leave.

The question whether an employer may discipline an employee while on FMLA leave does not arise frequently. But it can arise when, for example, the employee's misconduct occurs before he or she takes FMLA leave. It is clear that an employer cannot discipline an employee *because* he or she is on FMLA leave, but nothing in the law prevents an employer from pursuing disciplinary action unrelated to FMLA *while* an employee is on leave.

CASE STUDY: MISCONDUCT WHILE ON FMLA LEAVE

In a recent Sixth Circuit Court of Appeals case, the employer had a policy prohibiting employees from performing outside work without the employer's permission. The employee in the case requested and was granted four weeks' FMLA leave in connection with his wife's childbirth, but while on leave he managed a restaurant that his wife had recently purchased. The employer fired the employee when he returned from leave and the court upheld the firing. The court pointed out that the right to reinstatement under FMLA is not absolute, since an employer need not reinstate an employee who would have lost his job even if he had not taken FMLA leave. That was exactly the case here—the employee was fired for violating the company's outside work rule, not because he took FMLA leave.

The Sixth Circuit decision relied on the Department of Labor's FMLA regulations that list a number of circumstances under which an employer may refuse to reinstate or delay reinstatement:

- If an employee fails to provide a requested fitness-for-duty certification to return to work, an employer may delay restoration until the employee submits the certificate.
- An employee has no greater right to reinstatement or to other benefits and conditions of employment than if the employee had been continuously employed during the FMLA leave period.
- An employer may require an employee on FMLA leave to report periodically on the employee's status and intention to return to work.
- An employee who fraudulently obtains FMLA leave from an employer is not protected by FMLA's job restoration or maintenance of health benefits provisions.
  - If the employer has a uniformly-applied policy governing outside or supplemental employment, such a policy may continue to apply to an employee while on FMLA leave.

DOL regulations prohibit employers from discriminating against employees and applicants who have taken FMLA leave. So an employer may not base a job decision on the fact that an existing employee, or a former employee who is reapplying, exercised rights under FMLA. Similarly, if a job applicant took FMLA leave while with a *different* employer, the new employer cannot use that fact in deciding whether to hire.

Military Leave

The *Uniformed Services Employment and Reemployment Rights Act* (USERRA), adopted in 1994, requires employers to carry service members on leave status for benefit and seniority purposes while on active duty and to reemploy them when they return. USERRA also prohibits employers from discriminating against veterans and persons in the uniformed services. USERRA applies to all service members except those who receive dishonorable or bad conduct discharges, or who are discharged under less than honorable conditions.

It also protects volunteers as well as those ordered to active duty. To be eligible for USERRA protection, the service member must notify the employer that he or she has been called to active duty, unless he or she is precluded from doing so by military necessity, or unless it is otherwise impossible or unreasonable to do so.

Employees on active duty are considered to be on furlough or leave of absence. As such, they are entitled to whatever benefits other similarly situated employees receive. In addition, an employee on active duty:

- May (but cannot be required to) use any accrued vacation or other leave with pay.
- May elect to continue any employer-sponsored health insurance coverage for up to eighteen months. (For employees on active duty for less than thirty-one days, the employee can only be required to pay the portion of the premium normally charged to employees. For employees on active duty for more than thirty days, the employee can be charged up to 102% of the full premium.)
- May continue to contribute to any retirement plan to which he or she was contributing prior to active duty.
- Must be treated as continuing to work for the employer for purposes of computing the employer's pension plan funding obligation and benefits under any pension plan in which he or she participated. (This would be significant for defined benefit plans using a formula that includes a years-of-service component.)

A returning service member is entitled to be reemployed unless the employer can show that the employer's circumstances have so changed as to make reemployment impossible or unreasonable or that reemployment would impose an undue hardship. This right applies to service members who have been on active duty for as long as five years, and, in some cases, even longer.

The returning service member is entitled to be placed in the position in which he or she would have been employed but for the call to active duty (or in a position with equivalent seniority, status, and pay). Under this *escalator* provision, the employer must take into consideration any promotions or advancements the member would have received if he or she had continued to work.

If a member who has been on active duty for more than ninety days is not qualified for an escalated position, the employer must make reasonable efforts to help the member become qualified. For returning service members who became disabled while on active duty, the employer must make reasonable efforts to accommodate the disability.

To be eligible for reemployment, the returning service member must, after release from active duty, notify the employer of his or her intent to return to work. Strict time limits apply to this notice requirement.

- If the period of active duty was less than thirty-one days, the returning member must report to work on the first regular workday after release from duty (after allowing for an eight-hour rest period and safe transportation home).
- If the period of active duty was between thirty-one and 181 days, the returning member must apply for reemployment within fourteen days after release from duty.
- If the period of active duty was more than 180 days, the returning member must apply for reemployment within ninety days after release from duty.

These time limits can be extended for up to two years or more in cases of returning service members who are hospitalized or convalescing from an illness or injury suffered while on active duty.

Once the employer has reemployed a returning service member, the employer is restricted in its ability to discharge the member. Except for discharges for cause, members who have been on active duty for 180 days or less cannot be fired for a period of 180 days after reemployment. Members who have been on active duty for more than 180 days cannot be fired for one year.

Alert!

Docking the salary of exempt employees who are on temporary military leave of five days or less will cause loss of the exemption for *Fair Labor Standards Act* purposes. However, an employer may offset any compensation received by the employee for military service. (See Chapter 5 for more details.)

Other Types of Leave

State laws frequently have their own provisions regarding required leave. Be alert to the following possibilities in your state.

Extended Leave

Little FMLA laws are becoming increasingly popular at the state level, although eligibility and leave periods do not necessarily coincide with federal law.

Jury Duty

Federal law protects the jobs of employees who are serving as jurors in federal courts and most states provide similar protection for employees serving at the state level. Some states even require salary continuation during periods of jury service. Even where salary continuation is not required, it is common for employers to pay full salary or at least make up the difference between juror fees and regular salary. Docking the salary of exempt employees who are on jury service of five days or less will cause loss of the exemption for FLSA purposes, although an employer may offset any juror fees received by the employee.

Figure 8.1 contains a provision recommended for inclusion in employee handbooks regarding jury duty.

Figure 8.1: JURY DUTY

The following provision should be included in your employee handbook:

The Company encourages employees to fulfill their civic obligation to serve as jurors when summoned. The Company will not discharge, threaten to discharge, intimidate, or coerce any employee by reason of such employee's jury service, or the attendance or scheduled attendance in connection with such service.

Alert!

Asking an employee to lie about his or her availability for jury duty is a criminal offense.

Maternity and Paternity Leave

See Chapter 15.

Testimony

Some states protect the jobs of employees who are subpoenaed to appear in court as *witnesses* or who are attending court under a *victim's right* law. Docking the salary of exempt employees in these circumstances will cause loss of the exemption for FLSA purposes, although an employer may offset any witness fees received by the employee.

Paid Time Off

Some employers have abandoned the various forms of voluntary leave—vacation, sick leave, emergency leave, personal leave, etc.—and replaced them with a *Paid Time Off* or PTO plan.

Suppose, for example, that traditional company policy grants ten days paid vacation per year, ten days paid sick leave per year, three days leave without pay for a death in the immediate family, three days personal leave without pay, and up to three days hazard leave with pay for weather-related absences. Keeping track of all these categories is an administrative nightmare. Worse, determining in which category a particular day off should be placed imposes a substantial burden on supervisors and engenders endless bickering and hard feelings among employees.

After switching to a PTO plan, the company now grants twenty paid days off per year (6.67 hours each semimonthly pay period) that employees can use for any purpose. In addition to reducing administrative burdens and morale problems, the PTO plan discourages employees from taking sick leave, because doing so uses up vacation time. Instead, employees now schedule most of their leave in advance, giving the employer an opportunity to arrange for coverage or an opportunity to require that the leave be taken at a time more convenient for the employer.

PTO plans can be fine-tuned, depending on a particular employer's experience and needs. For example, a day of *scheduled* leave might cost the employee only six hours out of his or her PTO bank, but *unscheduled* leave might cost the full eight hours. The employer might also impose a cap on the amount of PTO that can be accumulated in the PTO bank. Allowing employees to draw prescribed amounts of PTO in cash in lieu of leave time tends to limit overall absences. PTO time can also be cashed out with *pretax* dollars in the form of employer contributions to a 401(k) retirement plan or cafeteria plan.

Other details need to be considered in implementing a PTO plan. For example, what happens to accumulated PTO at termination of employment—is it forfeited or cashed out? How is PTO time coordinated with FMLA—is the employee required to exhaust PTO before taking FMLA leave or may he or she take FMLA leave first? Of course, these same questions arise with any leave policy the employer may have.

PTO plans seem to have all the advantages over traditional leave arrangements. They are simpler to administer; they are more flexible; they can be fine-tuned to meet the employer's specific needs; and they discourage unscheduled sick leave. PTO plans deserve serious consideration.

Chapter

Deferred Compensation and ERISA

For a typical employer, the cost of employee benefits—together with other payroll costs like FICA and workers' compensation insurance—may be 25% or more of payroll. So, for every salary dollar promised an employee, the employer actually incurs at least $1.25—a significant factor when considering hiring an additional employee or raising an existing salary.

On the other hand, benefit plans help an employer attract and keep quality employees. Their costs are also generally tax deductible by the employer, like wage and salary payments. Some benefit plans enjoy especially favorable tax treatment. For example, even though the employer gets a current tax deduction for the cost of providing a cash benefit, the employee need not include the value of the benefit in current gross income for tax purposes. In other words, the benefit has a tax postponement feature. Where taxation of earnings on benefit contributions is postponed—called *inside build-up*—the benefit fund can grow much more rapidly than the employee's other investments. Many deferred compensation arrangements qualify for this favorable tax treatment.

If properly designed and administered, some plans give the employer a current tax deduction for the cost of providing the benefit, but the benefit is *never* taxed to the employee. Group health insurance and life insurance plans, for example, can fall in this category.

One of the risks of classifying workers as independent contractors is that if the IRS disagrees and re-classifies them as employees, these new employees may demand pension plan contributions for prior years. Worse, if a plan fails to include workers who should have been covered, the plan may lose its tax-qualified status. (See Chapter 7 for more information.)

These tax morsels come at a price. Employee benefit plans are highly regulated under tax and labor laws administered by the IRS and the U.S. Department of Labor. For example, a qualified plan cannot discriminate in favor of highly compensated individuals—it cannot give all the benefits to the boss and leave little or nothing for the employees. Qualified retirement plans must also meet strict funding and vesting requirements, so that the promised benefit is not illusory.

The design and operation of benefit plans are among the most complex tasks you are likely to face as an employer. It is best to hire an experienced benefits consultant who is familiar with the range of available options. A benefits consultant can project your future costs in managing and funding various plans, guide you through tax and labor law requirements, and be available to help with plan administration.

Deferred Compensation

Various arrangements fall under the general rubric of *deferred compensation*. In most cases, the employer will want the arrangement to qualify for the favorable tax treatment discussed above. These arrangements include:

- Pension plans;
- Profit-sharing plans;
- Employee Stock Ownership Plans (ESOPs);
- 401(k) plans;
- SIMPLE plans;
- Tax-sheltered annuities (403(b) plans); and,
- Cash balance plans.

Some common characteristics of each of these plans are: contributions to the plan within specified limits are deductible for tax purposes by the employer, but are not includible in the employee's gross income until later, upon actual receipt of benefits by the employee; the accumulated benefits must *vest* (become nonforfeitable) within a specified time period; and plan income is exempt from taxation. In the case of qualified retirement plans, the right to withdraw funds from the plan is restricted prior to retirement, which can be as early as age 59½. Withdrawals become mandatory when the plan participant reaches age 70½ or later retires. (Retirement plan participants who hold a 5% or greater ownership interest in the sponsoring employer must begin mandatory withdrawals at age 70½ even if they keep working.)

Pension plans generally fall into two broad categories—defined contribution plans and defined benefit plans.

Defined Contribution (Money Purchase) Plan

In a *defined contribution plan*, a separate account is established for each employee to which the employer (and sometimes the employee) make regular contributions according to an established formula such as a percentage of salary. When an employee retires, the employee's retirement benefit is whatever has been contributed to his or her account, plus any income the account has earned through investments (but minus any investment losses the account has suffered). 401(k) plans and profit-sharing plans are defined contribution plans.

An employer may automatically enroll its employees in a defined contribution plan, subject to each employee's right to opt out.

Defined Benefit Plan

In a *defined benefit plan*, there are no separate accounts for employees. Instead, there is simply a common fund out of which each retiring employee is entitled to a specified monthly benefit. The amount of the monthly benefit is usually based on a formula, such as years of service times the highest annual income, times some factor such as 1.5%, divided by 12. So for an employee earning $50,000 who retires after 30 years, the monthly benefit might be 30 x 50,000 x .015 / 12 = $1875. The employer is obligated to keep sufficient assets in the fund based on actuarial computations to enable payment of the benefits when they come due. (Figure 9.1 explains the differences between the two kinds of benefit plans.)

Figure 9.1: DIFFERENCE BETWEEN TWO TYPES OF PLANS

The major differences between defined contribution and defined benefit plans are as follows.

- *Separate account.* In a defined contribution plan, each employee has a separate account, whereas in a defined benefit plan there are no separate accounts but only a common fund.

- *Investment risk.* In a defined contribution plan, the employee wins if the market goes up and loses if the market goes down. In a defined benefit plan, the employer bears the investment risk.

- *Mortality risk.* If the employee lives for many years after retirement, he or she may use up all the funds in the defined contribution account. But if he or she had a defined benefit plan, the monthly annuity continues for life. In short, the employer bears the mortality risk in a defined benefit plan. The employee usually bears that risk in a defined contribution plan.

- *Insurance.* Defined benefit plans are insured by the federal Pension Benefit Guaranty Corporation, for which the employer pays an insurance premium. Defined contribution plans are not insured because there is no guaranteed benefit at retirement.

- *Settlement options.* Defined benefit plans simply pay the prescribed monthly benefit. In a defined contribution plan, the retiring employee can usually use the amount in his or her account to purchase an annuity, optionally (and subject to spousal consent, as discussed later) take the account in a lump sum, or roll it over to an individual retirement account (IRA) from which he or she may make periodic withdrawals.

- *Funding.* Defined contribution plans are always fully funded (assuming the employer actually makes the promised contribution), because the benefit is based on whatever is in the account. Defined benefit plans may become underfunded if, for example, investments do not turn out as expected or if retirees live longer than their life expectancies. For that reason, the employer must do an annual actuarial study of the plan and cover any shortfalls. Of course, if investments have performed better than expected, the employer's funding obligation will be reduced.

- *Loading.* Defined benefit plans that use a years-of-service/highest-pay formula to determine benefits are said to be backloaded because the size of the benefit produced by the formula tends to increase significantly in the last few years of employment.

> Defined contribution plans tend to be more front-loaded because the benefit amount grows at a more even rate.

Cash Balance Plans

Another item in the plan menagerie that has recently been in the news is the cash balance plan. Technically classified as a defined benefit plan, a cash balance plan has characteristics of both defined benefit and defined contribution plans. For that reason, cash balance plans are sometimes called *hybrids*.

Alert!

> When an employer converts from a defined benefit plan to a cash balance plan, employees lose the back-loaded boost they had anticipated from their defined benefit plan. Since this loss is borne most heavily by older workers who are near retirement, some have argued that such conversions amount to age discrimination.

In a cash balance plan, the employee establishes a hypothetical account for each employee. The account is hypothetical because there are no actual specific assets that belong to the employee. The account is really just a bookkeeping entry.

The employer credits the hypothetical account with a specific dollar amount each year, usually based on a percentage of the employee's salary. In addition, the employer credits the account with interest earned on the account balance—either a fixed interest rate or a rate tied to treasury bills or some other index.

EXAMPLE: An employer establishes a cash balance plan under which he credits 8% of salary and which is deemed to earn interest at 7% per year. For an employee who earns $35,000 per year, the balance in the hypothetical account will be $2,800 at the end of the first year (8% of $35,000). At the end of the second year, the

> balance in the account will be $5,796: the original $2,800, plus 7% interest on that amount ($196), plus another $2,800 credited at the end of the second year. When the employee retires, his benefit is based on whatever is then in the hypothetical account.

Because each employee does have an account—albeit hypothetical—and because the amount of the ultimate benefit depends on what is in the account at retirement, cash balance plans look like defined contribution plans. Other characteristics, however, make them look like defined benefit plans. For example, if the fund earns more than the interest rate promised to employees (7% in the above example), the employer's funding obligation is reduced, and therefore the employer bears the investment risk.

Profit-Sharing Plans

Profit-sharing plans allow an employer to share company profits with employees. At the same time, they give the employer some flexibility in determining how much to contribute to the plan. Although the employer's contribution must be substantial and recurring in order to maintain the plan, the employer can change the contribution from year to year to track business cycles. Profit-sharing plans are defined contribution plans, since each employee has an individual account and the ultimate benefit is a function of what is in the account. They are often used as retirement plans or at least as a component of a retirement plan, but they can also provide benefit payments at other times, such as after a fixed period of years, without regard to retirement.

401(k) Plans

401(k) Plans (so-called because they are authorized by Section 401(k) of the Internal Revenue Code) are a special type of defined contribution plan. Typically, the employee makes an election each year to contribute a certain percentage of salary. The employer then matches that election in some ratio, such as 100% of the employee's contribution up to 3% of the employee's salary and 50% of the employee's contribution that is between 3% and 5% of salary. (The elective component of the plan is sometimes called a *cash or deferral arrangement* or CODA.) Neither the employee's contribution nor the employer's match is subject to tax. In addition, 401(k) plans include a *profit-sharing* component, by which the employer agrees to pay some additional percentage of employee salaries that the employee can elect to take in cash (which is taxable to the employee) or in the form of an additional contribution to the plan (which is nontaxable).

SIMPLE Plans

SIMPLE plans (SIMPLE stands for Savings Incentive Match Plan for Employees) are available to employers with one hundred or fewer employees. All employees who receive compensation of $5,000 or more per year must be eligible to participate. SIMPLE plans may take the form of either 401(k) plans (discussed above) or Individual Retirement Accounts. In the IRA form, a SIMPLE plan must permit each eligible employee to elect to have the employer contribution (expressed as a percentage of compensation and subject to statutory limits) either paid to the employee in cash or paid into an IRA account. If taken in cash, the payment is immediately taxable to the employee. If taken as an IRA contribution, tax is deferred and the account is subject to usual IRA rules. The employer may also make a matching, tax deductible contribution to the IRA account.

For more information on SIMPLE plans, go to: www.dol.gov/ebsa/publications/simple.html.

Tax-Sheltered Annuities

Tax-sheltered annuities (sometimes called 403(b) annuities) are only available to organizations that are exempt from income tax under Section 501(c)(3) of the Internal Revenue Code, such as educational organizations, churches, public and private schools, and so on. (See Chapter 23 for a more detailed discussion.)

Nonqualified Deferred Compensation

The American Jobs Creation Act of 2004 added new section 409A to the Internal Revenue Code for taxing compensation *under non-qualified deferred compensation plans*. The effect of the provision is to ignore artificial arrangements for spreading out compensation over multiple years, and instead to tax compensation when it is actually earned.

For purposes of section 409A, a *deferred compensation plan* is any arrangement under which an employee or independent contractor receives a legally binding right to compensation in one year but is not in actual or constructive receipt of that compensation until a later year. Short-term deferrals of up to 2½ months after the end of a year are not considered deferrals, so that year-end bonuses that are not actually paid until February or early March are taxed to the employee in year two, not year one.

A *nonqualified* deferred compensation plan is any plan that provides for deferred compensation except a *qualified* employee plan (such as those discussed earlier in this chapter) and except a bona fide vacation leave, sick leave, compensatory time, disability pay, or death benefit plan. A *plan* is any arrangement or agreement with one or more persons. Compensation is *constructively received* when it is credited to an employee's or independent contractor's account or when it is otherwise made available to him or her.

Under section 409A, deferred compensation pursuant to a nonqualified deferred compensation plan is subject to *immediate taxation* to the recipient, plus a 20% additional tax, unless the compensation is subject to a *substantial risk of forfeiture*, or unless the plan complies with detailed requirements relating to the timing of elections, funding, and distributions. Although the law does not define substantial risk of forfeiture, it does give the example of compensation which is conditioned on the future performance of substantial services.

In general, compensation distributed after an employee or independent contractor terminates, becomes disabled, or dies is subject to taxation when received, rather than to immediate taxation in the year the right to receipt arose. In the case of termination of service by a *specified employee*, however, distributions cannot be made until six months after the termination. A *specified employee* is any officer of a corporation with publicly traded stock who is either a 5% owner and has annual compensation in excess of $130,000, or a 1% owner and has annual compensation in excess of $150,000.

Alert!

Severance agreements offered by public companies to its departing executives need to be drafted with the nonqualified deferred compensation rules in mind in order to avoid unanticipated tax consequences.

ERISA

The Employee Retirement Income Security Act (ERISA) was passed in 1974 in response to abuses in the handling of pension funds. Before ERISA, it was not unusual for employers to make grossly unwise investments with pension funds, to underfund pension plans, to adopt a drawn-out vesting schedule, or to borrow from pension plans to cover operating expenses and then be unable to pay promised benefits when the time came. Employers also sometimes fired their senior workers just before those workers were to retire and become eligible for benefits. Top-heavy plans that favored owners or upper management were also common.

To cure these abuses, Congress enacted ERISA. ERISA has parallel labor law and tax law aspects. For example, ERISA has minimum participation and vesting requirements. It contains detailed reporting and disclosure requirements. It imposes fiduciary (trustee) standards on plan administrators. It requires defined benefit plans to be fully funded, meaning that the employer must contribute sufficient amounts on a current basis so that the promised benefits will be available at retirement time. It even requires defined benefit plans to carry insurance against any shortfall in promised benefits should the plan terminate.

But ERISA goes far beyond pension plan abuses. Although it applies to employee benefit pension plans, it also applies to employee welfare benefit plans. Employee *welfare* benefit plans are defined as any plan, fund, or program established or maintained by an employer for the purpose of providing benefits for:

- Medical, surgical, or hospital care;
- Sickness;
- Accident;

- Disability;
- Death;
- Unemployment;
- Vacation;
- Apprenticeship or other training programs;
- Day care centers;
- Scholarship funds; or,
- Prepaid legal services.

In short, it applies to almost every ongoing plan or program an employer has for providing group benefits to employees. The only exceptions are plans that are maintained solely to comply with workers' compensation or unemployment insurance laws, plans maintained by tax-exempt churches or associations of churches, and certain unfunded plans.

Preemption

What makes ERISA particularly powerful is its *preemption provision*. By its own terms, ERISA supersedes any and all state laws relating to any employee benefit plan. One of Congress's purposes in enacting this preemption provision was to create a uniform body of *federal* law governing the administration of employee benefit plans.

CASE STUDY: BENEFITS SUBJECT TO ERISA

A grocery store chain in the New Orleans area issued vouchers to its retired employees, which they could use instead of cash to purchase goods at the chain's stores. When the chain decided to sell its business, it canceled the voucher arrangement and retirees who had been receiving the vouchers sued. The Fifth Circuit Court of Appeals ruled that the plan was subject to ERISA, so that the retirees were entitled to money damages for loss of their vested pension benefit.

On the other hand, the Supreme Court concluded that an employer policy of cashing out accrued vacation when an employee terminates was not covered by ERISA. In that case, the State of

Massachusetts brought criminal charges against the employer for violating that state's wage payment laws by refusing to pay certain employees for unused vacation. Since ERISA did not apply, the State was free to pursue criminal charges against the employer.

Subject to the exceptions mentioned above, ERISA requires every employee benefit plan to:

- Be in writing;
- Place its assets in a trust (except where the assets of the plan consist of insurance contracts or policies);
- Name one or more fiduciaries to administer the plan;
- Describe how the plan is to be funded;
- Describe the basis on which benefits are paid; and,
- Describe claim procedures.

Employers must provide employees with a *Summary Plan Description* (SPD) for every benefit plan covered by ERISA. SPDs describe plan eligibility requirements and they describe procedures for claiming benefits and for appealing benefit denials. SPDs must be provided within ninety days after an employee becomes a participant in the plan and after any significant modification of the plan. SPDs must also be provided every five years if there have been any amendments to the plan and every ten years if there have not been any amendments. The actual plan documents must be made available to participants and beneficiaries on request.

Employers must also file Form 5500 with the IRS each year for most types of benefit plans. The form is due on the last day of the seventh month after the end of each plan year. For plans that operate on a calendar year, the due date is July 31. The form calls for information as to the plan's financial condition, participation, and funding.

ERISA prohibits employers from interfering with employee rights under a plan or retaliating against employees for exercising plan rights. Employers are also prohibited from firing employees or taking other adverse action in order to avoid paying benefits. While an employer can, by amendment, reduce benefits under a plan (assuming the plan document permits such amendments) or even terminate a plan entirely, such actions cannot affect vested or accrued benefits.

Fiduciary Responsibilities

The fiduciary responsibilities imposed on persons who manage ERISA plans deserve mention. ERISA places managers in a special trust relationship with plan participants and beneficiaries. For example, plans must be managed in the best interests of participants and beneficiaries. They must segregate plan assets from the employer's operating funds. Plans are also prohibited from engaging in transactions with the employer. Employers and individual managers can be held personally liable for a breach of these fiduciary duties.

When an employer communicates with employees about an ERISA benefit plan, the employer may be acting in a fiduciary (trustee) capacity. If so, the employer will be held to a much higher standard of truthfulness, accuracy, and completeness than if communicating just in an employer capacity. The dangers are especially great for *Employee Stock Ownership Plans* (ESOPs), where company owners who also serve as fiduciaries routinely find themselves in conflict-of-interest situations.

Employers can also get into trouble in the area of pension plan investments. Suppose a plan allows the participating employee to direct investments within his or her account, or it provides the participant with choices among a number of mutual funds, each of which has a different objective or investment strategy. In general, employers should not give investment advice to their employees. Giving investment advice may make them liable as fiduciaries. However, plan sponsors have an obligation to provide *sufficient information* about investment choices so that the employees themselves can make informed decisions.

The Department of Labor has issued guidelines to help an employer walk the fine line between too much and too little information. Under DOL guidelines, an employer may provide the following in satisfaction of the affirmative obligation, without becoming a fiduciary:

- *Plan information*, such as the benefits of plan participation, the benefits of increasing plan contributions, the impact of pre-retirement withdrawals, investment alternatives, and historical return information;

- *General financial and investment information*, including investment concepts like diversification, risk and return, compounding, investment time horizons, and so on;
- *Asset allocation models* that provide hypothetical results based on differing assumptions of age, age to retirement, life expectancy, inflation rates, time horizons, risk profiles, and so on; and,
- *Interactive investment materials*, such as worksheets and software that enable the participant to estimate future retirement income needs and to assess the impact of different asset allocations.

When an employee becomes eligible for a pension plan distribution, plan administrators are also required to provide a written explanation of distribution options. An employee at a prominent chemical company, for example, successfully sued the company based on bad advice the company gave about the tax consequences of a roll-over distribution from one of its pension plans.

Spousal Rights to Pension Benefits

ERISA intentionally makes it difficult for pension plan participants to divert benefits from their spouses. The law requires that when a plan participant retires and he or she has a spouse, benefits must be payable in the form of a *joint and survivor annuity*—an annuity that will be paid to husband and wife jointly and that will continue to be paid (at a 50% rate) to the surviving spouse if the plan participant dies first. In order for benefits to be paid in some other fashion, such as to a different beneficiary or in a lump sum, the spouse must consent and the consent must satisfy the following statutory requirements:

- Be in writing;
- Designate some other specific beneficiary, which may not be changed without the spouse's further consent (unless the spouse expressly agrees to further changes without consent);
- Acknowledge the effect of the change; and,
- Be witnessed by a plan representative or notary public.

Courts require strict compliance with these spousal consent requirements and will not enforce a consent where requisite procedures have not been followed.

Issues arise when parties who are about to be married enter into a prenuptial agreement in which each party waives any legal claim he or she might otherwise have in the other's property, including claims to the other's pension benefits. Several courts have ruled that only a *spouse* can execute a valid consent, so that in a prenuptial agreement, where the parties are not yet married, a waiver of pension plan benefits is ineffective. Other courts have reached a contrary conclusion.

A similar issue arises in the case of a voluntary separation agreement where a divorcing couple resolves property and support issues, including claims to each other's pension plans. At least one federal court of appeals has indicated that ERISA's statutory requirements are not applicable in a divorce context, so that a voluntary separation agreement in which one spouse gives up any claim against the other's pension is effective so long as the agreement specifically refers to the plan involved.

Until the Supreme Court definitively resolves these issues, pension plan administrators are in a quandary. Suppose that a plan participant dies, and the participant's child claims benefits based on a separation agreement or prenuptial agreement that waives all spousal rights. However, the surviving spouse (who has since had a change of heart) also claims benefits, arguing that the waiver is invalid. If the plan administrator pays one of the claimants, the other might sue and force the administrator to pay again. So the safest course may be for the plan administrator to go to court and ask a federal judge to decide who is entitled—thereby incurring exactly the kind of expense and delay ERISA was designed to avoid.

Qualified Domestic Relations Orders (QDROs)

ERISA requires plans to contain a provision insulating plan benefits from an employee's creditors. In other words, if an employee fails to pay some personal obligation, is sued, and a court judgment is entered against the employee, the party who holds the judgment cannot go after pension plan assets to satisfy the judgment. But again, spouses get special protection. In a divorce proceeding, even if the parties have not reached agreement on how pension benefits should be allocated, the divorce court can issue a *qualified domestic relations order* (QDRO), awarding one spouse a portion (or all) of the other spouse's pension plan as alimony, child support, or simply as a division of marital property.

QUICK TIP

One way to avoid the uncertainty surrounding the effect of a voluntary separation agreement (but not a prenuptial agreement) is to ask the divorce court to bless the agreement by entering a QDRO incorporating the provisions of the agreement that address pension plan rights.

To be recognized as a QDRO, an order must be made pursuant to state domestic relations law that relates to alimony, child support, or marital property rights for the benefit of someone who qualifies as an alternate payee—a spouse, former spouse, child, or other dependent. A separation or property settlement agreement between divorcing spouses will not qualify as a QDRO unless the agreement's provisions otherwise satisfy ERISA requirements *and* the agreement is approved by an order of the domestic relations court. (The term *court* here includes administrative agencies if they have the power under state law to issue support orders.)

QDROs must:

- Contain the names and mailing addresses of the plan participant (employee) and each alternate payee covered by the order;
- Identify the plan to which the order applies;
- State the dollar amount or percentage interest of the alternate payee or at least the method by which the amount or percentage can be calculated; and,
- State the number of payments or time period to which the order applies.

QDROs cannot:

- Require a plan to provide the alternate payee with any type of benefit, option, or form not otherwise provided under the plan;
- Require the plan to provide increased benefits;
- Conflict with a previously issued QDRO; or,
- Order payments in the form of a joint and survivor annuity for the lives of an alternate payee and his or her subsequent spouse.

When presented with a QDRO that complies with the above requirements and prohibitions (there are some additional technical requirements that apply in special cases), a pension plan administrator must honor it. Every qualified pension plan is required to have written procedures for determining whether an order is a QDRO. Plans may, but are not required to, develop *model* QDRO forms to assist participants and potential alternate payees. Disputes as to whether an order is a valid QDRO are subject to resolution in federal court. Because ERISA preempts state law regarding pension plan administration, a state domestic relations court does *not* have the right (at least according to the U.S. Department of Labor) to determine whether its own order qualifies as a QDRO.

The Department of Labor takes the reasonable view that even before a QDRO is entered, the employer or plan administrator has an obligation to furnish a potential alternate payee (spouse, dependent child, etc.) with information about the pension plan, the participating employee's benefit status, and interest in the plan. No such information should be furnished, however, without first obtaining satisfactory evidence that a domestic relations proceeding is in fact pending and that the potential alternate payee is attempting to obtain a QDRO in that proceeding. It also makes for good employee relations to notify the participating employee that plan information has been requested.

Another aspect of ERISA's preemption provision is illustrated by a recent Supreme Court case. The case involved a Washington State statute that said a divorce decree had the effect of automatically revoking a beneficiary designation in favor of a former spouse. Presumably, the Washington legislature felt that after a plan participant gets divorced, he or she probably does not want an ex-spouse to receive plan benefits, even if he or she forgets to submit a beneficiary change. The Supreme Court invalidated the statute, saying that under ERISA the plan documents themselves govern the determination of who is the right beneficiary.

Top Hat and Excess Benefit Plans

Suppose that a company wants to hire away the star employee of one of its competitors and make that person its new CEO. The company is willing to pay whatever salary or bonus may be necessary to attract the star, but because of his or her tax status, the star does not really want or need more current taxable income. And making additional contributions to the company's qualified retirement plan for the star will not work because of the maximum contribution limits imposed by law. So the company promises to pay the new CEO deferred compensation on some future date. The amount promised may be a specified sum together with imputed earnings on that sum over the deferral period, or it may be tied to company performance or determined by some other formula.

Alert!

Before making any final commitments, the company should determine whether the star employee is bound by a noncompete agreement. (See Chapter 19 for a discussion of noncompete agreements.)

In terms of the tax consequence of this arrangement, all the new CEO is getting is a mere promise of compensation in the future (so long as the company doesn't *fund* the promise by setting aside amounts for the benefit of the CEO). Since no actual compensation is received by the CEO or subject to the CEO's control, he or she does not have to report the compensation as current income. At the same time, however, since all the employer has given is a mere promise, the employer gets no current deduction. Of course, when the CEO eventually receives the compensation (or once he or she is in *constructive receipt* of the compensation—defined as credited to the CEO's account or otherwise made available to him or her), it will have to be reported as income and the company may then claim it as a deductible expense.

Alert!

If the arrangement is considered a *nonqualified deferred compensation plan* (discussed earlier in this chapter), and it doesn't meet the requirements for deferring tax on the compensation, the compensation may be immediately taxable to the employee.

In terms of ERISA, since the arrangement is not a *plan* and it is unfunded, it is not subject to any ERISA requirements. But suppose the company decides to establish more formal deferred compensation arrangements for the benefit of a number of high-level company executives. Will that trigger the tax and labor law provisions of ERISA? ERISA itself offers two techniques for avoiding, or at least reducing, the compliance burdens and limitations imposed by the statute.

A *top hat plan* is an *unfunded* plan the employer maintains *primarily* for the purpose of providing deferred compensation to a select group of management or highly compensated employees. Top hat plans are exempt from ERISA's vesting, participation, funding, and fiduciary rules, but they are subject to ERISA's enforcement provisions. This means that an employee who is a beneficiary of a top hat plan can sue the employer in federal court to collect promised benefits.

An *excess benefit plan* is an *unfunded* plan the employer maintains *solely* for the purpose of providing benefits for certain employees in excess of the limitations on contributions and benefits imposed by Section 415 of the Internal Revenue Code. Excess benefit plans are not subject to either the substantive or the enforcement provisions of ERISA.

The italicized terms—*unfunded, primarily,* and *solely*—are critical. As used here, *unfunded* refers to whether the employer has actually set money aside, typically in a trust, to make good the promise of deferred compensation. If benefits are paid out of the employer's general assets and if employees have no greater rights to those assets than the employer's general creditors, the plan will be considered *unfunded*.

The purpose or purposes of the plan are also determinative. A top hat plan may have a number of purposes, including avoidance of various limitations imposed by the tax code. But in order to be an excess benefit plan, the plan must be limited to the single purpose of providing benefits in excess of I.R.C. Sec. 415 limitations.

Rabbi Trusts

Although top hat and excess benefit plans must be unfunded, the IRS has approved arrangements under which the employer can actually establish a trust as a *repository* for accumulating benefits, so long as trust assets remain subject to claims by the employer's creditors. The trust documents may establish broad investment policies, although specific investment authority must remain with the employer-designated trustee of the trust and cannot be given to the employee-beneficiaries. (This type of trust is known as a *rabbi trust* because the first IRS ruling on such an arrangement involved a retirement plan adopted by a congregation for its rabbi.)

To facilitate the adoption of rabbi trusts (and to reduce the IRS's burden of responding to ruling requests), the IRS in 1992 issued a Revenue Procedure that sets out a model trust form that employers may use.

While a rabbi trust may give participating employees some level of assurance that the employer will eventually make good on its promise of deferred compensation, employees need to realize that trust assets still remain subject to claims by the company's creditors and that the employees may end up with nothing if the company fails.

Chapter  10

Group Health and Other Voluntary Plans

▶ COBRA

▶ HIPAA

▶ Mandated Benefits

▶ Qualified Medical Child Support Orders

▶ Claims Administration

▶ Gender-Specific Coverage

▶ Stock Options

▶ Employee Stock Ownership Plans

▶ Other Plans

▶ Domestic Partners

Group health insurance competes with retirement plans as the most common type of employee benefit plan. A variety of funding arrangements are available. For example, the employer may pay the entire premium, in which case the plan is called *noncontributory*. Or the employer may adopt a *contributory* plan requiring the employees to contribute some of the premium. For qualified health insurance plans, whatever portion of the premium the employer pays is deductible to the employer. Even better, the employee does not include either the premium or the value of the medical services when received in his or her gross income.

Various risk-sharing and administrative arrangements also are available. For smaller companies, probably the most common arrangement is for the health insurer both to administer the plan and to assume the full risk, subject only to deductible and co-pay requirements. As companies get larger, they may want to undertake some of the administrative burdens, and they may also want to self-insure some or most of the risk. Some companies self-insure as to routine claims and buy a *stop loss policy* that kicks in when claims reach an unusually high level.

Companies that self-insure may self-administer. Alternatively, they may hire their stop loss carrier to administer the plan, or they may hire a third-party administrator (TPA) to handle claims and other administrative burdens. When the plan participants—the employee and any covered family members—choose their own health care providers and the insurance company reimburses the employee or pays the provider directly according to some policy formula, the plan is known as an *indemnity plan*.

In the last twenty years or so there has been explosive growth in a new type of plan known as *managed care*, driven largely by efforts to contain health care costs. In a managed care plan, the employer contracts with a *health maintenance organization* (HMO) or with an insurance company that has established a network of participating physicians, psychologists, hospitals, and so on. This network is sometimes called a *preferred provider organization* (PPO). The plan participant is required to stay within the network and pays nothing or only a nominal amount when medical care is received. If the participant *goes out of plan*, he or she may not be covered at all or may have a substantial co-pay obligation.

Managed care plans attempt to contain health care costs in other ways as well. For example, some plans use general practice physicians as gatekeepers who must approve referrals to specialists. Precertifications for hospitalizations are also common, both in managed care plans and in indemnity plans.

Group health plans usually impose a participation requirement that allows for cancellation of the group contract unless at least a minimum number of employees (such as 75%) participate in the plan. This helps assure that the group is broadly representative of the work force. It avoids *antiselection* where only less healthy employees elect to participate. Also, participation is usually limited to employees who work more than a specified number of hours per year, such as one thousand.

QUICK TIP

Provisions in group health plans that exclude or limit coverage for particular disabilities could violate the *Americans with Disabilities Act.* (See Chapter 17 for more on disability discrimination.)

Group health plans are subject to a variety of special requirements not applicable to other benefit plans. These special requirements—all highly technical—are discussed in the following sections. Employers should look to their health insurance company, experienced broker, or third party administrator for guidance through the group health plan labyrinth.

COBRA

Employers with twenty or more employees and who provide group health coverage need to know about one of the strangest acronyms in the employment field—COBRA. It stands for *Consolidated Omnibus Budget Reconciliation Act* (of 1985). The Act was really a catchall piece of legislation that just happened to include an amendment to ERISA. That amendment requires employers to continue health coverage for employees and their dependents who, for various reasons, would otherwise become ineligible.

Before COBRA, an employee who quit or was fired would automatically lose health coverage for him- or herself and for any participating family members. Similarly, a spouse's coverage would terminate on divorce, as would a child's coverage upon completion of his or her education or reaching a specified age. Most group policies had *conversion privileges*, which entitled the departing employee to purchase an individual policy, but the individual policies were usually very expensive and provided only limited coverage. Conversion privileges were usually not available to the divorced spouse or graduated child.

Alert!

For employees subject to *Title VII* of the federal *Civil Rights Act* or equivalent state law, pregnancy and childbirth must be treated as medical conditions under any health insurance plan maintained by the employer. (Review Chapter 14 for more detailed information regarding Title VII.)

COBRA changed all that. Now, when a *qualifying event* occurs, the employer must offer continuing coverage at the participants' cost to those who would otherwise lose benefits. The following are qualifying events that trigger COBRA coverage:

- The employee voluntarily quits;
- The employee is fired (except in cases of gross misconduct);
- The employee becomes ineligible for coverage because of a reduction in hours of work;
- The employee dies leaving a covered spouse or dependent;
- A covered spouse is divorced or becomes separated; or,
- A covered dependent ceases to be a dependent.

COBRA contains various deadlines within which notice must be given after the occurrence of a qualifying event. Once on notice that a qualifying event has occurred, the employer must, within fourteen days, offer continuing coverage. The employee, spouse, or dependent who is otherwise losing coverage then has sixty days within which to elect COBRA benefits.

What if a participant's coverage ends in anticipation of a qualifying event? For example, an employee with family coverage is in the midst of a divorce but, before the divorce is final, instructs his employer to drop his wife from the plan. Assuming the employee's instructions are consistent with plan requirements, and the employer is not on notice of a court order prohibiting the employee from dropping his wife's coverage, the employer has no choice but to comply. But, under IRS regulations, once the divorce is final, the employer must then give the usual COBRA notice to the employee's ex-wife. It does not matter that the wife was not participating at the time of the divorce, since she was dropped in anticipation of that event.

> **Alert!**
>
> Employers must continue health insurance coverage for an employee on leave under the *Family and Medical Leave Act* (FMLA) on the same basis as if the employee had continued to work. Health insurance continuation requirements may also apply to employees on military leave.

The cost of the continuing benefits must be paid 100% by the participant (the employee, spouse, or dependent), even if the employer was paying all or a portion of the premium before the qualifying event. The employer may also charge an additional 2% of the premium to cover administrative costs.

COBRA benefits do not continue indefinitely. For a terminated employee and his or her spouse and dependents, benefits last for only eighteen months. For a spouse or dependents who lose benefits due to divorce or separation from the employee or due to the employee's death, benefits last up to thirty-six months.

Many states have *little COBRA laws* that apply to employers who do not meet the twenty-employee threshold under federal law.

HIPAA

The federal *Health Insurance Portability and Accountability Act* (HIPAA) imposes a variety of requirements on group health plans in order to make health coverage more portable, so that when an employee changes jobs he or she will more quickly qualify for full coverage from the new employer. For example, HIPAA limits to twelve months the time period for which preexisting conditions may be excluded. The twelve-month limit is further reduced by the employee's *creditable coverage*, meaning coverage under a prior individual policy, under a prior group policy, under COBRA continuation benefits, or under Medicare or Medicaid.

Alert!

Department of Health and Human Services regulations under *HIPAA* impose strict confidentiality requirements on the handling of protected health information (PHI) relating to employees. (Chapter 18 provides more detailed information regarding employee privacy rights.)

To enable an employee to prove prior coverage, the previous employer or insurer must issue a *Certificate of Creditable Coverage* containing information about the prior plan and the employee's participation. HIPAA also requires plans to have special enrollment periods during which employees or dependents who previously declined coverage can sign up. Unlike COBRA, which applies to employers with twenty or more employees, HIPAA applies to all employers who have group health plans.

Note:

Additional information about HIPAA portability, including an optional form of Certificate of Creditable Coverage, is available at: www.dol.gov/ebsa/faqs/faq_consumer_hipaa.html.

Mandated Benefits

The federal *Newborns' and Mothers' Health Protection Act* prohibits group health plans from cutting off hospitalization benefits for a mother and her newborn child for the first forty-eight hours of hospitalization after a normal vaginal delivery and for the first ninety-six hours of hospitalization after a cesarean section.

The Act also prohibits health plans and insurers from offering financial incentives to mothers or health care providers to encourage hospital stays shorter than these minimum stays. Of course, in consultation with her physician a mother is free to leave sooner if it is medically appropriate. The Act does not require that births take place in a hospital.

The insurance laws of most states specify certain coverages that must be included in group health plans. Mental health coverage is a typical mandated benefit. Additional examples include chiropractic treatment and other treatments that have not always been considered in the health care mainstream. For the most part, the courts have upheld these requirements, despite claims that they are preempted by ERISA.

Qualified Medical Child Support Orders

ERISA requires that group health plans contain provisions to recognize *Qualified Medical Child Support Orders* (QMCSOs). QMCSOs are somewhat similar to QDROs (Qualified Domestic Relations Orders), discussed in Chapter 8, in that they give alternate payees—persons other than participating employees—rights with respect to an employer-sponsored benefit plan.

Under a QMCSO, an employee who has child support obligations may, as part of the obligation, be ordered to provide any available health insurance coverage for the dependent children. Assuming the employer's plan includes family coverage, delivery to the employer of such an order has the effect of requiring the employer to enroll the employee's dependent children. The employer may not disenroll the children unless the employee quits or obtains replacement coverage, or unless the employer eliminates family coverage from the plan. However, the employer is *not* required to provide any type or form of benefit or option not already provided under the plan. For example, if a plan limits participation just to employees and does not cover other family members, then a QMCSO cannot require the plan to begin providing family coverage.

> **Note:**
> The costs of enrolling a dependent child for coverage under a QMCSO are covered by deductions from the employee's pay.

Under ERISA's QMCSO requirements, a plan must have procedures in place for determining whether a court or administrative order entered in a domestic relations proceeding in fact qualifies as a QMCSO. To simplify the process, the U.S. Department of Labor has issued a standard set of forms to be used by state enforcement agencies (called IV-D agencies) in connection with QMCSOs.

Claims Administration

The Department of Labor has developed an elaborate set of regulations governing health plan claims procedures. Under these regulations, an insurer must process an initial claim:

- Within seventy-two hours for urgent care claims;
- Within fifteen days for preservice claims (with one fifteen-day extension allowed); and,
- Within thirty days for post-service claims (with one fifteen-day extension allowed).

Claimants have 180 days to appeal a claim denial, and the appeal itself must be decided:

- Within seventy-two hours for urgent care claims;
- Within thirty days for preservice claims; and,
- Within sixty days for post-service claims.

Plans are prohibited from imposing fees or costs as a condition to filing or appealing a claim. Appeals must also be decided by a person different from the decision-maker on the initial claim denial.

Where an appeal involves a medical judgment, such as the medical necessity of a particular procedure or drug, appropriate health care professionals must also be consulted. Finally, plans must:

- Provide participants with a full description of claim procedures;
- Provide specific reasons for claim denials, including identification of—and access to—guidelines or rules relied upon in denying the claim, along with all other documents and records relevant to the denial; and,
- Disclose the names of any medical professionals consulted as part of the claim process.

Gender-Specific Coverage

In 1978, Congress passed the *Pregnancy Discrimination Act* (PDA) amending Title VII of the federal Civil Rights Act. The PDA expands the definition of sex discrimination to include *pregnancy, childbirth, or related medical conditions*. Under the PDA, a group health plan must cover pregnancy, childbirth, and related medical conditions to the same extent the plan covers similar medical conditions. Abortions need not be covered except where the mother's life is endangered.

Alert!

Providing less comprehensive coverage for one gender than for the other may also violate federal antidiscrimination laws. (Chapter 15 covers gender discrimination in detail.)

The EEOC has ruled that an otherwise comprehensive health insurance plan that excludes coverage for prescription contraceptives violates Title VII's sex discrimination provision. At least one federal trial court has agreed with the EEOC. The idea is that unless a health plan is equally comprehensive for men and women, it discriminates on the basis of gender. However, in a recent federal court of appeals case, a plan that denied benefits for surgical fertility treatments was held not discriminatory, even though the surgical procedures are used only on women. The court reasoned that while the surgery itself is performed only on women, the underlying condition that the surgery abates could be male infertility, female infertility, or both, so that the exclusion is equally adverse to males and females.

Stock Options

More and more companies find it attractive to include, as part of their compensation package for key employees, some equity participation in the company. In a tight labor market, the opportunity to become a stockholder in the company may even be a necessary part of the recruitment and retention process. The idea is to provide an incentive to key employees by enabling them to share in the company's growth. The amount of stock involved is usually small enough that there is no significant effect on control of the company.

The company could simply give company stock to an employee as additional compensation or sell stock to the employee at some price that is below actual market value. However, any difference between the actual value of the stock and the amount paid by the employee will be income to the employee that is immediately taxable at ordinary income (not capital gain) rates. The employee may have to sell some of the stock in order to raise cash to pay the tax, defeating the purpose of the arrangement. Worse, if there is no market for the stock or the stock declines in value, the employee may be stuck with a big tax bill and have no way to pay it.

A more typical approach is to use *stock options* in which the company grants the employee a right, exercisable during a specified time period, to acquire company stock (or stock in a parent or subsidiary company) at a stated price, called the *option price* or *strike price*. While the *grant* of the option is not immediately taxable, the *exercise* of the option may or may not have tax consequences, depending on whether the arrangement qualifies as a *statutory* stock option or a *nonstatutory* stock option. But regardless of the tax consequences at the time the option is exercised, the grant of the option itself gives the employee a tax-free opportunity to participate in the growth of the company.

Statutory Stock Options

A *statutory stock option* is an option that qualifies as either an *incentive stock option* (ISO) under Section 422 of the Internal Revenue Code or as an *employee stock purchase plan* under I.R.C. Sec. 423.

Under an ISO, when the employee exercises an option, pays the option price, and acquires company stock, no taxable income is incurred (but the company gets no tax deduction, either). Should the employee later sell the stock (after satisfying applicable holding periods), he or she is taxed at capital gain rates on the difference between the option price and the selling price.

In order to qualify for this favorable tax treatment, the option must meet the following requirements.

- The option must be granted pursuant to a written plan and approved by the company's shareholders. The plan must specify the total number of shares that may be issued under the plan and must identify the employees or class of employees eligible to receive options. (The identity-of-the-employees requirement can be met if the plan simply says that the employees will be chosen by a specified person or committee.)
- The option must be in the form of a written agreement between the company and the employee.
- The option must be granted within ten years after adoption of the plan.
- The option must state that the option can only be exercised within ten years after being granted.
- The employee cannot be eligible to exercise more than $100,000 in options within any twelve-month period.
- The option holder must be an employee when the option is granted and must continue to be an employee until three months before the option is exercised. (Special rules apply to employees who die or become disabled.)
- The option holder can own no more than 10% of the voting stock of the company. (This requirement does not apply if the option price is at least 110% of the fair market value of the stock, and if the option cannot be exercised for at least five years.)
- The option price must be at least equal to the fair market value of the stock at the time the option is granted.

- The option cannot be exercisable by anyone other than the employee personally, and the option must be nontransferrable during the employee's lifetime. (Special rules apply to the exercise of options by a deceased employee's estate.)
- After the option is exercised, the shares themselves must be held for at least two years after the option was granted and for at least one year after the option is exercised.

Backdating

A number of public corporations have come under recent scrutiny for secretly *backdating* options. Normally, when an option is granted it is dated as of the date of the grant. That date determines the option's strike price, which is normally the price at which the company's stock was trading on that date. When an option is backdated, however, the option holder gets to pick the date of the option. By picking a date on which the company's stock was traded at a lower price, the option holder enjoys a lower strike price and maximizes his or her potential gain. This, of course, defeats the performance incentive aspect of the option grant. In addition, backdating exposes the company to shareholder suits for fraud, and it raises a host of tax and accounting problems.

QUICK TIP

ISOs are not subject to ERISA because their purpose is to provide a current incentive, much like salary, and not to defer compensation or provide retirement benefits.

Employee Stock Purchase Plan

Under an *Employee Stock Purchase Plan* (not to be confused with an Employee Stock *Ownership* Plan, or ESOP, discussed later), an employer grants options to its general work force in proportion to their compensation. The plan must exclude employees who own 5% or more of the company. It may exclude part-time and seasonal employees, employees who have worked less than two years, and highly-compensated employees. The option price cannot be lower than 85% of the value of the stock at the time the option is granted (or, alternatively, at the time the option is exercised).

Other restrictions apply, including a $25,000 per year limitation on the amount of stock for which a single employee can hold options. As with ISOs, the exercise of the option does not result in taxable income. The sale of stock acquired through the option receives capital gain treatment so long as applicable holding periods are satisfied.

Nonstatutory Stock Options

In a *nonstatutory stock option* (NSO), the tax advantages shift to the employer. Specifically, when the employee exercises the option and acquires company stock with a value higher than the option price, the employer can take a deduction for the difference. However, the employee must report the difference as ordinary income. An option will be nonstatutory if the option does not meet the statutory requirements listed earlier, or the option specifically states that it is not an ISO.

Although NSOs are not required to satisfy the conditions applicable to ISOs, a company may choose to impose certain conditions, such as holding periods, restrictions on transfer, and so on.

One disadvantage of an ISO is that the company must determine the fair market value of the stock subject to the option in order to set the option price. If the company's stock is publicly traded, the trading value is used. But if the company is privately held, hiring an outside valuation expert may be necessary. (The company need only make a *good faith effort* to value its stock. However, restrictions on transferability *cannot* be considered as reducing the value of the stock.) The ISO agreement can state that the company will issue a special class of stock, such as nonvoting stock, to satisfy the exercise of an option, but this further complicates the valuation process because of the need to value the special class of stock separately.

QUICK TIP

Businesses that grant NSOs to their employees must separately identify on the employees' W-2 forms any compensation received by the employees from the exercise of NSOs.

Once the employee exercises the option and acquires company stock, the employee can sell it immediately if the stock was acquired through an NSO. (This is subject, however, to any restrictions in the option agreement and to any securities law restrictions.) If it was acquired through an ISO, the employee can sell it after satisfying the ISO holding period requirements, any additional restrictions in the option agreement, and any securities law restrictions. But if the company is privately held, there is not likely to be any market for the stock. So in practical terms, the option plan must allow the employee to sell the stock back to the company. Such a repurchase obligation may entail yet another expensive valuation. If the employee sells back less than all the stock, he or she may be deemed to have received a taxable dividend.

Companies contemplating a stock option plan should consider the effect on employee incentive if the stock goes *down* instead of up. Employees whose primary compensation has been stock options may get discouraged and leave sooner than if their compensation had not included options. Companies should also consider their increased litigation exposure should a fired employee sue for wrongful discharge and claim not only the wages he or she would have received, but also the value of unvested stock options.

Publicly-traded companies should also be mindful of SEC rules designed to protect against *dilution in the dark*. Under these rules, companies are required to provide detailed information about their equity compensation plans in their annual reports to the SEC. The information is also required to be included in proxy statements whenever the company is submitting an equity compensation plan for approval by shareholders.

Employee Stock Ownership Plans

An ESOP, or *Employee Stock Ownership Plan*, is a form of a defined contribution plan in which the plan's primary investment is in stock of the employer company. (Under ERISA's self-dealing rules, most pension plans are prohibited from holding significant investments in the sponsoring company. ESOPs fall within an exception to these rules.) Since ESOPs, along with other qualified pension plans, must be managed for the exclusive benefit of participating employees and their beneficiaries, an ESOP is a way for employees to own the company or at least own a significant part of the company.

ESOPs have a number of advantages over other pension plans, particularly when the company is a closely-held corporation whose stock is not publicly traded. Among those advantages are the following.

- Employees are more highly motivated, since they have an ownership interest in the company and their productivity increases the value of their stock.
- The added control and bargaining power employees have through stock ownership may dissuade them from unionizing.
- When an ESOP acquires its stock by purchase of newly issued company shares, the company can, in effect, use pension plan contributions as a source of capital for company operations or expansion.
- When an ESOP acquires its stock by purchase from existing shareholders, the ESOP provides a market for those shares and provides liquidity to existing shareholders. (If the ESOP is acquiring at least a 30% interest in the company from existing shareholders, the selling shareholders may defer recognition of capital gain on those shares.)
- An ESOP can *leverage* its stock ownership by borrowing money from a bank or other lender to purchase stock, thereby providing additional capital to the company or liquidity to its selling shareholders. Future pension plan contributions by the company to the ESOP to service the loan are fully tax deductible; in effect, they enable the company to deduct otherwise nondeductible principal repayments.
- An ESOP provides continuity of ownership and management of the company. Without an ESOP, the death or retirement of a principal shareholder often means liquidation of the company or the involvement of new owners who are strangers to the company.
- Premiums for *key person* life insurance owned by an ESOP are fully tax deductible. (A key person is an employee whose death would cause substantial financial harm to the business.)

Employee ownership of company stock, whether obtained through the exercise of stock options or otherwise, requires attention to insider trading restrictions.

There are some disadvantages to an ESOP. When the company's stock is not publicly traded, the company must pay for expensive stock valuations to determine the fair market value of the stock being contributed or sold to the ESOP. These valuations are typically required on an annual basis.

Then there is the question of who will serve as trustees of the trust that holds the ESOP stock. Banks and other financial institutions are increasingly reluctant to assume the trustee role because of the fiduciary responsibilities and risks involved. But if company officers or directors are appointed as trustees, they may find it difficult to subordinate their own self-interest to the interests of participating employees (for whose benefit the ESOP is supposed to be managed).

The conflict of interest is heightened when the company is considering out-of-the-ordinary corporate actions, such as implementing a nonqualified deferred compensation plan for senior executives or responding to a merger proposal. In these instances, it may be necessary for the company to obtain a *fairness opinion* from an outside advisor as to the reasonableness of deferred compensation or the fairness of a proposed transaction.

Note:
ESOPs may not be for everyone, but their unique advantages deserve serious consideration.

Other Plans

Retirement and group health plans are probably the most significant employee benefits, both in terms of tax savings and in terms of popularity with employees. Other arrangements are available, however, and should not be overlooked. As with retirement and group health plans, these other arrangements generally must satisfy applicable tax and ERISA requirements.

Group Term Life Insurance

An employer may provide group term life insurance to employees either as part of a group health plan or as a separate plan. The first $50,000 in coverage is tax free to the employee. The premium for coverage in excess of $50,000 is taxable income to the employee.

Disability Insurance

Premiums on employer-sponsored group disability insurance if paid by the employer are deductible by the employer, but are not includible in the employee's income. However, if an employee becomes disabled and collects benefits under the policy, the benefits are taxable income to the employee. Alternatively, if the employee pays the premiums with after-tax dollars, then the benefits are not taxable to the employee.

Under one clever arrangement, the employer paid the disability insurance premiums but gave each employee an election between having the premium amounts included or excluded in the employee's gross income. The IRS concluded in a private letter ruling that if the employee becomes disabled in a plan year in which he or she has elected to *include* the premiums in gross income, then the benefits are not taxable. However, if the employee becomes disabled in a plan year in which he or she has elected to *exclude* the premiums, the benefits are taxable.

Long-Term Care Insurance

Premiums on employer-sponsored group long-term care insurance are deductible by the employer. If the coverage qualifies as medical care and the premiums are below certain limits specified in the Internal Revenue Code, the premiums are not includible in the employee's income. Benefits, when paid, are not taxable.

Cafeteria Plans

Sometimes referred to as Section 125 plans (because they are authorized under that section of the Internal Revenue Code), *cafeteria plans* give each employee a choice between taking cash or receiving qualified benefits such as health insurance, group term life insurance, long-term care insurance, etc. If the employee elects cash, he or she must report the benefit as taxable income. If he or she elects a qualified benefit, the benefit is excludible to the extent allowed by law.

Cafeteria plans are attractive in that they allow each employee to tailor benefits to his or her particular circumstances—as, for example, when an employee does not need health insurance due to coverage through his or her spouse's employer, but would like life insurance for which he or she cannot otherwise qualify because of a medical condition.

Alert!

Although the IRS permits employers to enroll employees automatically in cafeteria plans (subject to the employee's opting out), state wage-and-hour laws may prohibit an employer from making payroll deductions without the employee's express consent.

Flexible Spending Arrangements

Flexible Spending Accounts (FSAs) allow employees to put aside before-tax dollars to cover *dependent care expenses, uninsured medical expenses*, or both. Once an employer has approved inclusion of an FSA in its cafeteria plan, each employee individually designates a portion of income each year in the form of regular payroll deductions for payment into a special trust fund. The amount designated is up to the employee subject to any outside limits imposed by the plan, and is not includible in the employee's gross income for income tax purposes.

During the year, if the employee incurs dependent care expenses or medical expenses not covered by the health plan, the employee submits receipted bills to the administrator of the fund and is reimbursed. The reimbursement is also not included in gross income; so, the net effect is that the employee pays dependent care expenses and uninsured medical expenses with before-tax dollars rather than with after-tax dollars.

In the case of medical expenses, the tax result achieved with an FSA is similar to taking a deduction on the employee's tax return for uninsured medical expenses. However, medical expense deductions are limited to employees who itemize and are further limited to expenses that are greater than 7.5% of the employee's adjusted gross income. Therefore, from the employee's viewpoint, the practical benefit of an FSA is that it allows him or her to deduct *all* uninsured medical expenses, rather than just those that are above the 7.5% floor, *whether or not* he or she itemizes. Under an FSA, even nonprescription medicines, such as antacids, allergy medicines, pain relievers, and cold medicines qualify for tax-free reimbursement, even though such medicines cannot be deducted as an itemized medical expense.

The downside of an FSA for employees is that any money left in their accounts at the end of a plan year is forfeited to the employer. For that reason, employees should be conservative in their estimates of uninsured medical and dependent care expenses.

The downside for employers is that if an employee has substantial reimbursable expenses early in the plan year, before enough funds are accumulated to cover the expenses, the employer must advance the reimbursement to the employee. If the employee then quits, there will be no more payroll deductions and the employer will be left holding an FSA with a negative balance. To guard against this possibility, employers usually limit the size of each employee's FSA to no more than several thousand dollars.

Health Savings Accounts

A *Health Savings Account* (HSA) is an account established by an individual employee at a bank or other financial institution to pay the employee's current and future medical expenses. The employee establishes the account using IRS Form 5305-B and appoints the financial institution as trustee for the account. HSAs are used in conjunction with a *high deductible health plan* (HDHP)—any indemnity, HMO, or PPO plan that, with certain exceptions, has deductibles of at least $1,100 for self-only coverage or $2,200 for family coverage as of this writing. (These deductible amounts apply in 2007 and are indexed in later years for inflation.) To qualify, an HDHP must also have annual out-of-pocket limits of $5,500 for self-only coverage and $11,000 for family coverage (also indexed for inflation).

Contributions to an HSA may be made by the employer, the employee, or both, subject to maximum contributions from all sources (indexed for inflation) of $2,850 for self-only coverage and $5,650 for family coverage. An employer's HSA contributions are deductible expenses, just like wages or other fringe benefit payments, but are not includible in the employee's income. Similarly, the employee's contribution is excluded from his or her income. Earnings on the HSA are tax-free.

Like FSAs, distributions from an HSA to pay for the employee's qualified medical expenses, or the medical expenses of the employee's spouse or dependents (even if the spouse or dependents are not covered by the HDHP), are tax-free. Over-the-counter drugs qualify for HSA distributions, as do COBRA continuation premiums and certain long-term care insurance premiums. (Other health insurance premiums do not qualify.)

Unlike FSAs, HSAs do not have a use-it-or-lose-it feature. Amounts on deposit in an HSA can be carried over from year to year and applied to future medical expenses, even expenses incurred after the employee is no longer eligible to make contributions to the account.

The financial institution holding the HSA reports distributions on Form 1099 SA each year. The employee in turn reports contributions and distributions on Form 8889 filed with the employee's annual income tax return.

Employee Assistance Plans

Employee Assistance Plans (EAPs) are designed to provide counseling and related services to employees who have emotional or substance abuse problems. Typically, the employer contracts with an outside agency to provide the services.

Alert!

EAP records relating to substance abuse services are subject to special confidentiality provisions of federal law. (Chapter 18 discusses employee privacy in more detail.)

Child and Dependent Care Service Plans

These plans provide day care for an employee's child under thirteen years of age and for a spouse or dependents who are unable to care for themselves. The first $5,000 in benefits is excludible from the employee's income for tax purposes. Amounts in excess of $5,000 are includible.

Domestic Partners

The term *domestic partner* as used here refers to someone with whom your employee lives and has a voluntary, committed relationship, other than a spouse or relative. In general, benefit laws and antidiscrimination laws do not recognize domestic partnerships. For example, the federal *Defense of Marriage Act* (DOMA) defines *spouse* as someone of the opposite sex, so that a same-sex domestic partner has none of the protections or benefits provided to spouses under federal pension law. However, there are a few exceptions.

Disability

The federal *Americans with Disabilities Act* prohibits discrimination against an applicant or employee who is known to be *in a relationship with or be associated with* someone who has a disability. That language is broad enough to cover a domestic partner.

Sexual Orientation

A number of states and local jurisdictions prohibit discrimination based on sexual orientation. When a domestic partner is a person of the same sex as the employee, adverse treatment of the employee could give rise to a claim of discrimination because of sexual orientation.

Marital Status

Regardless of the genders involved, adverse treatment of an employee who has a domestic partner could give rise to a claim of discrimination because of marital status in violation of state or local law.

COBRA

COBRA benefits can include a domestic partner if the employer provides health insurance for domestic partners and if the employee has elected COBRA. However, a domestic partner has no independent right to elect COBRA benefits for him- or herself.

Establishing Benefits

Local governments and private employers are beginning to recognize domestic partners for benefit plan purposes. They do so because they see it as fair and equal treatment for their employees. Or they may agree to domestic partner coverage to stay competitive with other employers. Whatever the reason, domestic partner coverage poses a number of legal and practical issues that need to be addressed.

Who qualifies as a domestic partner?

Employers need to develop a clear definition of domestic partner. The definition might, for example, include some or all of the following requirements:

- Both persons in the relationship must be legally competent adults;
- The persons cannot be so closely related to each other that (aside from gender) they would be forbidden to marry under state law;
- The persons must have a committed, exclusive relationship and neither can be married or in a domestic partnership with someone else; and,
- The persons must live together and be financially interdependent.

The employer will also need to decide *whether to cover only same-sex partners or include opposite-sex couples* as well. In jurisdictions that prohibit sexual orientation discrimination, covering same-sex but not opposite-sex couples, or covering opposite-sex but not same-sex couples, could be discriminatory.

What proof will be required?

Once the definition of domestic partner is settled, the employer will have to specify what documentation will be required to recognize a person as a domestic partner. Is an affidavit from the two partners sufficient? Or will the employer also want to see such items as deeds or leases showing that the partners jointly own or lease their residence?

What benefits will be offered?

If domestic partners will be entitled to family coverage under the employer's group health policy, the employer will need to coordinate coverage with its insurer. Other benefits might include sick leave to care for an ill domestic partner, bereavement leave, the opportunity to participate in employer-sponsored recreational functions, health club memberships, conventions, business trips, and so on. (The *Family and Medical Leave Act* itself does not require employers to grant leave for the care of a domestic partner.)

Must an employer recognize same-sex marriages legally performed in another state?

The answer to this question appears to be no—at least for the time being. While each state is generally required by the U.S. Constitution to give *full faith and credit to*—that is, to recognize—the laws of every other state, the *Defense of Marriage Act* gives states the choice not to recognize another state's same-sex marriage. So if you are an employer in a state that does not recognize same-sex marriages, you need not do so either. (It remains to be seen whether this provision of the DOMA is constitutional.)

What are the tax implications of providing domestic partner benefits?

In general, an employer may claim an income tax deduction for the costs of a qualified benefit plan. In the case of health insurance provided to employees or to employees and their spouses or dependents, the employee need not treat the benefit as taxable income. However, the cost of providing health insurance to a domestic partner is taxable income to the employee since the domestic partner is not a spouse and, in most cases, cannot qualify as a dependent. Therefore, the cost of such coverage must be included in the W-2 form issued by the employer, and it must be reported on the employee's income tax return.

Chapter

Workers' Compensation

- ▶ Coverage
- ▶ Course and Scope of Employment
- ▶ Claim Procedure
- ▶ Benefits
- ▶ Second Injury Fund
- ▶ Rights against Third Parties

Prior to the adoption of workers' compensation laws, an employer could, at least in theory, be held liable in court for work-related injuries suffered by employees. The employer might have to pay damages if, for example, it failed to provide a safe place to work, or failed to provide a sufficient number of suitable fellow employees to accomplish the job at hand.

As a practical matter, however, the defenses available to the employer often prevented the employee from receiving any compensation for injuries. Those defenses included:

- *Fellow servant doctrine*, which insulated employers from liability where the injury was caused by the negligence of a fellow employee;
- *Contributory negligence*, which barred the employee from recovery if he or she contributed in any way to the cause of the injury; and,
- *Assumption of the risk*, under which the employee was held to have assumed the risk of injury normally associated with the particular job.

In essence, workers' compensation acts are *no fault* laws under which the employer is automatically obligated to pay compensation and benefits for each employee who suffers a work-related illness or injury, or who is killed in the course of employment. This obligation, which is usually funded by mandatory workers' compensation insurance, applies whether or not the employer was negligent and whether or not the employer could have raised one or more defenses to liability.

The trade-off for the employer is that workers' compensation benefits are the employer's *exclusive liability* for work-related injuries or illnesses. Unless the employer deliberately intended to injure or kill the employee, the employee cannot sue the employer in court; the employee cannot demand a jury trial; and the employee cannot obtain open-ended damages for pain and suffering.

Coverage

Workers' compensation acts broadly apply to all employers and, with few exceptions, all their employees. For purposes of these acts, the term *employee* means someone whose method of work the employer has a right to control. The acts apply to minors, even if they are employed unlawfully, and in some states to domestic workers in private homes.

State law typically defines *covered employee* broadly as any *individual while in the service of an employer under an express or implied contract of apprenticeship or hire*. The statutes then go on to list a number of exceptions and special provisions. For example, sole proprietors, partners, and officers of closely-held corporations may not be covered at all or they may have a right to *opt in* or *opt out* of coverage.

The acts do not apply to independent contractors or to *casual employees*—employees who work irregularly, for a brief period only, doing work not normally performed by employees of the employer.

Workers' compensation acts require employers to *secure compensation* for their covered employees by maintaining insurance through authorized insurance companies or through self-insurance. Insurance premiums are calculated as a percentage of payroll. The actual percentage varies for each employer based on factors such as the employer's industry classification and claim history. Employers may *self-insure* if they can demonstrate their financial ability to pay compensation. Self-insurers usually must put up security or a *bond* to cover their compensation obligations.

QUICK TIP

Workers' compensation programs are exempt from ERISA. (See Chapter 9 for more information about ERISA.)

State laws generally require employers to post a notice in the workplace as to the existence of workers' compensation coverage and the procedure to be followed after an injury or death. It is illegal for an employer to charge employees, such as by a wage deduction, for any part of the cost of providing workers' compensation. It is also illegal for an employer to retaliate against an employee for filing a compensation claim or for testifying in a compensation proceeding.

Personal Injury

Workers' compensation acts cover accidental *personal injury*, which is usually defined as:

- An accidental injury that arises out of and in the course of employment;
- An injury caused by the willful or negligent act of a third person in connection with a covered employee's employment;
- A disease or infection that naturally results from an accidental injury, such as frostbite or sunstroke; or,
- An occupational disease.

The acts typically *do not* cover injuries:

- That are intentionally self-inflicted;
- Resulting from the covered employee's attempt to injure or kill another or other willful misconduct; or,
- Resulting solely from intoxication while on duty and, in some states, from illegal drug use.

It is sometimes argued that the likelihood of injury in certain occupations is so great that when an injury does occur, it cannot fairly be called *accidental*. A professional football team, for example, sought to deny compensation to one of its offensive linemen who injured his ankle in a game. The team claimed that when injuries are customary, foreseeable, and expected—in other words, are simply part of the game—they are not accidental within the meaning of the workers' compensation statute. The Virginia Supreme Court rejected the team's argument, saying that just because an occupation is high-risk does not mean the compensation statute is inapplicable.

Course and Scope of Employment

Workers' compensation laws cover employees who suffer accidental injuries *arising out of and in the course of employment*. Sometimes it is difficult to tell whether an injury did or did not arise out of and in the course of employment.

Take, for example, an employee who is injured while commuting to or from work. The general rule (sometimes called the *going-and-coming rule*) is that employees are not covered while commuting. But there are exceptions. Despite the going-and-coming rule, coverage will be provided when:

- An employee is going from one of the employer's places of business to another during the workday;
- An employee is exposed to a special hazard, which the public-at-large is normally not exposed to, while gaining access to the employer's place of business;
- The means of transportation are provided by the employer, or the employee is being paid while commuting; or,
- The employer requires the employee to commute in a specified way or follow a specified route.

When an employee is on travel for the employer, he or she generally is covered, even if not specifically engaged in work at the time of the injury. This includes hotel bathroom falls, choking on a meal, suffering a criminal assault, or being injured in a hotel fire. Only if the employee is injured while on a *distinct departure* from work and on a *personal errand* will there be no coverage.

CASE STUDY: NO COVERAGE FOR AFTER-HOURS ASSAULT

A professional hockey player with an NHL team traveled to New York for a game with the New York Rangers. After the game he and some 20 other teammates went to dinner at a restaurant, paid for by their employer. While there, the player in question drank a substantial amount of beer and vodka. They then went to a club where they drank more beer and vodka. After the club closed and while the team members were out on a street near the club, the player in question tried to persuade a woman to accompany him in a limousine. The woman's companion then hit the player over the head with a bottle. The player was denied compensation for the resulting injury.

Claim Procedure

If an employee suffers a work-related injury or illness, he or she must both notify the employer and file a claim for compensation with the state agency that administers the compensation act. Once the employer learns of a compensable injury, the employer too must file a report with the state agency.

The time limits applicable to notification and reporting requirements vary from jurisdiction to jurisdiction. Failure to meet these deadlines may bar the employee's right of recovery, although the government agency that administers the law usually has authority to excuse a late filing.

After a claim is filed, the employer or its insurance carrier must either begin paying benefits or *controvert* (contest) the claim. If the claim is controverted, the government agency investigates, conducts a hearing if necessary, and then issues an award or denies coverage. Further appeal may be made to the courts. The parties are entitled to be represented by attorneys in a contested matter, but the amount of attorneys' fees charged the employee is often subject to approval by the administering agency.

Benefits

Workers' compensation acts provide for various categories of benefits, including:

- Disability benefits to the covered employee for lost wages or loss of earning capacity;
- Medical benefits;
- Death benefits to the employee's dependents;
- Funeral benefits; and,
- Vocational rehabilitation.

The actual amount of disability benefits is calculated from complicated statutory formulas based on the employee's average weekly wage. The following benefit formulas (subject to statutory maximums and minimums) are typical:

- *For temporary partial disability*—up to two-thirds of the employee's lost wage-earning capacity;

- *For temporary total disability*—two-thirds of the employee's average weekly wage;
- *For permanent partial disability*—up to two-thirds of the employee's average weekly wage. If the injury falls in one of the categories listed in the act (such as loss of a specific appendage, loss of a sensory organ, or loss of various combinations of appendages and sensory organs), the benefit continues only for the number of weeks specified in the law; and,
- *For permanent total disability*—two-thirds of the employee's average weekly wage.

Alert!

Although the meaning of *disabled* for workers' compensation act purposes is not the same as under the *Americans with Disabilities Act*, employers should be alert to the possibility that an injured employee might qualify as disabled under the ADA. If so, taking adverse employment action or failing to reasonably accommodate the employee could constitute illegal discrimination. A workplace injury can also trigger *Family and Medical Leave Act* obligations. (See Chapters 8 and 17 for more information on these topics.)

Workers' compensation premiums are deductible by the employer for federal income tax purposes. Benefits paid to an employee are exempt from income tax.

Terminating an employee for excessive absenteeism where the employee is out on disability as a result of a work-related, compensable injury is allowable in most states. However, although dismissal may be permitted, firing an employee who is out on work-related disability is fraught with peril. The potential problems include the following.

- The employee may claim that the termination was *abusive or in retaliation* for having filed a workers' compensation claim.
- If the employer is subject to the *Family and Medical Leave Act*, the employee may be entitled to FMLA leave.

- If the disabling condition is not merely temporary and if it substantially interferes with one or more major life activities, the employer's duty of reasonable accommodation under the *Americans with Disabilities Act* may be triggered.

Second Injury Fund

Suppose an employee has a serious, preexisting condition, but the applicant is nevertheless able to work. Some employers may be reluctant to hire the person, fearing that a subsequent injury on top of the earlier condition, even if minor, could disable the employee and expose the employer to liability for permanent disability benefits.

Recognizing that the workers' compensation system may inadvertently discourage the hiring of employees who have suffered prior injuries, many states have created a *second injury fund* that pays a portion of the compensation benefits due a re-injured employee.

Since the purpose of second injury funds is to discourage employers from discriminating against employment applicants who have suffered prior injuries, the question arises whether an employer who was *unaware* of a prior injury can obtain reimbursement from the fund after paying full benefits to a re-injured employee.

Some courts have adopted the rule that the employee's prior injury must be *manifest* for the employer to recover from the fund. As a practical matter, this means that the employer must either have actual knowledge of the prior injury at hiring time, or the prior injury must be obvious or documented in medical records available to the employer such that a reasonable person in the employer's shoes would have known about the prior injury.

The requirement that a prior injury be *manifest* for the employer to have access to the second injury fund in the event of a subsequent injury is one reason why an employer may require new employees to undergo medical exams.

QUICK TIP

The ADA prohibits preemployment physicals unless the employer has already made a conditional offer of employment to the employee. (Chapter 17 discusses disability discrimination more fully.)

Rights against Third Parties

Although workers' compensation acts prohibit an employee from suing his or her own employer for a work-related injury, the acts do not prohibit an employee from suing a third party who may have caused the injury.

> **EXAMPLE:** Suppose an employee is a passenger in his employer's truck that is being driven by a fellow employee in the course of a delivery. If the truck is hit at an intersection because another vehicle ran a red light, the employee-passenger can sue the driver of the other vehicle. However, if the accident occurred because the employee-passenger's fellow employee ran the red light, the employee-passenger may or may not be able to sue his fellow employee, depending on state law.

In the above illustration, regardless of how the accident occurred, the employee-passenger can of course collect workers' compensation benefits. But the employee-passenger is not allowed to invoke the legal doctrine of *respondeat superior* and attempt to hold his own employer vicariously liable.

State laws differ as to whether the injured employee has to elect between accepting compensation or suing the negligent third party. In some states, by accepting compensation the employee, in effect, assigns to the employer the right to sue the third person up to the amount of compensation paid by the employer. In other states, the employee may accept compensation and sue the third person, but if the employee's suit is successful, the employee has to reimburse the employer up to the amount of compensation paid by the employer.

If an injured employee enters into a settlement agreement with the third party and, in exchange for a cash payment, releases the third party from further liability, the employer may be able to raise the settlement as a defense to the employer's own workers' compensation obligation. The reason is that, by releasing the third party, the employee has also compromised the employer's *right of subrogation* to recover against the third party. So the employee should obtain the employer's consent (and the consent of the employer's workers' compensation insurance carrier) before entering into any settlement agreement with a third party.

Independent Contractors

Suppose an employer engages an independent contractor to perform some function at the workplace and, as a result of the independent contractor's negligence, an employee suffers an injury on the job. Certainly the employee can recover workers' compensation benefits, but can the employee sue the independent contractor as well? In other words, is the independent contractor considered so connected with the employer as to enjoy immunity from suit? Or is the independent contractor a third party who is subject to suit?

The answer usually depends on whether the independent contractor is a stranger to the employer's business or whether the independent contractor was performing an essential part of the employer's business. The following examples illustrate this concept.

EXAMPLE 1: A retail company hires an architect to design a warehouse for storing out-of-season merchandise. The architect negligently designs an overhead door at the warehouse that falls and injures one of the company's regular employees. The architect will in most instances be considered a *stranger* to the employer's business. The injured employee can sue him despite workers' compensation laws.

EXAMPLE 2: That same retail company hires a cleaning company to assist with store maintenance and to perform cleaning and janitorial functions, both during and after normal store hours. Here the cleaning company is performing an essential part of the employer's business and will not be subject to suit for negligence that results in injury to the retailer's regular employees.

Alert!

Health and safety laws require employers to provide medical first aid supplies and, in the absence of nearby medical facilities, assure the presence of a person trained in first aid. (See Chapter 12 for more on workplace safety.)

A related issue is the *dual capacity* doctrine. Take, for example, a hospital employee who is injured on the job and receives negligent medical treatment at the employer's hospital. Can the employee sue for the negligent medical treatment, or is the suit barred by the exclusivity provision of the workers' compensation statute?

A few states take the view that when an employee is acting in a capacity other than as the employer, the employer becomes a third party and is no longer immune from employee suits for negligence. Other states have ruled that when an employer negligently administers first aid to an employee who was injured on the job, the employer enjoys protection under the workers' compensation act not only for the initial injury, but also for the emergency medical treatment.

Chapter

Unemployment Insurance

- ▶ **Employer Contributions**
- ▶ **Coverage and Eligibility**
- ▶ **Misconduct and Quitting** *for Cause*
- ▶ **Claim Procedure**
- ▶ **Benefits**

Unemployment insurance benefits, together with workers' compensation, provide a safety net for employees. While workers' compensation protects employees who suffer loss of earning capacity through work-related injuries, unemployment benefits protect against involuntary job loss due to economic or other reasons not the fault of the employee.

The unemployment insurance system is a cooperative arrangement between the federal government and participating state governments. In essence, the federal government supervises the system, and state governments administer the system within federally-established guidelines. The system is financed through mandatory taxes (called *contributions*) imposed on covered employers by state unemployment insurance laws and, at the federal level, by the *Federal Unemployment Tax Act* (FUTA).

Each new business that has one or more employees must register under the unemployment insurance laws. Tax-exempt organizations described in Section 501(c)(3) of the Internal Revenue Code are exempt from FUTA, but not from state laws. (See Chapter 23 for more on nonprofit and tax-exempt organizations.)

Employer Contributions

At both the federal and state levels, an employer's unemployment insurance contribution is calculated as a percentage of wages paid in *covered employment* up to a cap. The amount of wages that are subject to tax is called the *wage base*. The federal wage base under FUTA is currently $7,000 per covered employee. Each state establishes its own wage base. In general, an employer is subject to the FUTA tax if it employs one or more individuals for at least twenty weeks, or pays wages of $1,500 or more per calendar quarter.

At the federal level, the tax rate applied to the wage base is normally 6.2%. However, the employer is entitled to credit its state unemployment tax against the federal tax (up to a maximum of 5.4% of taxable wages) *if* the state tax was paid on time. Therefore, the effective federal rate for most employers is 0.8%, or $56.00, per employee per year. (As of this writing, the 6.2% federal rate is scheduled to drop to 6.0%.) Federal unemployment tax is generally paid quarterly, with an annual return due on January 31.

At the state level, the tax rate depends on whether the employer is a *new employer* or whether the employer is entitled to an *earned rate*—a rate based partly on actual claims experience. A new employer is typically defined as an employer who has reported taxable wages for less than some specified period, such as three years. State unemployment contributions are usually due quarterly.

While earned rates are computed differently from state to state, in general they include these two factors: the employer's actual claims experience; and an adjustment or pooling charge to cover shortfalls in the benefit fund. Because of the experience factor, hiring and firing practices can have a significant impact on the amount of future unemployment tax due.

In order to determine an employer's claims experience, the state agency that administers unemployment insurance maintains a separate account for each covered employer. Although specific accounting practices differ from state to state, in general the account is charged with benefits that are paid out. The employer's earned rate is then determined based on benefits charged against its account over some prior period such as three years.

Base Period

The process of determining which employer to charge for particular benefits gets complicated. One concept that needs to be understood is *base period*. The base period is the most recent four of the employee's last five completed calendar quarters prior to the filing of the claim for unemployment benefits. If a claimant had only one employer during the base period, then 100% of the benefits are charged against that employer's account.

If a claimant had two or more employers during the base period, then, depending on the state, each base period employer is charged with a percentage of the benefits based on the ratio of the wages paid by that employer to the employee's total base period wages; or the employer for whom the claimant last worked for thirty days is charged with 100% of the benefit.

If an employee works in more than one state, the employer should typically report the wages for unemployment insurance purposes as follows:

- If all the employee's work is performed in one state, then the employee's wages are reported to that state;
- If substantial work (work that is not merely incidental, transitory, or occasional) is performed in several states, one of which is the employer's home office or a branch office, then that state is the state to which wages are reported; or,
- If no substantial work is performed in the state where the employer's home office or a branch office is located, then the employee's state of residence is the state to which wages are reported.

Unfortunately, these rules cannot always be clearly applied. In those instances, the employer should get competent advice or request a ruling from the state agencies involved.

Alert!

Employers are prohibited from deducting any part of their required contributions from employee wages. Agreements between employers and employees to waive unemployment insurance benefits are illegal.

Coverage and Eligibility

By definition, independent contractors are not employees. Therefore, compensation paid to them is not subject to unemployment tax. (However, compensation paid to an employee who is *misclassified* as an independent contractor is subject to tax.) Under federal law, general partners in a partnership and students who perform services for their schools are also excluded from coverage. Household employees and agricultural workers are specially treated. Each state has its own list of additional jobs not covered by the unemployment insurance laws.

Employers do not have to pay state unemployment tax for employees who are not covered and such employees are not entitled to claim benefits if they become unemployed.

In order to receive benefits, a claimant must first have been employed in a type of job covered by the unemployment insurance law.

Second, he or she must have been employed for at least two calendar quarters (not necessarily consecutive) within the base period. Third, he or she must have earned a specified minimum amount (which varies by state) during those two calendar quarters. In addition, the claimant must be *unemployed* (defined to mean not working at all for any wages) or be *underemployed* (working less than full-time and earning wages that are less than the benefit amount that would be payable to the claimant). The claimant must also be actively seeking work and must be available for and able to perform work. Failure to meet these qualifications or failure to accept suitable work will temporarily disqualify the claimant from receiving benefits.

Alert!

An employee who is out of work due to an injury or illness is ineligible for unemployment benefits since he or she is not able to work. However, he or she may be eligible for leave under the *Family and Medical Leave Act* and workers' compensation benefits. If the injury or illness is not work-related, benefits may also be available under any group disability insurance policy maintained by the employer.

If an individual receives a severance package or dismissal payments covering some period of time after employment ends, he or she may also be eligible for unemployment insurance depending on the form that the severance package takes. If an employer intends to offer a severance package, it makes sense to offer the package in the form of a specified number of weeks of continuing compensation and benefits. That should render the departing employee ineligible for unemployment insurance during the severance period. Even better, if the departing employee finds new work during the severance period, he or she may not make any claim at all.

Misconduct and Quitting *for Cause*

At the heart of unemployment insurance is the requirement that the person claiming benefits be out of work *involuntarily*, through no fault of his or her own. Therefore, state law often disqualifies an individual from receiving benefits if he or she is fired for misconduct or leaves work voluntarily without good cause.

Some states have gradations of misconduct, such as *aggravated misconduct*, *gross misconduct*, and *(ordinary) misconduct*. In states with gradations of misconduct, the most serious level may disqualify the employee from benefits entirely, whereas lesser degrees of misconduct may result in only temporary disqualification.

Normally, if an employee voluntarily quits, he or she is not entitled to benefits either. But unemployment insurance statutes usually specify that the disqualification only applies if the employee leaves work *without good cause*. Stated another way, if an employee voluntarily quits *with* good cause, he or she is not disqualified and may receive benefits.

In general, for there to be good cause, the cause must be connected in some way to the job the employee is leaving. A purely personal decision by the employee will not qualify. For example, leaving to take a better job, to become self-employed, to return to school, or to relocate with a spouse are not good causes. On the other hand, failing to pay the employee or maintaining discriminatory working conditions may amount to good cause depending on the circumstances.

QUICK TIP

If a reasonable person would find the working conditions intolerable, involving, say, severe and persistent discrimination, quitting to escape those conditions may be considered a *constructive discharge*. (See Chapter 4 for more information on constructive discharges.)

Employees on Strike

In general, benefits are denied to employees who are out of work because of a labor dispute at their worksite. However, a claimant is generally *not* disqualified despite the existence of a labor dispute at the worksite if the claimant is not personally involved in the labor dispute, and does not belong to a grade or class of workers whose members are involved in the labor dispute.

An individual who is receiving benefits may turn down a job that has become vacant because of a strike and still continue to receive benefits. Unemployment laws do not force workers to become strikebreakers.

Claim Procedure

An individual who loses his or her job or becomes underemployed must register for work and file a claim with the appropriate state agency. Since benefits are generally not paid retroactively, any delay in filing a claim results in loss of benefits.

When the state agency receives a claim, it notifies all the claimant's base period employers. All base period employers are asked to submit separation information to the state agency, giving the reason why the employment terminated, the last day of employment, the claimant's wage rate, and other information that might affect eligibility for or the amount of benefits.

> **Alert!**
>
> Providing false separation information is criminal. In addition, if the termination itself involved discrimination, an employer's subsequent attempt to disqualify a claimant for unemployment benefits could expose the employer to an additional claim of illegal retaliation.

Sometimes an employer will provide false or incomplete separation information in order to help the employee qualify for unemployment benefits. This, too, is problematic, because the employer's statements can be used against it should the employee later claim discrimination, abusive discharge, etc.

Once the state agency makes an initial determination of entitlement to benefits, the employer may contest benefits by appealing the determination to a hearing examiner. When the basis for the contest is employee misconduct, the employer normally must prove:

- That the employer had a clear, well-established work rule;
- That the employee knew about the work rule; and,
- That the employee willfully violated the work rule.

The employee then has an opportunity to show that the employer frequently failed to enforce the work rule.

One obvious reason for an employer to contest benefits (assuming there are reasonable grounds to do so) is to protect the employer's *earned rate*. Recall that employers other than new employers are entitled to be rated based (in part) on the employer's actual claims experience. Each benefit payment pushes that rate higher and increases the employer's required contribution for future years.

QUICK TIP

The employer will have an easier time proving the existence of a work rule and the former employee's awareness of the rule if the rule is contained in an employee handbook. It will also be beneficial if the employee signed an acknowledgment that he or she received and would read the handbook. (Chapter 2 provides more information on employee handbooks.)

A less obvious reason to contest a claim is to get a preview of any related claims the former employee may intend to bring against the employer. Suppose, for example, that the employee voluntarily quits but says in the claim for unemployment benefits that he or she had good cause to leave because he or she suffered racial discrimination on the job. Or suppose the employee says he or she was fired for refusal to perform some illegal act such as lying to an OSHA inspector. In those circumstances, the employer can reasonably expect to face not only an unemployment compensation claim, but also a charge of discrimination or a suit for abusive discharge.

If benefits are contested, the state unemployment agency must conduct a hearing at which the employee may testify, call other witnesses, and present documents. The employer, usually with the assistance of an attorney, can cross-examine the employee and his or her witnesses and can examine documentary evidence.

Benefits

Assuming the claimant qualifies for benefits, the amount of the benefit is determined by complicated statutory formulas based on the claimant's base period wages.

Benefits last up to twenty-six weeks, which may be extended in certain circumstances. After using up the maximum benefit, the claimant is ineligible for additional benefits until he or she has worked in covered employment.

Chapter 13

Workplace Safety

- Overview of OSHA
- Safety and Health Standards
- Record-Keeping
- Inspections and Citations
- FDA's Food Code
- Retaliation and Refusal to Work
- State Requirements
- Smoking
- Ergonomics
- Violence in the Workplace
- Disaster Planning

Workers' compensation laws largely eliminated employer liability for failing to provide a safe workplace. Occupational safety and health laws, such as the federal *Occupational Safety and Health Act* (OSHA), restore that liability by imposing detailed safety and health standards on employers, by authorizing unannounced inspections, by authorizing issuance of compliance orders and injunctions, and by imposing civil fines and criminal penalties for violations. While safety and health laws impose obligations on employees as well as employers, generally only the employer is subject to penalties.

Overview of OSHA

OSHA, passed in 1970, imposes on every employer the general duty to furnish to each of its employees employment and a place of employment which are *free from recognized hazards that are causing or are likely to cause death or serious physical harm*—the so-called *General Duty Clause*. To assure that obligation is met, OSHA requires every employer to comply with specific occupational safety and health standards promulgated by the Secretary of Labor. OSHA also imposes posting, record-keeping, and reporting requirements on employers.

OSHA requires the Secretary of Labor to issue safety and health standards in three categories:

1. *Established federal standards*, meaning standards that were in effect when the Act was passed, either as part of some other act of Congress, or contained in regulations of a federal agency;
2. *National consensus standards*, meaning broadly accepted standards adopted by nationally recognized organizations; and,
3. *Additional standards*, meaning additional occupational safety and health standards that the Secretary determines would serve the purposes of OSHA.

Employers are required to comply with all applicable standards issued by the Secretary. Many standards are industry-specific, such as those dealing with longshoring and the fishing industry. Many others are broadly applicable.

Safety and Health Standards

The standards adopted to date fill thousands of pages in the Code of Federal Regulations. A comprehensive analysis is not possible here. What follows is a brief discussion of a few standards of more general applicability or interest. Employers may want to contact their trade associations, or obtain copies of OSHA publications, for guidance as to specific standards or standards uniquely applicable to their industry or profession. Additional information is available at OSHA's website: www.osha.gov.

Generally Applicable Standards

As examples of generally applicable standards, employers are required to:

- Keep work areas clean, orderly, and sanitary, and keep floors clean and dry;
- Protect stairwells by guardrails and guard or cover other floor openings;
- Provide free and unobstructed exit from all parts of a building or other structure when occupied, mark exits by lighted signs, and maintain and test fire alarm and sprinkler systems;
- Provide readily accessible fire extinguishers; and,
- Provide medical first aid supplies and, in the absence of nearby medical facilities, assure the presence of a person trained in first aid.

Employers are also required to have an emergency action plan covering, at a minimum:

- Procedures for reporting a fire or other emergency;
- Procedures for emergency evacuation;
- Procedures to be followed by employees who remain to handle critical plant operations;
- Procedures to account for employees after evacuation;
- Procedures to be followed by employees performing rescue or medical duties; and,
- The names or job titles of employees who may be contacted for more information about the plan.

For employers with more than ten employees, the plan must be in writing and kept available in the workplace for review. Employers with ten or fewer employees may communicate the plan orally to employees.

Hazardous Materials

Handling of hazardous materials is the subject of extensive regulation. OSHA sets out detailed requirements for products such as flammable and combustible liquids, explosives, and liquefied petroleum gases. For highly hazardous chemicals (substances that are toxic, reactive, flammable, or explosive and are stored in sufficient quantities to cause a catastrophe if released), the employer must inform employees of the hazard involved and must consult with employees to develop safety management plans and training.

Closely associated with OSHA's hazardous materials standards are its hazard communication standards. Chemical manufacturers and importers are obligated to determine the hazards of each of their products. That information, along with protective measures for each product, is communicated downstream to distributors, who in turn distribute it to their customers. OSHA has developed a multi-page form for communicating this information, known as a Material Safety Data Sheet (MSDS). Use of the MSDS form itself is not mandatory, but the information it calls for must be provided. The MSDS form lists:

- Manufacturer's name, address, and emergency phone number;
- Specific chemical components that create the hazard;
- Physical and chemical characteristics of the product, such as appearance and odor, melting point, boiling point, and solubility in water;
- Fire and explosion hazards and any special fire-fighting procedures;
- Reactivity data, such as how stable the product is and any hazardous products of decomposition;
- Health hazards from exposure and recommended first aid procedures; and,
- Precautions for safe handling and use, such as what protective clothing should be worn.

All employers along the way, from manufacturer to end user, are required to communicate the MSDS information to their employees who come in contact with the product and to train their employees in handling the product. This communication and training program must be in writing; sample programs are available from OSHA. The hazardous products themselves must be appropriately tagged or marked.

Employers must have on hand, and make available to their employees, copies of the MSDS (or equivalent) for each hazardous chemical at the workplace. The burden is on the employer to contact the manufacturer and obtain any missing MSDSs. However, once obtained, the employer may rely on the accuracy of the form as furnished by the manufacturer.

Lockout/Tagout Rule

Another widely applicable standard is OSHA's *lockout/tagout rule*, designed to prevent the accidental startup of machines and equipment while being serviced, or the accidental release of hazardous energy. The standard requires that any machinery or equipment that is being serviced must be isolated from its energy source and the isolation device must be locked. If the device cannot be locked, it must be tagged with a warning such as DO NOT START. The lock or tag may be removed only by the person who put it in place. Before removal, he must conduct an inspection. After removal but before startup, he must notify affected employees that the machine or equipment is about to be placed back in service. The standard also requires employers to train their employees in complying with lockout/tagout procedures.

Personal Protective Equipment

OSHA has adopted a number of standards dealing with use of *personal protective equipment* (PPE). PPE standards are designed to protect the eyes, face, head, extremities, respiratory system, and the body generally. For example, when exposure to noise in the workplace exceeds specified maximum levels, or extends beyond specified maximum durations, protective devices must be worn to reduce effective exposure below permitted maximums. Respirators are required in dusty or smoky environments. Hard hats are a common sight at construction jobs. Detailed information is available at: www.osha.gov/SLTC/personalprotectiveequipment/index.html.

Who pays for personal protective equipment—the employer or the employee? In the past, OSHA regs required only that PPE must be *provided*. Some employers read these regs as allowing them to charge their employees for hard hats, wire-mesh gloves, ear plugs, etc. In November 2007 OSHA issued final regulations requiring the employers to pick up the cost of *all* PPE except:

- Nonspecialty safety footwear and nonspecialty prescription safety eyewear, provided the employer permits such items to be worn off the jobsite;
- Boots with built-in metatarsal guards;
- Logging boots;
- Everyday clothing;
- Clothing, creams, and other items used solely for protection from weather, such as winter coats, jackets, gloves, parkas, rubber boots, hats, raincoats, ordinary sunglasses, and sunscreen;
- Replacement PPE, when the replacement is necessary because the employee has lost or intentionally damaged the PPE; and,
- PPE voluntarily provided by the employee.

Blood-Borne Pathogens

The health care and medical research community may be particularly interested in OSHA's blood-borne pathogen standards. OSHA states the obvious when it says that HIV (human immunodeficiency virus) and HBV (Hepatitis B Virus) *merit serious concern* for workers occupationally exposed to blood, bodily fluids, human tissues and organs, and tissue and organ cultures. To comply with the standards, employers must first determine who faces occupational exposure. Obvious candidates are medical personnel in an operating room or who administer injections and are subject to needle-stick injuries. Less obvious are hospital laundry room workers, for example, who come in contact with contaminated bedding or clothing.

The next step is to inform those employees that they face occupational exposure to blood-borne pathogens. The employees must also receive training, to include:

- How to obtain copies of the OSHA regulation containing the standard;

- Information on the epidemiology, transmission, and symptoms of blood-borne diseases;
- An explanation of the employer's exposure control plan, and the use and limitations of workplace practices, such as personal protective equipment;
- The safety and efficacy of HBV vaccinations (which the employer must make available at no cost to all employees who face an exposure risk); and,
- Emergency procedures and how to report an exposure incident.

The employer must also follow *universal precautions*, which require that all blood and bodily fluids be considered potentially infectious. Universal precautions include proper labeling, decontamination and disposal procedures, and use of personal protective equipment such as gloves and eye protectors.

OSHA interprets its HBV "no-cost" rule as requiring employers to pay regular compensation to employees who receive treatment during off-duty hours for possible HBV exposure, and also pay the employees' travel expenses to receive the treatment. A federal appeals court recently upheld OSHA's interpretation.

Alert!

Safety considerations will justify placing limits on soliciting and distributing literature at the workplace. However, unless the rules are consistently enforced, the employer may be subject to unfair labor practice charges for prohibiting pro-union solicitations and literature. (See Chapter 24 for information on unions.)

Record-Keeping

Employers who employ more than eleven employees must maintain an annual log and summary of all *recordable occupational injuries and illnesses*. A recordable injury or illness is one that results in:

- A fatality;
- A lost workday;

- A transfer or termination of employment, or a restriction of work or motion;
- Medical treatment beyond mere first aid; or,
- Loss of consciousness.

The records are kept on an annual basis and each year's records must be retained for five years. OSHA provides a set of forms, instructions, and worksheets for satisfying record-keeping requirements, including *Form 300* (Log of Work-Related Injuries and Illnesses), *Form 300A* (Summary of Work-Related Injuries and Illnesses), and *Form 301* (Injury and Illness Incident Report). They are available at: www.osha-slc.gov/recordkeeping/OSHArecordkeepingforms.pdf.

Inspections and Citations

OSHA inspectors (called *Compliance Safety and Health Officers*) are authorized to enter and inspect any workplace at all reasonable times to assure compliance with OSHA standards. The inspections are unannounced—it is illegal for anyone to forewarn an employer that an inspection will take place—and may include interviewing employees in private, taking photographs and environmental samples, and reviewing records. A representative of the employer and an employee representative may accompany the inspector during the inspection.

An inspection may be initiated by OSHA itself, or it may be conducted at the request of an employee who believes that a safety violation exists. It is illegal for an employer to retaliate against an employee for complaining about an OSHA violation, or for giving testimony or otherwise cooperating in an OSHA matter.

Inspections and other proceedings under OSHA present the risk that an employer's trade secrets will be disclosed. The act, as well as Department of Labor regulations, contain special provisions to protect the confidentiality of trade secrets. Inspectors also need appropriate security clearances to inspect areas containing classified information, and they must comply with the employer's health and safety rules, such as wearing personal protective equipment.

Employers may refuse to admit an OSHA inspector and insist that he or she obtain a search warrant. Putting an inspector to this added burden obviously does not create a cooperative atmosphere and it may in fact encourage the inspector to perform a more detailed, intrusive procedure. Nevertheless, there are times when the employer should insist upon a warrant. For example, if the employer suspects that a violation exists, a brief delay may provide just the opportunity needed to fix the problem. A delay might also be needed if a particular company official who should be present during the inspection is away. The company might also want advice from its attorney before permitting the inspection. If an inspector anticipates that the company will insist on a warrant, the inspector may obtain one beforehand, thus defeating any advantage the employer had hoped to gain from delay.

At the conclusion of the inspection, the inspector must inform the employer of any apparent health and safety violations. The employer also has an opportunity to point out conditions or procedures related to the apparent violations. After the inspection, the inspector submits a report to OSHA's local Area Director. If the report indicates a violation, the Area Director issues either a *citation* or a *notice of de minimis violation* (a violation that has no direct or immediate relationship to health or safety). Citations and notices must be issued within six months of the inspection.

The Secretary of Labor may also go to federal court for an injunction to stop any practices or procedures that pose an imminent threat of death or serious physical harm. Citations must describe with particularity the nature of the alleged violation, including a reference to the safety or health standard allegedly violated. The citation must also fix a reasonable time within which to abate the violation. Employers are required to post a copy of the citation at or near the site of the violation for at least three days or until the violation is abated, even if the citation is being contested.

In addition to the citation, OSHA's Area Director also notifies the employer of a proposed penalty. (No penalty is proposed for de minimis violations.) Civil penalties can range up to $70,000 per violation, depending on the seriousness of the violation and whether it is willful. In assessing civil penalties, the Area Director is also required to consider the size of the business, the employer's good faith, and any history of previous violations. Failure to correct a violation can result in an additional civil penalty of up to $7,000 per day. The Act also provides for criminal penalties in cases of willful violations resulting in the death of an employee.

The employer has fifteen working days after receipt of notice to contest the citation, the proposed penalty, or the time allowed for abatement of the violation. Contests are initially handled through administrative proceedings, followed by a right of appeal to the courts.

FDA's Food Code

The federal Food and Drug Administration's Food Code is a set of model regulations offered by the FDA for adoption by state and local government agencies that have public health responsibilities. The regulations in turn govern food service industry procedures. Unless adopted by other government agencies, the Food Code itself is not a binding regulation. The Food Code (which the FDA updates every two years) is available at: www.cfsan.fda.gov/~dms/primecon.html.

Jurisdictions that have adopted the Food Code are listed at: www.cfsan.fda.gov/~ear/fcadopt.html#adopt-03.

Retaliation and Refusal to Work

OSHA prohibits retaliation against an employee because the employee filed an OSHA complaint, testified in a OSHA proceeding, or exercised any other rights afforded him or her by the statute. However, the statute itself does protect an employee who walks off the job out of safety concerns. In that situation, the employee's remedy is to notify his employer of the danger and, if the employer fails to take appropriate action, to request an OSHA inspection. The statute does not authorize *unilateral self help*.

There may be situations, however, where the employee faces an impossible choice of either immediately complying with a supervisor's instructions and risking serious injury or death, or not complying and being fired. In other words, the right to complain may simply not be a viable remedy. For those situations, the U.S. Department of Labor has adopted regulations that say if the employee, with no reasonable alternative, refuses in good faith to expose himself to the dangerous condition, he will be protected against subsequent discrimination.

The condition causing the employee's apprehension of death or injury must be of such a nature that a reasonable person, under the circumstances then confronting the employee, would conclude that there is a real danger of death or serious injury and that there is insufficient time, due to the urgency of the situation, to eliminate the danger through resort to regular statutory enforcement channels. In addition, in such circumstances, the employee, where possible, must also have sought from his employer, and been unable to obtain, a correction of the dangerous condition.

In a 1980 decision, the Supreme Court upheld this regulation in a case where an employee refused to work on a steel mesh that other workers had fallen through and suffered injury or death. Later court decisions have emphasized that the specific requirements of the regulation must be met—that the employee be acting reasonably and in good faith, that the danger be both real and serious, and that the employee have no opportunity to address the danger through regular channels.

The National Labor Relations Act (NLRA) protects workers who voice safety concerns, or who engage in a job action to protest safety conditions. Under the NLRA, an employer may not take adverse action against employees who engage in concerted activity by complaining about safety issues or other job-related conditions. The NLRA also provides that employees who quit work in the good faith belief that their workplace is abnormally dangerous are not deemed to be on strike. That provision has been interpreted to mean that, like workers who are on strike to protest an unfair labor practice, workers who are absent for safety reasons may not be permanently replaced. (In contrast, workers who are on strike for purely economic reasons may be permanently replaced. See Chapter 24 for more on unions.)

CASE STUDY: PROTECTED JOB ACTION

In a 1962 Supreme Court decision involving a factory in Baltimore, seven employees walked off the job on a bitter cold January day because their work area was unheated. The area was often uncomfortably cold anyway (a matter of repeated complaint) and, on the day in question, the furnace that usually supplied some heat had broken down. The Supreme Court ruled that the job action was protected under federal labor law, so that the employer had no right to fire the workers.

> In more recent cases, fear of exposure to asbestos in an apartment complex and fear of exposure to radioactive depleted uranium dust have justified employee refusals to work.

State Requirements

The Occupational Safety and Health Act provides that individual states may assume responsibility for occupational safety and health matters by developing a plan that is *at least as effective* as OSHA itself. State plans are subject to review and approval by the U.S. Secretary of Labor.

At this writing, the following states, along with Puerto Rico and the Virgin Islands, have approved state plans:

- Alaska
- Arizona
- California
- Connecticut (covers public sector employees only)
- Hawaii
- Indiana
- Iowa
- Kentucky
- Maryland
- Michigan
- Minnesota
- Nevada
- New Jersey (covers public sector employees only)
- New Mexico
- New York (covers public sector employees only)
- North Carolina
- Oregon
- South Carolina
- Tennessee
- Utah
- Vermont
- Virginia
- Washington
- Wyoming

For a current listing, go to: www.osha.gov/fso/osp/index.html.

Once a state plan has received final approval, enforcement of workplace safety and health matters shifts to the state.

Smoking

Most of the issues relating to smoking involve the rights of non-smokers to be free from second-hand smoke. Many states and local jurisdictions have laws requiring employers to restrict smoking in the workplace. Some employers have responded by prohibiting smoking altogether. Others have designated a specific area for smoking that is sealed from the remainder of the workplace, or that is under negative pressure so that smoke-filled air does not escape.

Aside from state and local law obligations, employers could conceivably face liability to nonsmokers:

- Based on a violation of OSHA's General Duty Clause;
- Under workers' compensation laws if an allergic employee suffers a temporary disability from cigarette smoke;
- Under the Americans with Disabilities Act, on the theory that an employee who is allergic to cigarette smoke is disabled and is entitled to reasonable accommodation; and,
- For unemployment insurance benefits, if the nonsmoker claims he is entitled to quit for cause to avoid a smoke-filled, unsafe workplace.

A prudent employer will adopt and enforce a smoking policy designed to protect the health of nonsmokers.

Do employees have a right to take smoke breaks? With few exceptions, most state laws do not entitle employees to any breaks at all, so that a break policy (including cigarette breaks) is a matter within the employer's discretion. An employer who does permit short breaks cannot (in the view of the U.S. Department of Labor) exclude that time for purposes of computing hourly workers' wages.

Even though employers do not have to permit smoke breaks, they are prohibited by laws in some jurisdictions from discriminating against smokers, provided the smokers limit their smoking to off-duty hours.

QUICK TIP

For unionized shops, smoking policy is a subject of mandatory bargaining.

Ergonomics

Ergonomics is the branch of science that studies the relationship between workers and their work environment. While some have dismissed the entire field as poorly grounded in fact, there is increasing evidence that the traumatic effects of repetitive motion and poor positioning over prolonged periods are cumulative and can result in discomfort, pain, and even disabling injury.

Ergonomic issues affect employers in a number of ways. Discomfort and pain obviously decrease performance and may result in lost time. If a connection with the work environment can be shown, lost time may result in a workers' compensation award. Serious, disabling injuries may also trigger obligations under the Americans with Disabilities Act.

Computers get some of the blame. Keyboard and mouse designs have prompted claims of carpel tunnel syndrome, eye fatigue, headaches, and neck and back pain. OSHA has developed nonmandatory guidelines for use of video display terminals (VDTs), which are available at: www.osha.gov/SLTC/computerworkstations_ecat/checklist.html.

The U.S. Department of Labor has pushed for mandatory OSHA ergonomic standards, but its efforts have so far been delayed or overturned by Congress. Despite Congressional resistance, OSHA never abandoned the field and has been studying ergonomics ever since. As part of that process, it announced in April 2002 a protocol for developing industry- and task-specific guidelines. As of this writing it has issued voluntary guidelines for nursing homes, retail grocery stores, and poultry processing. Shipyards will be the focus of the next set of industry-specific guidelines, according to OSHA. The guidelines, along with additional ergonomics information, are available at: www.osha.gov/SLTC/ergonomics.

Although the guidelines are nonbinding, in the sense that OSHA will not rely on them for enforcement purposes, employers still have a duty under the General Duty Clause of the Occupational Safety and Health Act to provide a safe workplace. Despite their nonbinding status, the guidelines could conceivably be used to show that an employer has violated the General Duty Clause.

Employers should anticipate that ergonomics litigation will increase and that federal or state safety standards in some form will eventually be adopted.

Violence in the Workplace

According to the Occupational Safety and Health Administration, homicide is the second leading cause of fatal occupational injury in the United States. OSHA also reports that nonfatal violence is a widespread and growing phenomenon, particularly in jobs involving the exchange of money with the public (retail, home delivery, etc.), working alone, working late at night, guarding valuable property, and working in a community setting (taxicab drivers, health care workers, etc.)

OSHA does not have any specific standards for workplace violence. OSHA points out, however, that the General Duty Clause—that every employer furnish employment free from recognized hazards—may itself impose duties on employers whose workers are at risk.

Whether or not employers owe a specific legal duty to prevent workplace violence, it makes good business sense to offer at least a minimum level of protection. Employers should consider these steps:

- Be alert to any *history of violence* in applicants for employment;
- Adopt, disseminate, and enforce a policy that any *violence or threats of violence* by employees will be met with dismissal;
- Prohibit employees from bringing *weapons* of any kind to the employer's place of business or from carrying weapons during working hours (except where state law bars such a prohibition);
- Prohibit employee use or possession of *alcohol and illegal drugs*, or being under the influence of alcohol or drugs, while on the job;
- For larger employers, require photo *ID badges* for all employees;
- *Secure* nonpublic work areas and *limit access* to those with keys/ passcards;
- *Secure all areas* after normal working hours;
- Provide *adequate lighting* for storage and garage areas;
- Provide *cell phones* to employees who work off-premises;
- As necessary, contract with a *security firm* to provide security personnel, remote monitoring, emergency phones, alarms, etc.;

- Restrict distribution of *employee directories*, particularly if they contain home addresses, home telephone numbers, names of spouses or children, or other personal information;
- Establish an employee assistance program (EAP) and encourage its use; and,
- Alert employees to any *special risks* the job may present; develop policies for responding to emergencies; train employees in recognizing and responding to emergencies; and invite employees to express their concerns.

Disaster Planning

Recent events have focused attention on responding to disasters of both the terrorist and the natural kind. While complete protection is impossible, advance planning can minimize injury and death.

Building Owners

An employer who owns the building in which the workplace is located must, of course, maintain the building in compliance with local and state safety codes. This may include, for example, fire alarm and sprinkler systems, fire extinguishers, and exit lights. Emergency exits must be accessible and unlocked.

Building owners can take additional steps which, though not required, may go a long way to protecting employees. The National Institute for Occupational Safety and Health (NIOSH), which is part of the federal Centers for Disease Control and Prevention, has issued its Guidance for Protecting Building Environments from Airborne Chemical, Biological, or Radiological (CBR) Attacks, available for at: www.cdc.gov/niosh/bldvent/2002-139D. html.

NIOSH's recommendations regarding CBR attacks include the following:

- Preventing access to outdoor air intakes, such as by relocating them on secure building roofs;
- Securing roofs and other areas where mechanical equipment is located;
- Isolating lobbies, mailrooms, loading docks, and storage areas;

- Securing return air grilles;
- Restricting access to information about building operations and systems;
- Installing high-efficiency filters in the HVAC system; and,
- Developing a response plan for a CBR emergency, such as shutting down the HVAC system entirely.

Other Employers

Employers who are not directly responsible for building maintenance and operation can also prepare for disasters, by means such as:

- Maintaining duplicate employee information (names, addresses, payroll data, emergency contact, etc.) off-site;
- Establishing a phone tree to alert employees about whether to report to work;
- Determining in advance (in consultation with local disaster planning agencies) which emergencies require evacuation of the workplace and which require sheltering in place;
- Conducting practice drills for various types of emergencies;
- If evacuation is appropriate, such as in response to a fire emergency, establishing a gathering point for all employees so that an accurate count can be obtained and emergency personnel can be informed whether all persons are accounted for; and,
- Identifying persons with disabilities or who may have special needs in an emergency and assigning appropriate personnel to assist them.

QUICK TIP

The EEOC has ruled that an employer may inquire about a worker's disability so that the employer can assist the worker in a disaster. However, it is up to the worker to decide whether assistance is necessary. Any information obtained about the worker's disability or need for assistance is subject to special confidentiality requirements.

Bird Flu Pandemic

Experts say that Bird Flu—technically, Influenza type A virus, sub-type H5N1—is likely to mutate and become transmittable from human to human. When that happens, a pandemic will almost certainly occur. While seasonal flu occurs just about every year, Bird Flu, if it strikes, will be much worse, more like the so-called Spanish Flu of 1918. This is so in part because Bird Flu is a new strain for which natural immunities do not exist, and in part because Bird Flu appears to trigger an overwhelming (and often deadly) immune response, called an *inflammatory cascade* or *cytokine storm*. In contrast to seasonal flu, which takes its greatest toll among the elderly, the very young, and others with compromised immune systems, Bird Flu is likely to take a significant toll on healthy young adults.

It makes good business sense for employers to take whatever steps they can to protect their work force. They may also have a legal obligation to do so under federal and state occupational safety and health laws. This means limiting the spread by good sanitation practices and social distancing. For example, employers should:

- Educate employees as to means of transmission, symptoms, treatment, etc.;
- Encourage frequent hand washing;
- Suspend social customs like hand shaking;
- Encourage employees to clean work areas frequently with alcohol wipes;
- Provide and encourage use of hand sanitizers;
- Provide and encourage use of face masks or respirators;
- Spread employees out over work areas and stagger their shifts;
- Cancel face-to-face meetings;
- Require symptomatic or exposed employees to stay away from the workplace;
- Implement a telecommuting policy for as many employees as possible (see Chapter 20 for more on telecommuting);
- Limit nonessential travel, especially to regions where flu is prevalent; and,
- Isolate employees who are returning from flu-prevalent regions.

Despite these efforts, employers are still likely to face substantial reductions in their work force. To prepare for that, they need to identify critical functions that must be performed; provide backup for those critical functions, such as cross-training of employees; and postpone or eliminate noncritical functions. If the business is one that can switch to a related product or service, employees will need to be trained in providing that product or service. A restaurant, for example, might add home-delivery services, which will affect staffing—fewer waiters, but more delivery personnel. Delivery employees will need to learn safe food-handling practices and how to process credit card payments off-site.

Businesses will also need to develop alternatives to face-to-face communications. Experience with recent disasters shows that land line and mobile telephone systems may either be down or unreliable due to overload. Alternatives might include:

- Email via computers and mobile devices;
- Company intranets;
- Virtual private networks (VPNs);
- Text messaging (also called SMS for short message service) via mobile devices;
- Instant messaging; and,
- Voice over Internet Protocol (VoIP).

Each of these systems needs to be put in place and tested before the pandemic hits. For example, if email will be an important form of communication, employees' home email addresses will have to be collected and distributed and listservs should be created and kept current.

Chapter

Discrimination in General

The Civil War made clear that slavery would no longer be tolerated in the United States, but it did little to remedy rampant discrimination. It was not until 1964, through the efforts of Presidents Kennedy and Johnson and after bitter Congressional debate, that the first significant antidiscrimination laws were passed. Since then, numerous protections have been added, not only at the federal level, but also at state and local levels.

This chapter addresses employment discrimination in general, including religious discrimination. Subsequent chapters deal with discrimination on account of gender, age, and disability.

Title VII of the Civil Rights Act

The *Civil Rights Act of 1964* is the first modern piece of federal legislation to address discrimination generally. The Act deals not only with discrimination in employment but also with discrimination in public accommodations. The Act was amended in 1991 to clarify and strengthen certain provisions and to expand the range of available remedies to include compensatory and punitive damages in cases of intentional discrimination.

Title VII of the Act addresses *employment discrimination*. It applies to all employers who have fifteen or more employees and to employment agencies and labor unions. The *Equal Employment Opportunity Commission* (EEOC) (created by Title VII), together with cooperating state and local agencies, enforce Title VII at the administrative level by investigating charges, recommending remedies, and conciliating disputes between employers and employees. The EEOC can also bring suit against employers in federal court. EEOC guidelines interpreting Title VII are a useful resource.

At the heart of Title VII is the following provision:

It shall be an unlawful employment practice for an employer:

(1) to fail or refuse to hire or to discharge any individual or otherwise to discriminate against any individual with respect to his compensation, terms, conditions, or privileges of employment, because of such individual's race, color, religion, sex, or national origin; or,

(2) to limit, segregate, or classify his employees or applicants for employment in any way which would deprive or tend to deprive any

individual of employment opportunities or otherwise adversely affect his status as an employee, because of such individual's race, color, religion, sex, or national origin.

Those two paragraphs have generated whole libraries of commentary and thousands of court decisions. Many of the Supreme Court's landmark cases during the last forty years have involved Title VII. It would be impossible to digest that body of material here. What follows is a brief overview of Title VII principles and a discussion of some of the more important issues employers are likely to face.

Title VII is not limited to traditional minorities. Everyone—whites as well as blacks, males as well as females, Christians as well as Jews—is protected. In other words, Title VII does not protect *special groups* from adverse employment decisions. Rather, it prohibits an employer from using *certain criteria* when making decisions. So, for example, a more qualified white male who is passed over for promotion in favor of a less qualified black female has a good Title VII claim if the employer was motivated by race or gender.

CASE STUDY: REVERSE DISCRIMINATION

The discrimination that a nonminority member suffers when an employer discriminates in favor of a minority member is sometimes called reverse discrimination. Although the Supreme Court has made clear that such favoritism is plain and simple discrimination, the Court's current views on this topic are not entirely clear. In a pair of widely-publicized decisions involving the University of Michigan, the Court ruled that the University's law school may consider race as a plus factor in evaluating individual applicants to the law school. According to the Court, the law school had a legitimate educational interest in assembling a diverse student body. Since employers, too, have a legitimate interest in a diverse work force, the Court's reasoning would seem to be applicable to employment as well as higher education. It remains to be seen, however, just how the Michigan decisions might be applied to the workplace.

Disparate Treatment and Disparate Impact

Discrimination under Title VII is sometimes classified as either *disparate treatment* discrimination or *disparate impact* discrimination. The first category includes what immediately comes to mind—intentionally making a personnel decision, such as refusing to hire or promote a particular individual because of race, color, gender, etc. That type of discrimination is prohibited by Title VII. So, too, is an employer practice of grouping employees by race, color, gender, etc., and treating the groups differently. Employment ads that indicate a preference for or against a particular race, color, or sex are also illegal, whether or not any actual discrimination is shown.

Disparate impact discrimination is a bit more subtle. Suppose an employer adopts a policy that on its face seems neutral, but that turns out to have an adverse impact on a particular ethnic group or gender. Take, for example, a private security company that has a minimum height and weight requirement for its patrol officers, the net effect of which is to exclude most females, but almost no males.

Other practices that could give rise to disparate impact claims include minimum education or experience requirements that do not serve a legitimate business purpose; use of test scores in hiring or promoting if the test is culturally biased or is not related to job performance; or blanket exclusion of applicants with criminal records or whose wages have been garnished.

Terms, Conditions, and Privileges of Employment

Title VII prohibits discrimination in hiring, firing, compensation, and other terms, conditions, and privileges of employment. Ready examples of what is meant by *terms, conditions, and privileges* of employment include shift assignments, fringe benefits such as vacation, sick leave, insurance programs, and access to facilities such as the cafeteria and fitness center. Courts have ruled that the *intangible work environment* is covered by Title VII as well. Under those rulings, an employer who promotes or tolerates a workplace environment filled with demeaning racial or sexual slurs can be sued by the target of those slurs and by others who find the environment offensive, if a *reasonable person* would find the environment offensive.

Trivial or inconsequential workplace actions by the employer will not support a Title VII action. The Supreme Court has said that a job action must amount to a *significant change in employment status*. The action must also be *objectively detrimental*, not just something a particular employee dislikes. As one court put it, not everything that makes an employee unhappy is an actionable adverse action, nor are changes that make a job less appealing but that do not affect a term, condition, or benefit of employment.

QUICK TIP

A less-than-favorable evaluation, a minor change in duties, or a change in title, with no effect on pay or status, even for allegedly discriminatory reasons, is not illegal. But if the evaluation leads to a loss of bonus or a demotion and the employee can show discriminatory motive, a good Title VII claim will result.

Bona Fide Occupational Qualification

An employer charged with discrimination on the grounds of sex, religion, or national origin (but not discrimination on the grounds of race) may, in theory, raise a defense of *bona fide occupational qualification* (BFOQ). However, the defense is very narrowly interpreted and as a practical matter is rarely available. In the airline industry, for example, a carrier who fails to hire male applicants as flight attendants under the belief that passengers expect females in that role does not have a good BFOQ defense. On the other hand, an employer may rely on the BFOQ exception in hiring actors for male roles and actresses for female roles.

Testers

Private organizations and even the EEOC sometimes use *testers* to obtain evidence of discrimination in the workplace.

EXAMPLE: Suppose an employer who is suspected of having racially discriminatory hiring practices advertises a job opening. Two testers—one white, one black—apply for the job and give fake credentials that appear to be substantially similar. The employer interviews the black candidate first but says he needs to check references before making any offer. He then interviews the white candidate and makes an offer on the spot. If this pattern is repeated several times, the employer will have a difficult time explaining his actions in the discrimination suit that is sure to follow.

It should be noted that claims of discrimination by testers, and by the organizations that employ them, do not always fare well in court, since the testers were not really candidates and they cannot really claim to have been denied a job. According to recent press reports, the EEOC is also under pressure from Congress to stop using testers.

Retaliation

Title VII also prohibits *retaliation* against an employee who has complained about discrimination or who has assisted another complainant, such as by testifying on his or her behalf.

Whenever a discrimination charge is pending—even an informal one that is still at the internal investigation stage—employers should exercise extraordinary caution in making personnel decisions that affect the complaining employee or others involved in the matter. Any adverse action taken after the initial charge has been made is likely to generate a charge of retaliation.

The Supreme Court has recently made clear that in order to constitute retaliation, the retaliatory acts must be *material* and *adverse*. However, unlike discrimination itself, the retaliation need not affect the terms or conditions of employment. Under this ruling, an act can qualify as retaliatory even if it is completely unrelated to the job, so long as it would dissuade a reasonable employee from filing a discrimination charge.

QUICK TIP

The term *employee* as used in Title VII includes *former employees*. Therefore, it is illegal for a company to, for example, give a bad reference to a former employee in retaliation for the former employee's filing a charge of race discrimination after he or she was fired.

Covered Employers

Title VII defines *employer* as a person or organization engaged in an industry affecting commerce who has fifteen or more employees for each working day in each of twenty or more calendar weeks in the current or preceding calendar year.

The term *industry affecting commerce* means any activity, business, or industry in commerce in which a labor dispute would hinder or obstruct commerce or the free flow of commerce—in other words, just about any activity in which an employer might engage. (Title VII is tied to the Commerce Clause of the U.S. Constitution because all federal legislation must be based on one or another of the powers granted the federal government by the U.S. Constitution.)

Determining who are employees for purposes of the fifteen-employee threshold is critical to a claim of discrimination. If the threshold is not satisfied, a Title VII claim is subject to being dismissed. And, of course, the person making the claim must be an employee to invoke federal antidiscrimination laws in the first place.

The discrimination laws themselves are not at all helpful in answering the question of who are employees. They typically define *employee* as an individual employed by an employer. In the Supreme Court's words, that is a mere nominal definition that is completely circular and explains nothing.

One issue is how to deal with individuals who are carried on the employer's books as employees, but who are not physically at work for a full twenty weeks. In a 1997 Supreme Court case, the employer had between fifteen and seventeen employees on its payroll for at least twenty weeks, but during eleven of those weeks, it was not actually compensating fifteen or more employees. The difference resulted from the fact that two of its employees were part-time who worked fewer than five days per week.

The Court ruled that the employer was subject to Title VII, adopting what has become known as the *payroll method* for counting employees. Under that method, if an employee appears on the employer's payroll records, he or she is counted whether or not he or she is actually being compensated on a particular day. In short, part-time employees, full-time employees, and presumably persons on leave all count.

QUICK TIP

The employee-counting question is broadly applicable to a wide range of federal employment-related laws, even though they may have different numerical thresholds.

Professional Corporations

Yet another issue involves shareholder-directors of professional corporations, such as doctors, lawyers, and so on. While they may be classified as employees for federal tax and pension plan purposes, they also manage the professional corporation. (Professional corporations and other types of business entities are discussed in Chapter 1.)

CASE STUDY: SHAREHOLDER-DIRECTORS AS EMPLOYEES

In a recent Supreme Court case called Clackamas, an Oregon medical clinic was sued for discrimination by the clinic's bookkeeper. The bookkeeper argued that the clinic met the fifteen-employee threshold so long as four of its physician-shareholders were counted. The bookkeeper pointed out, for example, that the physician-shareholders had employment contracts, they were salaried, and they were treated as employees for tax purposes. The clinic claimed otherwise—that the physician-shareholders were really more like partners in a partnership and should therefore not be counted. Citing EEOC regulations, the Court in Clackamas listed the following six factors to be considered in determining whether a shareholder-director of a professional corporation is an employee for discrimination purposes:

• Whether the organization can hire or fire the individual or set the rules and regulations of the individual's work;

• Whether, and if so, to what extent, the organization supervises the individual's work;

• Whether the individual reports to someone higher in the organization;

- Whether, and if so, to what extent, the individual is able to influence the organization;

- Whether the parties intended that the individual be an employee, as expressed in written contracts; and,

- Whether the individual shares in the profits, losses, and liabilities of the organization.

Whatever the merits of the Clackamas decision, the six factors the Supreme Court listed are highly fact-specific. Having to deal with these additional factors adds further uncertainty to discrimination claims and increases associated costs and delays.

Extraterritorial Application

Activities by employers outside the U.S. could certainly affect commerce within the U.S. But the Supreme Court has held that Title VII does not have *extraterritorial application*, so that U.S. citizens employed abroad, even U.S. citizens employed by U.S. employers, have no Title VII protection. Title VII itself exempts aliens employed outside the U.S., and it permits employers operating in a foreign country to comply with that country's law even if compliance amounts to a violation of Title VII.

Religious Discrimination under Title VII

Title VII makes it illegal for an employer to discriminate against an employee on the basis of his or her religion. *Religion* includes all aspects of religious observance, practice, and belief. This means, for example, that an employer cannot refuse to hire an applicant because the applicant is a member of a particular religious sect any more than the employer can refuse to hire an applicant on the basis of the applicant's race or gender. Harassment based on religious beliefs or practices is also a violation of Title VII.

But special rules apply to religious discrimination. The First Amendment to the U.S. Constitution says that "Congress shall make no law respecting the establishment of religion, or prohibiting the free exercise thereof." Based on the First Amendment, the courts have developed the so-called *ministerial exception* to Title VII, under which religious organizations may discriminate in connection with the selection and employment of their own clergy.

The term *clergy* has been broadly defined by the courts to include lay employees whose primary duties consist of teaching, spreading the faith, church governance, supervision of religious orders, or participating in religious ritual and worship. So, for example, a nun who was an assistant professor of canon law at Catholic University could not sue for sex discrimination when she was denied tenure. And a lay music teacher at a Catholic elementary school who directed a church choir also could not complain of sex discrimination because, as the court recognized, music is important in the spiritual and pastoral mission of the church and plays an integral role in religious tradition. Even for nonclergy, religious organizations may discriminate against employees on *religious grounds*. (See Chapter 23 for more on religious organizations and discrimination based on religion.)

Title VII also requires employers to *reasonably accommodate* their employees' religious observances and practices. In this respect it is similar to the *Americans with Disabilities Act* (discussed in Chapter 17), which requires reasonable accommodation of employees with disabilities. As with the ADA, the burden is on the employee to ask for a reasonable religious accommodation.

One difference between disability accommodation under the ADA and religious accommodation under Title VII is that under the ADA, the employer must, in effect, conduct a dialogue with a disabled employee to arrive at what is reasonable. Under Title VII, the employer gets to choose how to accommodate the employee's religious observance and practice and need not consider the employee's suggested accommodations.

The employer is excused from accommodating a religious practice if the accommodation would impose an undue hardship. While anything more than a minimal cost to the employer will qualify as an undue hardship, the hardship must be real and not merely speculative or hypothetical in order to excuse the employer from accommodating.

Following are examples of cases in which employees or applicants claimed that the employer failed to accommodate their religious observances or practices.

Sabbath Day

A number of cases have involved work on a Sunday or other Sabbath day. The courts have ruled that an employer must attempt to accommodate a good faith belief prohibiting work on Sabbath, such as by allowing the employee to switch with another employee or by having a flexible leave policy that allows the employee to choose the Sabbath as a leave day. However, the employer does not have an absolute duty to accommodate such religious beliefs. If, due to the employer's workload, weekend work is necessary, and if excusing some employees completely from all weekend work would create disruption within the workplace, or would violate established seniority rules or a union contract, the employer may insist that employees participate in weekend work schedules despite their religious scruples to the contrary.

Religious Garb

If there is a good business reason, such as interference with job performance or safety concerns, an employer may prohibit employees from wearing religious garb, such as crucifixes, yarmulkes, or chadors. Otherwise, the employer is likely obligated to accommodate the practice. One way to accommodate might be to transfer the employee from a position that deals with the public to a position that does not. (Dress codes are discussed in Chapters 2 and 15.)

Abortion and Birth Control

Two cases in this area provide a good illustration of what is, and what is not, required of an employer. In one case an anti-abortion activist took a religious vow always to wear a particular button depicting a fetus and containing anti-abortion slogans. The button was disturbing to many of her coworkers for reasons unrelated to religious beliefs. Her employer offered her the option of covering the button while at work, wearing a different button that contained the slogans but not the fetus, or removing the button when she left her immediate work area. She refused all of these options and was fired. In her Title VII suit for religious discrimination, the court held that the employer had offered a reasonable accommodation and was justified in firing her when she rejected the accommodation.

In the second case, an orthodox Jewish pharmacist, who was unwilling to sell condoms on religious grounds, applied for a job at a drugstore. The drugstore refused to consider his application and was sued for discrimination. The court agreed with the pharmacist, noting that the drugstore made no effort whatever at accommodation and that the drugstore's claim of undue hardship, had it tried to accommodate, was merely speculative.

Praying and Preaching

To what extent may an employee actively promote his religious beliefs to fellow employees? In one case a management-level employee who had become an evangelical Christian wrote a letter to her supervisor stating that because of certain unidentified actions the supervisor had taken, he needed to "get right with God." The supervisor's wife saw the letter and took it to mean that her husband was having an affair. The same employee wrote a second letter to a subordinate of hers, suggesting that the subordinate's illness was punishment for premarital sex. The employee's firing over the letter-writing was justified, said the court, because the employer had no obligation to accommodate such inappropriate behavior by an employee with management responsibilities, even if the behavior was religiously motivated.

In another case, a born-again Christian occasionally prayed in his office with other employees and he made isolated references to his Christian beliefs. The court ruled that tolerating these trifling incidents imposed no hardship on the employer and could not justify termination.

Refusal to Comply with Tax Laws

When an applicant for employment refused, on religious grounds, to provide his Social Security number, the prospective employer was justified in rejecting his application. The court held that the prospective employer was not required to accommodate the applicant by violating IRS regulations or by seeking a waiver from the IRS.

Other Antidiscrimination Laws

Although Title VII is by far the broadest and most significant federal antidiscrimination law, it is not the only one. Other federal laws apply in more limited circumstances.

Section 1981

A Reconstruction-era statute guarantees to all persons within the United States "the same right...to make and enforce contracts...as is enjoyed by white citizens." (Lawsuits brought under this statute are known as *Section 1981 actions* because the statute is codified at Title 42, Section 1981, of the United States Code.) Congress has amended the statute to cover not only the formation and enforcement of contracts, but also the making, performance, modification, and termination of contracts, and the enjoyment of all benefits, privileges, terms, and conditions of the contractual relationship.

Section 1981 is an important statute. Even though Title VII also prohibits racial discrimination, Title VII is limited to employers with fifteen or more employees. Section 1981 has no such limitation. In addition, claims under Section 1981 are not subject to the abbreviated time limits set by Title VII and they can be filed in court without first going through the administrative procedures applicable to Title VII.

Immigration

When Congress passed the *Immigration Reform and Control Act* in 1986 making it illegal for employers knowingly to hire persons who are not eligible to work in the U.S., Congress included a provision prohibiting discrimination on the basis of citizenship or national origin. The prohibition applies to employers with four or more employees. Title VII, in contrast, prohibits national origin discrimination by employers with fifteen or more employees, and it does not address citizenship status at all.

Military Service

Federal law prohibits any employer from discriminating against employees and applicants for employment on account of their military service. Persons who are members of the uniformed services, who have applied to become members, or who have obligations to one of the uniformed services are protected against discrimination in hiring, retention, reemployment, promotion, or the granting of any employment benefit.

QUICK TIP

Nondiscrimination clauses are frequently contained in construction and other contracts with government agencies. (See Chapter 22 for more specific information.)

Financial Discrimination

Federal law prohibits an employer from discharging an employee whose earnings have been subject to garnishment for any one debt, regardless of the number of levies made or proceedings brought to collect it. Discrimination against a person who has filed for bankruptcy is also prohibited.

State and Local Prohibitions

Most states and many local governments have their own laws prohibiting discrimination on grounds of race, color, and so on. These laws are not just duplications of federal law, since they often prohibit additional forms of discrimination not covered by federal law, such as ancestry, marital status, sexual orientation, transgendered individuals, and genetics. These laws also reach smaller employers not covered by Title VII.

Professional Codes of Ethics

The *Codes of Ethics* of some professional groups contain nondiscrimination clauses. A professional who discriminates in employment may become subjected to disciplinary proceedings before his or her state licensing board and may suffer suspension or revocation of his or her license to practice.

Discrimination Based on Genetics

By use of *genetic testing*, it is possible to calculate the probability that persons who are now symptom-free will develop a variety of disabling or fatal disorders. The *Human Genome Project* and related biomedical research continue to increase the number of conditions known to be genetically linked. While the existence of some genetic markers increases only slightly the statistical risk that an associated disease will become manifest, other genetic markers are virtual guarantees of eventual sickness or death.

> **Alert!**
>
> To the extent that a genetic marker is associated with a particular race or nationality, discrimination on the basis of genetics may violate other employment discrimination laws.

Under the new federal *Genetic Information Discrimination Act* (GINA), due to become effective in late 2009, employers will be prohibited from discriminating against employees on the basis of genetic information. With limited exceptions, it will also be illegal under GINA for employers to request or obtain genetic information about an employee or his or her family members.

A growing number of states also prohibit employers from using genetic information when making employment decisions, or bar use of genetic information in connection with the rejection of applicants for health insurance or the pricing of health insurance policies.

Even aside from GINA and similar state laws, requesting genetic information could expose the employer to liability in other ways.

ADA

The federal *Americans with Disabilities Act*, which applies to employers with fifteen or more employees, has long prohibited all *pre-employment medical examinations* (except drug testing). (See Chapter 17 for more on the ADA.) A test for genetic markers undoubtedly falls within this prohibition and is therefore illegal.

HIPAA

The *Health Insurance Portability and Accountability Act* (discussed in Chapter 10) prohibits a group health insurance plan from establishing eligibility rules based on *health status-related factors*, which includes genetic information. Also under HIPAA, genetic information cannot be used to conclude that a person has a preexisting condition. The conclusion can only be based on a diagnosis of the condition itself.

Health and Human Services Department regulations under HIPAA prohibit group health plans from disclosing protected health information to plan sponsors, except to enable plan sponsors to carry out plan administration functions that the plan sponsor performs. This would cover any genetic information obtained by the group plan. The plan documents of employer-sponsored plans must contain a provision prohibiting employers from using protected health information for any employment-related action or decision. Again, this would cover genetic information, but only to the extent the information was obtained from the group plan.

Executive Order 13145

Executive Order 13145 prohibits all executive departments and agencies of the federal government from collecting *protected genetic information* about its employees or basing employment decisions on such information. Protected genetic information is defined as:

- information about an individual's genetic tests (that is, analysis of DNA, RNA, chromosomes, proteins, or certain metabolites in order to detect disease-related genotypes or mutations);
- information about the genetic tests of an individual's family members; and,
- information about the occurrence of a disease or medical condition or disorder in an individual's family members.

The Executive Order is limited to federal employment; it does not apply to the general work force.

Contingent Workers

The term *contingent worker* is loosely defined as any worker who is outside the employer's core work force of full-time, long-term employees. As used here, the term refers to independent contractors, part-time employees, job-sharing employees, temporary employees, leased employees, and joint employees.

In general, independent contractors are not covered by the employment provisions of the nondiscrimination laws because they are not employees. However, the *misclassification* of a true employee as an independent contractor is as disastrous for nondiscrimination law purposes as it is for tax and benefit entitlement purposes. (Independent contractors are discussed in more detail in Chapter 7.)

All other categories of contingent workers—part-timers, job-sharers, telecommuters, etc.—are fully protected by the nondiscrimination laws. For example, a company whose staff includes temporary workers furnished by an agency cannot direct the agency to furnish (or not to furnish) temps of a particular race or gender. Nor can the company accept temps from an agency when the company knows that the agency itself discriminates in selecting persons to be temps.

For certain categories of contingent workers, such as leased or joint employees, it is not always clear who the actual employer is— the staffing firm, the company that controls the actual worksite, or both. The EEOC has developed an elaborate set of definitions to determine who the employer is for purposes of applying the federal nondiscrimination laws. The definitions turn on such factors as who does the hiring and firing, who handles payroll, who controls the employee's day-to-day work environment, and so on. While it may be possible in any particular circumstance for either the staffing firm or the worksite owner to avoid being tagged as the employer, any company that tolerates or commits discrimination against a member of its work force is exposed to substantial risk.

Record-Keeping

Under EEOC regulations, employers with 100 or more employees are required to file an *Employer Information Report* (Form EEO-1) each year. Form EEO-1 calls for a breakdown of the employer's work force by race, sex, and national origin. The EEOC does not prescribe any particular records that must be kept to support the information contained in Form EEO-1.

Note:

A sample form and instructions are available at: www.eeoc.gov/ stats/jobpat/e1instruct.html.

EEOC regulations permit employers to collect post-employment records of race and national origin (unless doing so is prohibited by state law), but the EEOC recommends that any such records be kept separate from other personnel data, such as evaluations. Any records that are prepared to support submission of Form EEO-1 must be saved for at least one year.

Alert!

Additional record-keeping requirements apply under wage-and-hour laws, income and withholding tax laws, laws regulating pension and other benefit plans, safety and health laws, and laws regarding the employment of non-U.S. citizens.

Statutes of limitations—the time period within which an employee or enforcement agency can bring a claim—should also be considered in establishing record retention policies. Those statutes differ from state to state and they may even vary for different types of claims. Although charges of Title VII discrimination must be initiated within a relatively brief time period (one hundred eighty days or three hundred days, depending on the particular federal, state, or local agency that has jurisdiction), other types of claims may be filed as late as three or more years after the events take place. A five-year retention policy—that is, a policy of retaining all employment-related documents and information for five years after an employee terminates or an applicant is rejected—may seem a bit excessive, but can prove very helpful.

The retention policy should apply not only to documents and information that relate to individual applicants and employees, but should also include items such as employee handbooks and policy directives that have become out-of-date or superseded. That way, the employer can show what the rules were at a particular time, even if the rules have since changed.

Employment Practices Liability Insurance

Most standard premises liability insurance policies or *comprehensive general liability (CGL) insurance* policies exclude claims arising out of employment matters. That means that if you are sued for abusive discharge, for race or sex discrimination, or for employment-related defamation, your insurance carrier will not provide a defense attorney and it will not pay any judgment against you. Unless, that is, you have *Employment Practices Liability (EPL) insurance.*

A number of companies offer coverage that picks up where the usual exclusion leaves off. While the coverage may be expensive, it is probably a good idea to at least discuss EPL insurance with your insurance broker and find out whether it is available and at what cost. Even if you eventually decide not to buy coverage, the process of looking into it may highlight shortcomings in your employment practices.

Chapter  15

Gender Discrimination

Sex discrimination in employment, along with discrimination based on race, color, religion, or national origin, is covered by Title VII. It is just as illegal for an employer to reject an applicant on gender grounds as it is to reject the applicant on racial or religious grounds. Establishment of a glass ceiling, which limits promotion opportunities for women but not for men, is also illegal under Title VII. In other words, all the Title VII principles that apply to discrimination based on race, color, religion, and national origin generally also apply to gender-based discrimination.

But sex discrimination has some unique features. For one thing, sex discrimination is covered by two additional federal laws—the *Equal Pay Act* and the *Pregnancy Discrimination Act*—which do not apply to other forms of discrimination. For another, while the differences between persons of varying races, religions, or national origins are superficial at best, there are real biological differences between men and women. Finally, while the term *sex* as used in Title VII was probably intended to mean *gender*, the term can also refer to activity that has nothing to do with discrimination.

The special aspects of sex discrimination are discussed in the following sections of this chapter.

Equal Pay Act

In addition to its minimum wage and overtime pay provisions, the federal *Fair Labor Standards Act* as amended by the *Equal Pay Act* prohibits employers from paying males and females at different rates for the same work. And while executives, administrators, and professionals, among others, are exempt from the minimum wage and overtime pay requirements of the FLSA, they are *not* exempt from its equal pay requirements.

So an employer who intentionally discriminates by paying males more than females for equal work not only violates Title VII, but also violates the Equal Pay Act.

Pregnancy

In 1978, Congress enacted an amendment to Title VII known as the *Pregnancy Discrimination Act* (PDA). As a result of the PDA, Title VII now defines *because of sex* as including:

because of or on account of pregnancy, childbirth, or related medical conditions; women affected by pregnancy, childbirth, or related medical conditions shall be treated the same for all employment-related purposes, including receipt of benefits under fringe benefit programs, as other persons not so affected but similar in their ability or inability to work.

In other words, discrimination because of pregnancy, childbirth, or a related medical condition is sex discrimination, so that an employer cannot refuse to hire a pregnant woman or a woman of childbearing age because of her pregnancy or because of the possibility she may become pregnant.

Nor may an employer have special rules for pregnant women. For example, sick leave must be available to pregnant women on the same basis as it is to others. Similarly, employers who have health or disability insurance plans must cover pregnancy-related expenses and disabilities the same as other medical expenses or disabilities.

Title VII does not require an employer to cover *abortions* in its group health insurance policies, except where the mother's life would be endangered if the fetus were carried to term and except where medical complications have arisen from an abortion. However, Title VII permits a plan to cover abortions.

Breast-feeding

A number of states require employers to grant breaks to breast-feeding mothers so they can express milk. The laws typically require employers to provide private, sanitary areas for that purpose.

QUICK TIP

The federal *Newborns' and Mothers' Health Protection Act* prohibits group health plans from cutting off benefits for a mother or her newborn child after less than forty-eight hours of hospitalization following a normal vaginal delivery. This Act also prohibits cutting off benefits after less than ninety-six hours of hospitalization following a cesarean section. (Review Chapter 10 for more on group health insurance.)

Alert!

For employers with fifty or more employees, extended leave without pay for complications of pregnancy and childbirth, and to care for newborn children, may be required by the *Family and Medical Leave Act*. (See Chapter 8 for a discussion of FMLA.)

Forced Leave

Generally an employer may not require pregnant women to take leave at a specified point in their pregnancies unless the employer can demonstrate a *business necessity* or *bona fide occupational qualification* (BFOQ) for the rule. Compulsory leave policies for school teachers have routinely been held to violate Title VII. On the other hand, several cases involving the airline industry have held that mandatory maternity leave for flight attendants was justified by passenger safety considerations.

Job Reassignment

An important Supreme Court case involved the use of lead in battery manufacturing. Lead poses substantial health risks, including risks to fetuses carried by pregnant women who are exposed to the substance. When the manufacturing company discovered high lead levels in the blood of a number of its pregnant employees, the company adopted a policy barring all women of child-bearing age from jobs involving exposure to lead unless they could document that they were incapable of having children.

The Supreme Court held that the policy amounted to sex discrimination despite the company's benign motives. The Court said that the policy could not be justified as a BFOQ, since there was no evidence that pregnant women were less able than others to manufacture batteries. The Court concluded that the question of fetal safety should be for the mother, not the company, to decide, and it dismissed as only a remote possibility the company's fear of suit by children with birth defects attributed to fetal lead exposure.

EEOC Position

The EEOC takes the position that since pregnancy and childbirth are conditions unique to women, refusal to grant special leave to a pregnant employee may amount to sex discrimination.

In other words, according to the EEOC, the employer had better grant leave (assuming it is medically justified) unless the employer can show that the job cannot remain vacant and it cannot be filled by a temporary replacement. As of this writing, it remains to be seen whether the EEOC's position will be upheld in the courts.

Paternity Leave

If an employer grants maternity leave, at least one court has indicated it does not have to also grant *paternity* leave. However, for employers with fifty or more employees, fathers as well as mothers can qualify for leave under the FMLA.

Harassment in General

When the authors of Title VII added the word *sex* to the list of characteristics that an employer could not consider in making personnel decisions, they probably intended the term to be synonymous with *gender*. In other words, employers cannot consider gender when establishing pay rates or deciding whether to hire, promote, or fire, just as they cannot consider other characteristics, such as race or color, deemed irrelevant to job performance.

But the courts and the EEOC have ruled that sexual harassment is also a form of discrimination prohibited by Title VII. According to the EEOC, unwelcome sexual advances, requests for sexual favors, and other verbal or physical conduct of a sexual nature constitute sexual harassment when:

- Submission to such conduct is made either expressly or implicitly a term or condition of employment;
- Submission to or rejection of such conduct by an individual is used as the basis for employment decisions affecting such individual; or,

- Such conduct has the purpose or effect of unreasonably interfering with an individual's work performance or creating an *intimidating, hostile, or offensive working environment.*

The illegality of some forms of sexual harassment can probably be explained by traditional Title VII analysis. Take, for example, a male company supervisor who requests a female subordinate to sleep with him, promising her a promotion if she does and threatening to fire her if she does not. This type of sexual blackmail is discriminatory because the supervisor does not make the same request of any male subordinate. In other words, the supervisor has imposed on a female employee—because of her sex—a term or condition of employment that he has not imposed on a similarly situated male. Sex discrimination of this type has sometimes been called *quid pro quo* harassment.

Hostile Environment

The courts and the EEOC have gone beyond *quid pro quo* harassment, ruling that Title VII is violated by a *hostile environment* as well. To illustrate, suppose the branch manager of a bank requests sex from a teller who works for him, he touches her sexually, and he makes sexual jokes and comments directed to her or in her presence, *but he never promises any tangible job benefit, nor threatens to take any away.* The courts have held that the mere creation of an intimidating, hostile, or offensive work environment is a form of sex discrimination because, in effect, the employee must tolerate the hostile environment in order to keep her job. And if the employee finds the environment so hostile that she actually quits, she may have been constructively discharged and have a claim of *quid pro quo harassment* as well. (Constructive discharge is discussed in Chapter 4.)

The above example involves a male seeking sex from a female. But make no mistake—a male who is threatened with dismissal or harassed by a sex-seeking female supervisor has just as good a claim. The EEOC even takes the position (not well supported in the case law) that when an employee is promoted because she sleeps with the boss, *other employees* who do not get the promotion suffer sex discrimination.

QUICK TIP

Although harassment is most often associated with sex discrimination, harassment based on any discriminatory factor—race, color, religion, national origin, age, or disability—is also illegal if it is sufficiently severe to create a hostile work environment.

Same-sex harassment is also illegal under Title VII. In a case involving a male roustabout on an oil rig who was repeatedly subjected to sex-related, humiliating actions against him by other male members of the crew—including physical assaults and threats of rape—the Supreme Court ruled that sexual harassment *of any kind* is prohibited.

An offensive environment must be *severe* and *pervasive*, but it need not be so intolerable as to force the employee to quit or to cause the employee to suffer psychological injury. It is an environment that the complaining employee finds offensive and that a reasonable person would find objectionable as well. (In other words, the environment must be both subjectively and objectively offensive to support a Title VII claim.)

A super-sensitive employee, for example, who takes offense at the retelling of an off-color TV episode, does not have a good claim. But note that the offended employee need not be the specific target of the harassment in order for the environment to be considered hostile. The routine exchange of pornographic email among a willing group of employees may create a hostile work environment for another employee who is not involved in the exchange but who is simply exposed to the material.

Workplace Civility Code

A number of courts have ruled that Title VII is not intended as a code of workplace civility. For example, there should be no Title VII violation when the work environment is equally offensive to both male and female employees. This occurred in a strange case involving a supervisor who sought sexual favors from two subordinates, who happened to be husband and wife. The court in this situation found no violation of Title VII because Title VII is premised on eliminating discrimination. Inappropriate conduct that is inflicted on both sexes or is inflicted regardless of sex is outside the statute's ambit.

CASE STUDY: DETERMINING DISCRIMINATORY SEXUAL HARASSMENT

A security guard supervisor working under contract at the Environmental Protection Agency disciplined two other guards at the site. The two guards, apparently infuriated by the discipline, launched a retaliatory campaign against the supervisor that began by repeated slashing of his tires. Later they taunted him in a sexual manner that included a variety of lewd gestures and comments.

In response to the supervisor's Title VII claim, the court ruled that the harassment he complained about, although tinged with offensive sexual connotations, was not based on his sex. The supervisor did not claim, for example, that the two guards were homosexual or that they were seriously proposing to have sex with him. Nor did the supervisor show that the guards were motivated by general hostility to males in the workplace. Instead, according to the court, the guards were motivated by a workplace grudge having nothing to do with sex.

On the other hand, the U.S. Court of Appeals for the Ninth Circuit (headquartered in San Francisco), ruled in effect that even equal opportunity harassment could result in employer liability. In that case, a senior official with an office of the National Education Association was rude, overbearing, obnoxious, loud, vulgar, and generally unpleasant. Significantly, none of the official's conduct was of a sexual nature.

The Ninth Circuit said that even if male and female employees were being treated the same, a reasonable woman may well have a more negative reaction than her male counterpart to the official's conduct. In other words, according to the court, because women by nature may feel more intimidated or threatened than men by a supervisor's obnoxious behavior, even when that behavior is directed equally at all employees, women enjoy less desirable working conditions and they therefore suffer sex discrimination. (Some would argue that this decision promotes the very gender stereotype that Title VII was intended to abolish.)

How can an employer possibly distinguish between sexual harassment that is discriminatory and sexual harassment that is not? The short answer is that there is no safe way to make that distinction. And despite pronouncements that Title VII was not intended as a workplace civility code, that is exactly what it may have become. At the risk of incurring substantial liability, employers have little choice but to prohibit all teasing, horseplay, banter, and other conduct with sexual overtones for fear that a court may view the conduct as discriminatory harassment.

Employer Liability for Harassment

Employer liability for sexual harassment has been a controversial issue in the courts. The controversy was heightened by the 1991 amendment to Title VII that added *compensatory and punitive damages* as available remedies in cases of intentional discrimination.

The Supreme Court has ruled that an employer is *always* liable for a hostile work environment created by a *supervisor* when the discrimination takes the form of a *tangible employment action*—defined as a significant change in employment status. Usually, but not always, a tangible employment action results in economic injury because it relates to matters such as hiring, firing, failing to promote, reassignment with significantly different responsibilities, or a significant change in benefits. The theory is that when a supervisor takes a tangible employment action with respect to a subordinate, he or she is exercising authority delegated by the employer company, and the company is automatically responsible for how that authority is exercised.

In a hostile environment case where no tangible job action is involved, the employer is only *presumed* liable for a supervisor's harassment. The employer may have an *affirmative defense* against such a claim, and avoid liability, if the employer can show that it had and enforced a *policy* against sexual harassment and the complaining employee *unreasonably failed* to take advantage of preventive or corrective opportunities provided by the employer.

In order to evoke this affirmative defense, the employer must have and *enforce* a policy against sexual harassment. It is not enough simply to have a written policy in place. Many courts have recognized that employers must educate their work force about the policy, such as by conducting periodic training for both managers and rank-and-file employees.

Nonsupervisor Conduct

Workplace sexual misconduct is not limited to a supervisor's mistreatment of subordinates. The employer can also be liable for tolerating a hostile work environment created by an employee's fellow employees and even nonemployees, such as customers, if the employer knows (or should know) about the offensive work environment but fails to take appropriate remedial action. In effect, the law requires employers to make reasonable efforts to provide a working environment free from hostile or offensive harassment. The law does not necessarily care who is doing the harassing.

Protective Policies

Employers have tried different techniques to protect themselves from claims. Some employers require that employees who are involved in an office romance, particularly if the romance is between a higher-level supervisor and a lower-level employee, sign a *love contract* setting out the ground rules for the relationship. The contract might have the parties acknowledge, for example, that the relationship is consensual and that it can be terminated by either party at any time.

However, those measures seem extreme and may expose the employer to liability for invasion of privacy. The bottom line is that an employer must have an *effective* sexual harassment policy. While no list of dos and don'ts can completely protect employers from sexual harassment claims, the suggestions in Figure 15.1 should go a long way.

QUICK TIP

The complainant's own conduct is relevant when investigating a claim of sexual harassment, such as whether the complainant willingly participated in the activity that he or she now claims was offensive. However, an investigation that focuses primarily on the complainant's own conduct may be viewed as retaliatory and may subject the employer to additional claims of discrimination.

Sexual Orientation

Title VII coverage does not extend to discrimination based on being gay or lesbian. A recent case involved a homosexual male nurse who worked for a hospital in Indianapolis. The nurse complained that one of his physician supervisors made fun of his homosexuality, yelled at him during telephone conversations, and otherwise treated him poorly, all of which were based on his sexual orientation. The nurse was eventually fired, allegedly because of his complaint, although the hospital said it was for making an unauthorized entry in a patient's chart.

The court ruled that Congress used the term *sex* in Title VII to mean a biological male or biological female and not one's sexuality or sexual orientation. Therefore, according to the court, harassment based solely on a person's sexual preference or orientation (and not on one's sex) is not an unlawful employment practice under Title VII. And even if the nurse's firing was in retaliation for his complaint of harassment, the nurse still did not have a valid Title VII claim since the underlying conduct—harassment based on sexual orientation—was not itself covered.

Alert!

While Title VII may not prohibit discrimination based on sexual orientation, many state and local laws do.

Figure 15.1: HARASSMENT POLICY

To reduce the risk of a successful sexual harassment claim, an employer should, at the least:

- Establish a *written* nondiscrimination policy, including a specific policy against sexual (and all other forms of) harassment. The policy should define sexual harassment. It should be published in the employee handbook and posted conspicuously at the workplace. *In the absence of a written policy, an employer has no chance at all of defending against a claim of hostile environment sexual harassment by a supervisor against a subordinate.*

- Include in the policy various means by which an employee can complain *in confidence* about sexual harassment. The complaint route should not be limited to the employee's immediate supervisor, since he or she may be the harasser.

- Consider installing an *anonymous hotline* or an *interactive website* for employees to report harassment and other types of workplace problems.

- Conduct regular *training seminars* on sexual harassment, attendance at which should be mandatory. (It usually makes sense to have separate sessions for supervisors and nonsupervisory personnel.)

- Keep careful *records* of who attended each training session and what material was presented.

- Plan in advance *who* will be in charge of investigating complaints of sexual harassment and *how* the investigation will be conducted. (Making those determinations after a complaint is received will cause delay and could result in the harassment policy being ruled unreasonable or ineffective.)

- On receipt of a complaint of sexual harassment, review your *Employment Practices Liability Insurance Policy* and give notice of the complaint to your insurance carrier.

- If the complaint involves sexual assaults or other criminal conduct, suggest that the complaining party make a police report.

- Investigate *all* complaints of sexual harassment *promptly, thoroughly, and objectively*. Consider hiring experienced employment counsel to supervise the investigation.

- Include an interview with the complaining party in the investigation. Get as much detail from him or her as possible about what happened, when and where it happened, and who else saw or knows about the harassment. Also, ask the complainant how he or she would like the matter to be resolved (without making any promises about what action will be taken).

- Treat as confidential all information developed during the investigation. However, do not promise confidentiality, since complete confidentiality is probably not possible. Be careful about prohibiting your work force from discussing the matter, since that may constitute an unfair labor practice.

- Make a contemporaneous, detailed written record of the investigation.

- If the investigation shows that the complaint is justified, take *immediate and appropriate* corrective action against the harasser. Inform the complaining party about the action taken and ask whether there is anything further he or she wishes to bring to the employer's attention.

- For serious, ongoing incidents, consider temporarily reassigning the alleged harasser or complaining party, or placing one or both of them on temporary leave with pay, to prevent additional incidents pending your investigation. (This could be a perilous step, if the reassignment or leave is construed as retaliation against the complainant or defamation of the alleged harasser.)

- If the investigation shows the complaint to be unfounded, inform the complaining party and the accused harasser and close the investigation.

- Do not take disciplinary action against the complainant unless it is clear that he or she intentionally lied about the matter. (Retaliation against an employee for exercising rights protected by law, such as the right to complain about harassment, constitutes illegal discrimination.)

Other Issues

Title VII's prohibition of sex discrimination gives rise to additional workplace issues from time to time, described below.

Dress Codes

A few federal court cases have ruled that employers have a certain amount of latitude in adopting dress and grooming standards that are not entirely gender neutral, and that minor differences in personal appearance regulations do not constitute sex discrimination under Title VII. As a caveat, however, the dress codes must be enforced even-handedly between men and women.

Many of the dress code cases have involved hair length. A few have involved earrings. The issue typically arises when a male employee is disciplined for violating policies that prohibit long hair for men but not for women, or that prohibit earrings on males but not females. The courts have said that while long hair and earrings on men may be fashionable in some circles, an employer may legitimately wish to present a more conservative image and need not tolerate the outer bounds of current fashion. But if the business justification for a gender-specific dress code is to present a more conservative image, application of the dress code to employees who have no contact with the public makes no sense.

Alert!

A dress code policy that prohibits clothing or accessories associated with particular religious beliefs or practices may constitute religious discrimination under Title VII. (Review Chapter 14 for more information on religious discrimination under Title VII.)

Contraceptive Coverage

The EEOC has ruled that an employer-sponsored health insurance plan that provides comprehensive benefits, including drug coverage but excluding contraceptive drugs, violates Title VII of the federal *Civil Rights Act*. A federal court in Washington State has reached the same conclusion. That court ruled that while Title VII does not require employers to offer any particular type or category of benefit, any resulting plan must not discriminate based on sex-based characteristics and the plan must provide equally comprehensive coverage for both sexes.

Infertility Treatments

A group health plan that denied benefits for surgical procedures to implant embryos was held nondiscriminatory, even though the particular treatment is only performed on women. A court reasoned that even though the surgical procedure was limited to women, it was not discriminatory because the underlying condition that the surgery was attempting to abate could be male infertility, female infertility, or both. In other words, the exclusion was equally adverse to males and females.

Transgender Issues

Employees who identify with and adopt a gender opposite to his or her traditional biological gender present unique problems.

For example, the Eighth Circuit Court of Appeals has ruled that a Minneapolis teacher who was a biological male but who considered himself a female could use the women's faculty restroom despite objection by a woman faculty member. The case was based in part on Minnesota law, however, and does not necessarily indicate how other courts might rule.

In another case, from the Second Circuit Court of Appeals in New York, an employee who suffered from *gender dysphoria* (discomfort with gender of birth) and underwent sex-change surgery was not entitled to reimbursement from her group health plan. Since the surgery was not medically necessary, the plan's denial of benefits was not a violation of Title VII.

Retirement Plans

An employer cannot provide smaller monthly retirement payments to women just because women, on average, live longer than men and collect benefits for a longer time.

Physique

A number of cases have involved size and strength differences between men and women. If an employer sets minimum height and weight standards that tend to exclude most women applicants but few men applicants, the standards will be deemed discriminatory unless the employer can show a business necessity for the standards.

Chapter 16

Age Discrimination

The purpose of the federal *Age Discrimination in Employment Act* (ADEA) is to *promote employment of older persons based on their ability rather than age* by prohibiting age-based discrimination against employees and job applicants. Consistent with that purpose, the ADEA only applies to persons 40 years of age or older, so that an age-based decision affecting a person under 40 does not violate the ADEA.

Alert!

Many states and local jurisdictions have their own age discrimination laws that apply to all employees, not just those 40 years of age or older.

Hiring or promoting a 35-year-old employee instead of a 45-year-old *for reasons other than age* is perfectly legal. However, the employer should identify the objective, job-related, nondiscriminatory criteria used in making the decision. In making personnel decisions, employers should avoid using terms such as *dead wood, fresh faces, new blood,* or *more energy.* These terms are often viewed as evidence of *discriminatory intent* and will hurt the employer in defending an age discrimination claim.

Harassment with respect to age can constitute age discrimination—just as harassment with respect to race or sex can violate Title VII. Employers should not tolerate workplace jokes or teasing aimed at older employees, their medical conditions, or other factors common to age.

There has been some doubt just how the ADEA works in certain circumstances. For example, is favoring a 45-year-old over a 60-year-old illegal, even though both workers are within the protected, over-40 class? Alternatively, may an employer favor a 60-year-old over a worker aged 45?

In 1996, the Supreme Court answered the first question, ruling that when an older worker is replaced by someone younger because of age, it does not matter that the younger worker is also in the 40-and-older protected class. A case of age discrimination can be based just on a significant age difference even though both workers are over 40, said the Court.

More recently the Supreme Court answered the second question as well. The Court ruled that an employer practice that *favors older workers* is permitted under the ADEA, even though it discriminates against younger workers who are in the 40-and-over protected class. In the Court's words, the ADEA does not *look both ways*.

Covered Employers

The ADEA covers most employers with twenty or more employees. Specifically, it covers employers engaged in an industry affecting commerce who have twenty or more employees for each working day in each of twenty or more calendar weeks in the current or preceding calendar year. The coverage provisions track Title VII, except that the employee threshold for Title VII is fifteen employees instead of the twenty-employee threshold of the ADEA. (See Chapter 14 for a discussion of the meaning of *industry affecting commerce* and the methodology for counting employees.)

Exceptions

As with Title VII, there is an exception in the ADEA for a *bona fide occupational qualification* (BFOQ); however, the exception has been very narrowly applied by the courts. For example, an airline had a rule that its flight engineers must retire at age 60 on the theory that many persons over that age have limitations that preclude safe operation of aircraft. The airline argued that it would be impractical, if not impossible, to examine all flight engineers and identify those with limitations. A jury found the rule illegal under the ADEA and awarded damages. The Supreme Court let the jury verdict stand, saying that it was not enough for the airline to have a *rational basis* for its policy. Instead, the airline had to prove that its policy was *reasonably necessary* to the normal operation or essence of the particular business. (Ironically, the Federal Aviation Administration long had a rule that pilots must retire at age 60. Congress recently raised that age to 65.)

The ADEA also permits an employer to have a *bona fide seniority system* provided it is not intended to evade the purposes of the ADEA. A seniority system cannot be used to justify involuntary retirements.

The ADEA has other exceptions that make the Act unique among federal antidiscrimination laws. For one, the ADEA does not apply to persons under age 40, so age discrimination against persons younger than 40 is not illegal under the ADEA. (As pointed out above, it may be illegal under state or local laws.)

Although the Act generally prohibits compulsory retirements based on age, *bona fide executives* or *high policy makers* may be forced to retire. A bona fide executive is a person who exercises substantial managerial authority over a significant number of employees and a large volume of business. A high policy maker is an employee other than a bona fide executive who plays a significant role in developing and implementing corporate policy. The Act allows forced retirement of a bona fide executive or high policy maker if the person held the position for two years preceding retirement, is at least 65 years old, and is entitled to annual retirement benefits of at least $44,000 based solely on employer contributions.

QUICK TIP

The definition of a bona fide executive for ADEA purposes is different from the *Fair Labor Standards Act's* definition in connection with exemption from overtime requirements. (Chapter 5 addresses overtime requirements.)

State and local governments are also permitted to establish mandatory retirement ages for firefighters and law enforcement officers.

Benefit Plans

Almost all retirement plans make age-based distinctions. Plans stating that employees who have attained a specified age (such as 65) may retire and begin receiving benefits are lawful. However, employers must use caution when changing the terms of plans to ensure that benefits are not being taken from a class of persons protected by the ADEA.

For example, when an employer *converts* from a defined benefit plan to a cash balance plan, employees lose the back-loaded boost they had anticipated from their defined benefit plan. Since this loss is borne most heavily by older workers who are near retirement, some have argued that such conversions amount to age discrimination.

Proving Age Discrimination

Although an older worker may be the victim of age discrimination, the worker still has to prove that the adverse employment decision was age-based. It is often difficult to find direct evidence of discriminatory motive. In the more usual case, the boss's motive is unclear (or at least unexpressed), and circumstantial evidence is all that is available.

One type of circumstantial evidence is a significant age differential between the fired person and his or her replacement. Courts have come up with a variety of answers as to what is significant, ranging from three years to ten years. Five to seven years seems to be emerging as a standard, so that an age differential of less than that should not provide circumstantial evidence of age discrimination. But even when the age difference is less than five years, an employee could still prevail in court if he or she has *other evidence of* age discrimination.

Release of ADEA Claims

A *release* is a type of contract by which one party gives up a legal right or claim in exchange for valuable consideration—usually money. In general, no special form of contract is required to release most types of claims, including discrimination claims.

ADEA cases are different. Unlike other employment-related disputes, the release of an ADEA claim will be ineffective unless the employer follows very specific procedures spelled out in the law. For example, the employee must be advised in writing to consult with an attorney before signing the release. Then, the employee must be given at least twenty-one days to consider the release before signing it. Also, the employee must be given an additional seven-day rescission period after signing it to change his or her mind.

The law does not require the employee to actually wait twenty-one days before signing the release. The employee can sign earlier, so long as his or her right to take a full twenty-one days is not restricted. However, the seven-day period after signing cannot be shortened.

The Supreme Court has ruled that where a release did not comply with ADEA requirements, an employee who received severance pay in exchange for a release of her ADEA claim was entitled to keep the severance pay and still sue her employer for age discrimination. Therefore, an employer who has required a release of all claims in exchange for a severance package should not begin making severance payments to the 40-plus employee until the seven-day rescission period has expired.

If a release of ADEA claims is requested in connection with an exit incentive or other employment termination program offered to a group or class of employees, the twenty-one-day period increases to forty-five days. In addition, the employer must provide all persons in the class or group with a description of the class or group. The employer must also inform them of the job titles and ages of all employees eligible or selected for the program. The ages of all employees in the same job classification or organizational unit who are not eligible or selected for the program must also be disclosed.

Chapter

17

Persons with Disabilities

- Definition of *Disability*
- Medical Examinations
- Duty of Reasonable Accommodation
- Other Prohibited Conduct
- Direct-Threat Defense

The latest entrant in the field of federal antidiscrimination law is the *Americans with Disabilities Act* (ADA). The statute is intended to be a *clear and comprehensive mandate for the elimination of discrimination against individuals with disabilities.*

In the employment context, the ADA applies to employers who have fifteen or more employees. It prohibits discrimination against a *qualified individual with a disability* with respect to application procedures, hiring, promotion, discharge, compensation, training, and other terms, conditions, and privileges of employment. A *qualified individual* is a person who, with or without reasonable accommodation, can perform the essential functions of the job he or she holds or for which he or she is applying.

Definition of *Disability*

As used in the ADA, *disability* means a physical or mental impairment *that substantially limits one or more major life activities*. The ADA, as amended by the ADA Amendments Act signed by President Bush in 2008, provides specific examples of *major life activities*, including caring for oneself, performing manual tasks, seeing, hearing, eating, sleeping, walking, standing, lifting, bending, speaking, breathing, learning, reading, concentrating, thinking, communicating, and working. Also included are bodily functions, such as functions of the immune system, and digestive, bowel, bladder, neurological, brain, respiratory, circulatory, endocrine, and reproductive systems.

An impairment that is episodic or in remission is a disability if it would substantially limit a major life activity when active. However, *transitory* or *minor impairments* are not disabilities. The Act defines *transitory* as an impairment with an actual or expected duration of six months or less.

The physical and mental impairments that can give rise to a disability would fill a medical encyclopedia. Generally speaking, any condition that can be diagnosed by a physician or psychotherapist is an impairment within the meaning of the ADA. If the impairment does not substantially limit one or more major life activities, however, it is not a disability for ADA purposes. Figure 17.1 contains a list of conditions that are not considered impairments for ADA purposes.

Figure 17.1: EXCLUSIONS FROM ADA COVERAGE

By statute, the following conditions are not considered disabilities for ADA purposes:

- homosexuality and bisexuality;

- transvestism, transsexualism, pedophilia, exhibitionism, voyeurism, gender identity disorders not resulting from physical impairment, or other sexual behavior disorders;

- compulsive gambling;

- kleptomania;

- pyromania; and,

- psychoactive substance abuse disorders resulting from current illegal use of drugs.

Diagnoses that are not generally accepted in the medical community will not trigger ADA obligations. For example, several courts have held that *multiple chemical sensitivity syndrome* falls in this category.

It is important to note that the existence of even a significant impairment does not necessarily render a person *disabled*. There is no such thing as a *disability per se* under the ADA since each impairment, no matter how serious, must still be shown as substantially limiting a major life activity. An individualized, case-by-case inquiry is required to determine whether, as a result of the impairment, a particular employee is in fact substantially limited in one or more major life activities.

Alert!

Employees who suffer temporary illnesses and injuries from their employment, even though they are not disabled under the ADA, may be entitled to workers' compensation benefits. (See Chapter 11 for more information on workers' compensation.)

Special rules apply to substance abuse. Addiction to drugs or alcohol is an impairment that may trigger ADA coverage, depending on the particular individual's circumstances. However, employers may discriminate against current, illegal drug users and persons who traffic in drugs at the workplace, whether or not they are addicted. Employers may also prohibit intoxication or use of alcohol at the workplace and may impose discipline for poor performance or absenteeism related to alcohol use, even if the employee is an alcoholic.

Medical Examinations

The ADA has special rules for medical examinations. Prior to actually offering employment, an employer may *never* require an applicant to undergo a medical exam. While testing for illegal drugs is not considered a medical exam and is permitted prior to making a job offer, just about every other form of preoffer medical test is illegal.

When the employer actually offers employment, the offer may be conditioned on the results of a medical exam if:

- All entering employees in the job category are subject to examination;
- The exam requirement can be shown to be job-related and consistent with business necessity;
- The resulting medical information is separately maintained and treated as confidential; and,
- The results are not used to discriminate against persons with disabilities.

The EEOC defines medical examination as a procedure or test that seeks information about an individual's physical or mental impairments or health. In determining whether a test is medical or nonmedical, the EEOC looks to the following factors.

- Is it *administered by a health care professional* or someone trained by a health care professional?
- Are the results *interpreted by a health care professional* or someone trained by a health care professional?

- Is it designed to *reveal an impairment or physical or mental health?*
- Is the employer trying to determine the candidate's *physical or mental health or impairments?*
- Is it *invasive* (for example, does it require the drawing of blood, urine, or breath)?
- Does it measure a candidate's performance of a task (permitted), or does it measure the candidate's *physiological* responses to performing the task (not permitted)?
- Is it normally given in a *medical setting* (for example, a health care professional's office)?
- Is *medical equipment* used?

According to the EEOC, a psychological test that is designed to identify a mental disorder or impairment is medical, whereas a psychological test that measures only personality traits such as honesty, preferences, and habits is not.

Closely related to medical examinations are disability-related inquiries. In general, an employer may not ask an applicant or employee about a disability and may not ask questions designed to elicit information about a disability. An employer may, however, ask whether an applicant or employee can perform job functions, ask whether an employee has been drinking, and ask about current illegal drug use.

CASE STUDY: SICK LEAVE POLICY VIOLATED ADA

The prohibition against disability-related inquiries invalidated one employer's sick leave policy. The policy required employees who were absent on sick leave to furnish a medical certification that included a general diagnosis of the condition that gave rise to the absence. The court ruled that since some diagnoses are bound to reveal underlying disabilities, the policy violated the ADA.

Of course, once an applicant or employee discloses information about a disability and requests an accommodation, the employer not only may make disability-related inquiries, the employer is *required* to.

QUICK TIP

The EEOC has ruled that an employer may inquire about a worker's disability in connection with disaster planning, so that the employee's need for special assistance can be identified in advance. However, it is up to the worker to decide whether assistance is necessary.

Duty of Reasonable Accommodation

Included within the ADA's definition of *employment discrimination* is failing to make reasonable accommodations to the known physical or mental limitations of an otherwise-qualified applicant or employee. *Otherwise qualified* means a person with a disability who, with or without reasonable accommodation, can perform the essential functions of the particular position he or she holds or is applying for.

The key concept here is *essential*. The employee has to be able to perform at least the essential functions of the job for ADA protections to apply. In determining what is essential and what is merely marginal, the employer's judgment is given substantial weight.

QUICK TIP

An employer should determine the essential functions of a particular position, and write them down, before advertising or interviewing for the position. A determination of essential functions after a disabled applicant has been rejected carries less weight.

To discriminate means to fail to make reasonable accommodations for the known physical or mental limitations of an otherwise-qualified applicant or employee. Under this definition, the employee has the burden of identifying his or her disability and requesting the accommodation, unless the need is obvious. The employer does not have an obligation to inquire about a non-obvious disability and, in fact, is prohibited from doing so. The employer may, however, make general inquiries as to the ability of an applicant or employee to perform job-related functions.

Alert!

When an employer suspects a psychological impairment which manifests as moodiness, rudeness, short temper, etc., the employer should address only the unacceptable behavior and leave it to the employee to raise the matter of any underlying disability.

Reasonableness of Requested Accommodation

If an employee informs the employer of a disability and requests the employer to accommodate, the employer must do so unless the accommodation would impose an *undue hardship*—that is, if the accommodation would be significantly burdensome or expensive.

It is often difficult to know whether a requested accommodation is reasonable or is an undue hardship. The ADA gives some examples of what is reasonable. For one, the employer's facilities must be readily accessible and usable. Wheelchair ramps may have to be installed and doorways and restroom facilities may need to be enlarged. Other examples might include:

- Restructuring jobs;
- Modifying work schedules;
- Relaxing workplace rules;
- Making reassignments to vacant positions; and,
- Modifying or replacing existing equipment.

The list of what is reasonable goes on, but it is not limitless. The courts have ruled, for example, that an employer has no duty to grant indefinite leave, since the ADA covers people who can perform the essential functions of their job presently or in the immediate future. Nor is an employer required to create a new position tailored to an employee's abilities.

The courts have also ruled that, generally speaking, an employer is not required to accommodate a disability by allowing the disabled worker to telecommute. The reason is that most jobs require the kind of teamwork, personal interaction, and supervision that simply cannot be performed at home without compromising the quality of the employee's performance. Only in an extraordinary situation might a work-at-home accommodation be reasonable. (Telecommuting is discussed in Chapter 20.)

Assignment to Vacant Position

One form of reasonable accommodation involves assignment of a disabled employee from a job he or she cannot perform to a vacant position he or she can perform. However, seniority systems will normally prevail over a disabled employee's interest in being assigned to a particular position. It is unreasonable, said the Supreme Court, to require an employer to violate a seniority system to accommodate a disability. Seniority systems, whether imposed under a collective bargaining agreement or unilaterally imposed by management, provide important employee benefits by creating and fulfilling employee expectations of fair and uniform treatment, job security, and predictable advancement based on objective standards, said the Court.

Alert!

The ADA Amendments Act, which became effective Jan. 1, 2009, instructs the courts to give a broader, more expansive reading than they have before. In light of this instruction, some earlier court decisions—particularly those of the Supreme Court—may no longer be good precedent.

QUICK TIP

The seniority problem is further complicated when a union asks for copies of the disabled employee's medical records to determine whether a company's decision to override normal seniority rules is justified. Both the EEOC and the National Labor Relations Board take the position that disclosure of the records is a matter for good faith collective bargaining. However, in *special circumstances* the disabled person's ADA rights will trump a seniority system. If an employee could show, for example, that the employer made frequent exceptions to its seniority system, then one more departure to accommodate a disabled employee might well be reasonable.

Effect of Remedial Measures

The courts have ruled that where a person is able to mitigate the effects of an impairment by the use of medication, a prosthetic, or other device, such that the person is not substantially limited in any major life activity, the impairment is not disabling and the person does not qualify for ADA protection. The ADA Amendments Act overrules those decisions and instructs the courts, when determining whether an impairment is a disability, to disregard the ameliorative effects of most mitigating measures, such as medication, medical equipment or appliances, low-vision devices, prosthetics, hearing aids, mobility devices, oxygen therapy, and assistive technology. The only exceptions are eyeglasses and contact lenses, which *may* be considered in determining whether an individual is disabled.

Note:

At least one court has indicated that failure to follow the advice of a doctor (when following the advice could have relieved an otherwise disabling condition) may bar an employee's ADA claim. The EEOC, however, disagrees with this view.

In understanding when the duty of reasonable accommodation applies, it is helpful to list the various degrees of impairment.

- An impairment that does not substantially limit any major life activity—*not covered* by the ADA.
- An impairment that substantially limits one or more major life activities, but the individual involved is able to perform all the essential functions of his or her job without any accommodation or with reasonable accommodation—*covered* by the ADA.
- An impairment that substantially limits one or more major life activities, and the individual is not able to perform one or more essential functions of his or her job, despite reasonable accommodation—*not covered* by the ADA.

What employers need to remember is that when a disabled employee or applicant for employment requests an accommodation, the employer must engage in a good faith interactive process with the employee to identify accommodations that might enable him or her to perform the essential functions of the job. It could be that no accommodation will actually work, or that while a particular accommodation might work, it is unreasonable. Should that be the case, the employer is free to terminate the employee or reject the applicant. However, if the employer fails to engage in an interactive process or delays doing so, the employer will almost certainly lose any ADA suit that follows.

Other Prohibited Conduct

The ADA includes in its definition of disability *having a record* of being impaired and being *regarded as* impaired. In other words, an employer cannot reject an applicant because he or she has a history of being impaired or because he or she is considered impaired, even if not actually so.

The question arises whether an employer is required to provide reasonable accommodation to an employee or applicant who is merely *regarded as* disabled and, if so, just what that accommodation might be. The ADA Amendments Act now makes clear that an employer need not provide reasonable accommodation to an individual who is covered by the ADA solely under the *regarded as* prong of the Act.

Another form of discrimination prohibited by the ADA arises where an applicant or employee is known to be in a relationship or be associated with *someone else* who has a disability. Suppose an employer knows that a job applicant's spouse or domestic partner has a chronic condition that, the employer fears, may distract the applicant or require extra time off. A refusal to hire for that reason violates the ADA. As noted above, however, excessive absenteeism need not be tolerated.

Many states and local governments have their own disability discrimination laws, which are similar to the ADA. California, for example, defines *disability* as an impairment that limits one or more major life activities as contrasted with the ADA's *substantially limits*. State and local laws often have thresholds lower than the ADA's fifteen-employee requirement.

Direct-Threat Defense

The ADA allows employers to exclude persons who pose a direct threat to the health or safety of the disabled person or to others in the workplace when the threat cannot be eliminated by reasonable accommodation.

The food industry, for example, may exclude persons from food handling who have infectious or communicable diseases that are transmitted to others through the handling of food if those persons cannot otherwise be reasonably accommodated. The ADA also permits enforcement of state and local laws dealing with food handling by persons with infectious or communicable diseases. The Secretary of Health and Human Services is required to publish a list of such diseases and the manner in which they are transmitted. See: www. cfsan.fda.gov/~dms/fc01-a3.html#a3-2.

Other situations in which the *direct-threat defense* applies include a worker with diabetes and hypertension who is at risk for coma and stroke and who seeks employment as a bus driver; or a restaurant employee with epilepsy who is at risk for seizures and seeks a promotion to cook where he or she would be working with dangerous appliances and equipment. In both these situations, the employer may rely on the ADA's direct threat defense and refuse to place the worker in the position sought.

The direct-threat defense is unique to the ADA and does not spill over to other areas of discrimination law.

The conclusion that a direct threat exists cannot be based on ignorance or irrational fear. When AIDS first came to public attention, but before the means of transmission were well understood, some employers simply fired or refused to hire infected individuals. The courts held that practice to be illegal under the ADA.

Chapter

Employee Privacy

Privacy is the right to be left alone. When someone's privacy has been wrongfully invaded, he or she may have a claim for damages. The types of invasions that can give rise to a claim for damages are:

- Unreasonable intrusion upon the seclusion of another;
- Appropriation of another's name or likeness;
- Unreasonable publicity given to another's private life; and,
- Publicity which places another in a false light before the public.

Invasions of privacy do not usually arise in the employment context. After all, the workplace and the equipment in it belong to the employer. Those assets are there to promote the employer's business, not the employee's. When an employee is at the workplace using the employer's equipment, he or she is supposed to be acting for the employer's exclusive benefit. His or her performance is constantly being evaluated, and normally there is no expectation that his or her activities are personal and private.

There are, however, exceptions.

Private Places

Most employees would expect their bodies, pockets, purses, wallets, and briefcases to be private and not open to inspection by their employer. If an employer intends to inspect those private places, a compelling business reason must exist and a clear written statement of this intention should be established and disseminated to all employees. In the diamond mining industry, for example, body cavity searches might be justified. Technicians working with lethal viruses might reasonably be put through decontamination at day's end. Perhaps retail workers should expect to have their packages inspected as they leave the store premises.

Less clear are places such as an employee's desk. An employer's right to go through an employee's desk without the employee's permission depends on the circumstances. If the employer has an announced policy of doing so, or if the employee shares the desk with others and could have no reasonable expectation of privacy, then the employer probably has the right. But if there is no announced policy, if the employer does not make it a practice of inspecting desk drawers, and if employees routinely lock their desks without objection from the employer, then the employer may not have the right.

CASE STUDY: EMPLOYER MAY CONSENT TO POLICE SEARCH OF OFFICE

The Internet service provider for a Montana company notified the FBI that one of the company's employees had accessed child pornography websites from a company computer. The FBI investigated and, in the process, obtained a copy of the suspect employee's hard drive. Doing so involved obtaining a key to the employee's private office, entering the office, and opening the computer's outer casing to gain access to the hard drive. When later prosecuted for child pornography, the employee tried to exclude the contents of the hard drive as evidence against him. The U.S. Court of Appeals for the Ninth Circuit allowed the evidence to be used, ruling that the company retained control over the employee's office and computer and could therefore consent to the search and seizure.

Sensitive Records

Employers frequently acquire highly sensitive, personal information about their employees, such as:

- Drug test reports;
- Results of medical exams;
- Information about physical or mental disabilities that need to be accommodated under the *Americans with Disabilities Act*;
- Medical information about the employee or employee's family in support of leave requests under the *Family and Medical Leave Act*;
- Workers' compensation records;
- Health insurance utilization records;
- Substance abuse treatment records in connection with employee assistance programs;
- Tax and financial information; and,

• Information about family problems, divorces, separations, and
  so on.

The confidentiality of some of this information is guaranteed by
law. Even if no specific law applies, employees expect such information to be kept confidential and to be used strictly for its intended
purpose. Employers should live up to those expectations. Sensitive
records should be kept in a secure area and access should be limited
to those with a legitimate need to know. Where sensitive information is stored electronically, appropriate computer security systems
should be installed to prevent unauthorized access.

ADA

The *Americans with Disabilities Act* prohibits pre-employment medical examinations (except drug tests) and prohibits inquiries as to
disabilities. The ADA permits an employer to conduct post-hiring
medical exams so long as certain requirements are met, including
the requirement that information obtained regarding medical condition or history be collected, be maintained on separate forms and
in separate medical files, and be treated as a confidential medical
record. (See Chapter 17 for a more detailed discussion of medical
examinations under the ADA.)

Drug and Alcohol Abuse Treatment

Substance abuse records may only be disclosed with the patient's consent, in cases of medical emergency, or when authorized by court
order based on a showing of good cause for disclosure. This means
that, in the absence of consent by the patient, even a subpoena issued
to an employer is insufficient to justify disclosure. Instead, the party
desiring the records must obtain a specific court order for disclosure.

HIPAA

There are extensive regulations implementing the privacy requirements of the *Health Insurance Portability and Accountability
Act*. The regulations are expressly applicable only to health plans
(except for plans with fewer than fifty participants that are self-
administered solely by the sponsoring employer), health care clear-
ing houses, and health care providers that electronically transmit

health information. However, employers are affected by the regulations in important ways.

Health insurers and HMOs are prohibited from disclosing *protected health information* (PHI) to employers who sponsor health plans, except to enable plan sponsors to carry out plan administration functions that the plan sponsor performs, and then only upon certification that the plan documents have been amended as required by the regulations.

Employers in turn must:

- Amend their plan documents to set out the permitted and required use of protected health information;
- Require others who gain access, such as agents and subcontractors, to comply with use and disclosure restrictions;
- Provide for return or destruction of information that is no longer needed;
- Provide for separation between the group plan itself and the plan sponsor; and,
- Describe those employees or classes of employees who have access to the information.

Alert!

Employers are specifically prohibited from using protected health-care information for any employment-related action or decision. (See Chapter 24 for more on collective bargaining.)

Surveillance

An employer may install surveillance cameras around the workplace, as long as the cameras are located in places where there is no reasonable expectation of privacy. Having a stated legitimate business reason for installing cameras—safety in garage areas or to stop employee theft—is a good idea. Cameras installed in private areas, such as restrooms, would be difficult to justify.

In a unionized shop, the installation of surveillance cameras is a matter for mandatory bargaining. Surveillance to determine who is supporting a union organizing effort is an unfair labor practice. (See Chapter 24 for more on collective bargaining.)

Surveillance outside the workplace is slightly different. Take, for example, an injured employee who is on leave and collecting workers' compensation benefits. If the employer has a reasonable suspicion that the employee is malingering and hires an investigator to videotape the employee surreptitiously outside the workplace, there is no invasion. The employer has a legitimate business purpose in conducting the surveillance and does so in an unobtrusive manner. However, if the employer instructs the investigator to interview all the employee's neighbors, golfing buddies, and bowling team, as well as take the video, the employer may have invaded the employee's privacy.

Some companies take surveillance to a whole new level by inquiring into or investigating an applicant's or employee's after-hours leisure activities and lifestyle in making employment decisions. Claiming a desire to hold down health insurance costs, absenteeism, or negligent employment suits, companies have been known to inquire about tobacco and alcohol use, participation in dangerous sports like motorcycle racing or sky diving, and even sexual activities. Balancing the invasive nature of these inquiries against the questionable value of the information obtained suggests that such practices are ill-conceived. Some states prohibit an employer's using information about lawful after-hours activities to make employment decisions.

Electronic Monitoring

Under the federal *Electronic Communications Privacy Act* (ECPA), it is illegal to intentionally intercept a wire, oral, or electronic communication. *Intercept* means the aural or other acquisition of the contents of any wire, electronic, or oral communication through the use of any electronic, mechanical, or other device. Telephone conversations, voice mail messages, face-to-face conversations, and email (while being transmitted) are all protected by the ECPA. Employers are subject to the ECPA just like any other interceptor.

The ECPA prohibition does not apply when one of the parties to the conversation has consented to an intercept. So at least under federal law, if two persons are engaged in a telephone or face-to-face conversation, one of them may record the conversation without the consent or even the knowledge of the other.

A provision of the ECPA exempts telephone equipment so long as the equipment is being used in the ordinary course of business. Extension telephones and speaker phones, for example, normally qualify under this exemption, even though they can be used to intercept electronic communication.

Many states have enacted laws similar to the ECPA. Be warned, however, that unlike the ECPA, which is a *one-party consent* statute, some states have *two-party consent* statutes. In a two-party consent state, both parties to the conversation (or all parties if there are more than two) must consent to the intercept. State two-party consent statutes are not preempted by the ECPA and are fully enforceable.

Some companies find it helpful to record telephone conversations between employees and customers for quality control or verification purposes. If the company is doing business in a two-party consent state, it must get the consent of both the *employee* and the *customer*. The employee's consent will be presumed if the employer notifies the employee of its intentions to record the communication beforehand. (It is a good idea to give the notice in writing and have the employee sign a receipt. A monitoring policy should also be stated in the employee handbook.) As for the customer, the employer should have a recorded announcement at the beginning of each telephone conversation that the conversation may be monitored. If the customer proceeds with the conversation, his or her consent is also presumed. Even in one-party states, it is a good idea to let both the employee and the customer know in advance that conversations may be monitored.

Stored Communication

The ECPA also prohibits unauthorized access to stored communications (as distinguished from real-time, ongoing communications), but it has an exception for the provider of the communications service. This exception probably allows an employer to access employee emails that are backed up on the employer's own email server, as well as logs showing an employee's Internet surfing habits.

Alert!

Posting employee photographs or other personal information about employees on a company website, if done without their permission, may not only be a privacy violation, it may also increase the risk that employees will become crime victims—identity theft, violence, and so on.

Word-processing and other data files stored on the employer's network server or on the employee's workstation hard drive are not covered by the ECPA since they are not *communications*. However, even as to materials that are exempt from or not covered by the ECPA or comparable state statutes, employers need to be concerned about common-law privacy rights. As with searches of private places, the test is whether the employee had a reasonable expectation of privacy. To dispel any possible expectations of privacy, the employer should make clear in its employee handbook that the entire computer network, including individual workstations, belongs to the employer and that the employer may, at any time and without notice, inspect any files stored, processed, or transmitted on company computers.

Personal Use of Equipment

Some companies go so far as to prohibit any personal use of communications equipment, such as telephones and email. While such a policy is perfectly legal, it is difficult to enforce. Failure to enforce a policy consistently can give rise to employee expectations that the policy is one in name only. It probably makes more sense to recognize that some personal use will inevitably take place and to adopt a policy limiting personal use to no more than a few minutes a day. The policy should also prohibit any improper or illegal use.

Alert!

Prohibiting employees from using the company email system for concerted activity relating to union organizing or conditions of employment could constitute an unfair labor practice. (See Chapter 24 for more on unions and labor relations.)

If an employer discovers a computer file that appears to be personal and in violation of company policy, the employer should normally not study its contents except to determine that the file is in fact personal. Studying the file's contents beyond that point serves no legitimate business purpose, since the employer's interests are normally sufficiently served by instructing the employee to remove the file and imposing appropriate discipline. If the employer reasonably suspects that the employee is using office computers to engage in some illegal activity, such as gambling, theft of trade secrets, or distribution of pornography, further inspection of the file's contents may be justified.

Lie Detectors

With very limited exceptions, a federal law known as the *Employee Polygraph Protection Act* (EPPA) prohibits use of lie detectors in employment situations. The term *lie detector* as used in the federal statute includes not only polygraph equipment (which measures pulse, respiration, and perspiration), but also any other device, such as a voice stress analyzer. The EPPA goes so far as to prohibit an employer's even requesting or suggesting that an employee submit to a lie detector test. Discharging an employee for refusing to submit to a test is abusive and subjects the employer to civil damages.

Exceptions

Exceptions to the EPPA include tests administered by federal, state, and local government employers and tests administered by the federal government to employees of government contractors in connection with security, counterintelligence, and law enforcement functions.

Exceptions for private employers include the following.

- *Ongoing investigation.* An employer may request its employee to submit to a polygraph test in connection with an ongoing investigation involving economic loss or injury to the employer's business such as theft, embezzlement, misappropriation, or an act of unlawful industrial espionage or sabotage. The employee must have had access to the property that is the subject of the investigation and the employer must have a reasonable suspicion that the employee was involved in the incident or activity under investigation.

- *Security personnel.* Prospective employees may be required to undergo polygraph tests in connection with employment as armored car personnel, personnel engaged in the design, installation, and maintenance of security alarm systems, and security personnel whose functions include protection of facilities that have a significant impact on public health or safety (nuclear power plants, public water supply, etc.).

- *Controlled substances.* Prospective employees who will be involved in the manufacture or distribution of controlled substances may be required to undergo polygraph tests. In addition, an existing employee may be required to undergo a polygraph test in connection with an ongoing investigation involving loss of a controlled substance if the employee had access to the substance.

The EPPA goes on to specify a variety of requirements and procedures that must be met in order for the exemptions to apply. As a practical matter, most private employers will simply rule out lie detectors as a workplace tool.

Drug Testing and Drug-Free Workplaces

Employers and employees have sharply competing interests over drug and alcohol testing. On the one hand, an employer has a strong, sometimes compelling interest in maintaining a drug- and alcohol-free workplace: the employer is legitimately concerned with the safety of employees, customers, and the public generally, and with the effect of drug and alcohol abuse on job performance, accident rates, and absenteeism. Some employers, such as those regulated by the U.S. Department of Transportation (discussed below), are even required to test for drugs and alcohol under certain circumstances.

In contrast, employees have privacy rights. They object to employer scrutiny of their off-hours conduct. They question the accuracy of testing procedures. And they worry about the confidentiality of unrelated medical information obtained in the testing process. Public sector employees and employees in regulated industries additionally have a constitutional right against unreasonable searches and seizures by the government.

Employers who decide to have a drug testing program should engage an outside consultant to set up the program and perhaps even administer it on an ongoing basis. This will help assure that the program is run professionally and in accordance with any applicable law, that drug screens are accurate and reliable, and that medical information obtained in the process is handled appropriately. Using an outside consultant may also help insulate the employer from liability should a breach of confidentiality occur or should an employee be falsely reported as an illegal drug user.

QUICK TIP

The *Americans with Disabilities Act* excludes current, illegal drug use from the disabilities that must be reasonably accommodated. Although the ADA prohibits medical exams prior to an offer of employment, a test for illegal drugs is not considered a medical exam. It may take place before an offer of employment is made. (See Chapter 17 for more information relating to employees with disabilities.)

Alert!

Employer records relating to substance abuse treatment are subject to special confidentiality provisions under federal law.

Department of Transportation

Employers in the various transportation industries regulated by the U.S. Department of Transportation (DOT) (aviation, mass transit, interstate pipelines, railroads, shipping, and trucking) are required to establish drug and alcohol policies for employees performing safety-sensitive jobs. Under these requirements, covered employees are prohibited from using, possessing, being under the influence of, or being impaired by drugs or alcohol while performing their jobs.

Covered employees are subject to drug and alcohol tests:

- As part of their employment application process (drug testing required; alcohol testing permitted);
- When there is a reasonable basis to suspect drug or alcohol abuse;
- On a random basis; and,
- Following an accident.

DOT regulations set out in detail the components of a comprehensive drug-testing program with particular emphasis on fairness to the employees, collection and testing procedures, and record-keeping. Employers outside the transportation industry who are contemplating such a program should be guided by these regulations, found at: www.dot.gov/ost/dapc.

DOT regulations have come under constitutional attack as a violation of the employees' Fourth Amendment right to be free from unreasonable searches and seizures. The Supreme Court has ruled, however, that while the Fourth Amendment applies to drug and alcohol testing conducted pursuant to government regulation, such testing is not unreasonable even in the absence of a search warrant and even absent any basis to suspect the individual being tested.

Employers need to keep in mind certain federal-level restrictions applicable to their drug and alcohol programs. The *Americans with Disabilities Act* generally prohibits any pre-employment medical examinations. Although pre-employment tests for illegal drugs are expressly permitted under the ADA, pre-employment tests for alcohol are not.

The ADA also generally prohibits discrimination against, and requires reasonable accommodation of, people with disabilities— including addictions. While people with drug and alcohol addictions fall within these general ADA provisions, an employer:

- *May* discriminate against current users of illegal drugs;
- *May* discipline employees for use or possession of drugs or alcohol at the workplace in violation of company policy, even if the use or possession is the result of addiction; and,
- *Need not* tolerate poor work performance or behavioral issues, even if they are the result of addiction.

Employee Mail

Federal law prohibits obstruction of mail correspondence. If a letter arrives addressed to a former employee that is obviously personal— the envelope is the size and shape of a greeting card, the address is handwritten, it is addressed to the former employee *in care of* the company, it has a handwritten, nonbusiness return address, and it was hand-stamped rather than metered—then the employer's clear duty is to forward it unopened to the former employee.

However, if the envelope has all the earmarks of a business correspondence, including a preprinted return address of one of the company's customers, most employers would not hesitate to open the letter, but their right to do so is not so clear.

An appropriate provision in the employee handbook should help resolve the matter. The provision might say:

Mail arriving at the company's place of business that reasonably appears to be business mail intended for the company may be opened by any authorized company employee, even if it is addressed to some other specific employee or former employee. By accepting employment, an employee grants permission to the company to open mail in accordance with the foregoing, and that the permission continues throughout the employment and after it ends.

Consumer Reports

Federal law regulates the use by employers of credit and investigative reports prepared by consumer reporting agencies. The federal *Fair Credit Reporting Act* (FCRA) defines a consumer reporting agency (CRA) as a person or entity which, for a fee, assembles or evaluates credit information or other information on consumers for the purpose of regularly furnishing consumer reports to third parties (such as employers).

In general, employers may obtain consumer reports from CRAs, including investigative reports, to assess character and general reputation for purposes of evaluating, promoting, reassigning, or retaining an applicant or employee. The law places limits on how far back the credit reporting agency may go for various types of information, but those limits do not apply when highly compensated positions are being filled.

When requesting a consumer report, the employer must inform the applicant or employee in writing that such a report is being requested and must obtain the applicant's or employee's written authorization to obtain the report. The authorization should be a separate, stand-alone document and not be imbedded in the employment application or some other form. The applicant or employee may in turn make a written request to be informed of the full nature and scope of the report being requested, and the employer must then furnish that information.

If the employer intends to make an adverse employment decision based wholly or partly on the consumer report, the employer must first inform the applicant or employee of this intention. In addition, the employer must supply the applicant or employee with the name and address of the CRA that made the report, a copy of the report, and a statement explaining the applicant's or employee's rights under federal law to challenge the accuracy of the report. The Federal Trade Commission, which enforces the FCRA, has developed a form statement of employee rights under federal law that satisfies the employer's FCRA obligations. A copy is available from the FTC at: www.ftc.gov/os/statutes/2summary.htm.

Pursuant to a 2003 amendment to the FCRA known as the Fair and Accurate Credit Transactions Act (FACTA), the FTC has adopted regulations governing the disposal of consumer information. The FTC's *Disposal Rule* requires employers and others who have such information to properly dispose of it by taking *reasonable measures to protect against unauthorized access or use*. Examples of reasonable measures include burning, pulverizing, or shredding papers containing consumer information; and implementing and enforcing policies for erasure of electronic media containing consumer information.

> **Note:**
> Additional information about the FCRA and FACTA is available at: www.ftc.gov.

Criminal Records

The EEOC and some courts have taken the view that using *criminal convictions* as a basis for employment decisions has a *disparate impact* on certain minorities. (Disparate impact discrimination is discussed in Chapter 14.) Nevertheless, employers are generally free to inquire about and base decisions on conviction records so long as they can show a reasonable business purpose for doing so. In order to establish a reasonable business purpose and reduce the risk of a successful disparate impact claim, employers should adopt a policy that includes the following:

- Only relatively *recent convictions* are considered;
- The policy is *crime-specific*, in only excluding applicants for crimes which, if committed during employment, would have a significant negative impact on the employer's business (for example, a financial institution asking about convictions for dishonesty, or a retail establishment asking about theft and shoplifting convictions);

- The policy is *position-specific* (in the financial institution example, only applicants who will be dealing with customers' or the employer's funds are excluded); and,
- The employer has a *factual basis* for the policy, such as statistics showing that the rejected applicants, as a class, are significantly more likely than the general population to commit the crimes the employer is concerned about.

Asking about arrest records is much more likely to result in a successful disparate impact claim. In general, employers should not ask about or consider arrest records.

Driving Records

The federal *Driver's Privacy Protection Act of 1994* prohibits state motor vehicle departments from disclosing a driver's *personal information* without the consent of the person involved. Personal information is defined as information that identifies an individual, including an individual's photograph, Social Security number, driver identification number, name, address, telephone number, and medical or disability information. Excluded from the definition is information on vehicular accidents, driving violations, and driver's status.

When an employer decides to check driving records, the simplest procedure is to require the employee or applicant personally to obtain the record. As always, the decision should be supported by a reasonable business purpose and should be invoked on a nondiscriminatory basis.

Identity Theft

Identity theft is a serious and growing national problem. According to some reports, the top cause of identity fraud is theft of records from employers or other businesses that maintain personal information on individuals. The information that employers necessarily obtain as part of the employment relationship—name, birthdate, address, and Social Security number—is the very information that enables an identity thief to commit crimes. Employers need to safeguard that information. Failure to do so could result in legal liability. Figure 18.1 lists steps employers can take to protect employee personal information.

Figure 18.1: **PROTECTING PERSONAL EMPLOYEE INFORMATION**

- Keep records containing employee information in a *secure room* or file area and separate from other company records.

- If employee information is maintained electronically, be sure the files are *protected by a password*. Change passwords frequently, particularly when an employee with password access leaves the company.

- Consider *encrypting* any employee information that is electronically stored; also, consider isolating the information from the office computer network and from the Internet.

- Perform thorough *background checks* on all employees who have access to personal employee information.

- Do not allow access by *unauthorized employees*, particularly temps who sometimes take jobs for the sole purpose of obtaining identity theft data.

- Do not use *Social Security numbers* for identification purposes or on employee badges; in addition, do not print Social Security numbers on paychecks or other documents that could be available to the general public. (In some states, it is illegal for an employer to print Social Security numbers on checks or use Social Security numbers for employee identification purposes.)

- Limit distribution of *company directories* and allow employees to exclude personal information—home addresses, phone numbers, spouse's and children's names, and so on.

- Develop a *records retention policy* that requires destruction of all obsolete records; in addition, shred obsolete records, rather than merely discarding them.

- Ask *vendors* who have access to personal information about your employees—your payroll service, third-party benefit plan administrators, etc.—what steps they have taken to safeguard the information.

- Consider requiring *contractual provisions* with vendors obligating them to maintain appropriate safeguards, to notify you immediately about unauthorized access or other problems, and to indemnify you if one of their employees compromises your information.

Chapter

Employee Loyalty

- ▶ Competing with an Employer
- ▶ Trade Secrets
- ▶ Computer Fraud
- ▶ Loyalty by Contract
- ▶ Remedies for Breach of Contract
- ▶ Employee Dishonesty

Every employee owes a common-law duty of loyalty to his or her employer. The duty is an implicit part of the employment relationship unless the employer and employee agree otherwise. Under this duty, an employee is bound to serve his or her employer diligently and faithfully, to refrain from knowingly or willfully injuring the employer's business, and to avoid any conflict between the employer's interest and the employee's own self-interest.

Corporate officers and directors have heightened duties of loyalty to their employers. Officers and directors are generally considered fiduciaries, meaning that they must act for the benefit of their employer. They may not use corporate facilities or assets for personal gain. An even higher standard of loyalty and fiduciary duty is sometimes applied to trustees of charitable, nonprofit organizations. (See Chapter 23 on nonprofit organizations.)

Competing with an Employer

In the absence of a contract that restricts an employee's right to compete with his or her former employer, the duty of loyalty ends when the employment relationship ends. So an employee is perfectly free to quit and go with a competitor or start a competing business.

As a general rule, an employee may make plans to compete while still employed. This includes gathering information, consulting with advisors, developing a business plan, creating a business entity, arranging for financing, negotiating to purchase a rival business, and even letting existing customers and fellow employees know about his or her intentions.

But when the employee goes beyond the planning stages or engages in some unfair, fraudulent, or wrongful conduct, he or she has crossed the legal line. Figure 19.1 lists examples of improper conduct by an employee.

Figure 19.1: EXAMPLES OF IMPROPER EMPLOYEE CONDUCT

Improper conduct may include:

• actually beginning business in competition with a current employer;

- misappropriating employer's trade secrets;

- pirating confidential customer lists;

- soliciting current customers or fellow employees for the new business;

- conspiring to bring about a mass resignation of key employees;

- usurping business opportunities, such as by diverting new business or asking a customer to delay a purchase until the employee's new company is operating; or,

- destroying current employer's records or computer files.

Trade Secrets

As a supplement to common-law duties of loyalty, most states have adopted the *Uniform Trade Secrets Act*, which prohibits the *misappropriation of trade secrets* by *improper means*. A *trade secret* is defined as information that has economic value because it is not generally known to others and that the employer makes reasonable efforts to keep secret. Examples include a closely-guarded process like the formula for a soft drink, or a computer operating system's source code. *Improper means* includes theft, bribery, misrepresentation, breach of duty to maintain secrecy, and espionage. So if an employee steals information or documents while still employed, for example, in anticipation of leaving that job and going with a competitor, the company will have a claim under the Uniform Trade Secrets Act.

QUICK TIP

Theft of a trade secret is also criminal under the federal *Economic Espionage Act.*

The Uniform Trade Secrets Act authorizes the courts to issue an injunction prohibiting an employee from misappropriating trade secrets.

However, under the statute, there must be an *actual or threatened* misappropriation. Normally, to base an injunction on threatened disclosure, the courts at a minimum require evidence of intent to disclose.

Courts in a few states have adopted a legal doctrine known as *inevitable disclosure*. Under that doctrine, even when there is no actual or threatened disclosure, the court may issue an injunction against a former employee who had access to highly confidential, specifically identified trade secrets, if the employee's old and new companies are in direct competition, and if the employee's old and new jobs are so similar as to make disclosure of the secrets inevitable. Other courts have rejected the inevitable disclosure doctrine.

Computer Fraud

The *Computer Fraud and Abuse Act* (CFAA) is a potentially powerful weapon in an employer's hands. The CFAA covers virtually any computer that is connected to the Internet.

Under the CFAA, it is criminal for anyone to access a protected computer without authority or to exceed authorized access. Trafficking in passwords or similar information is also a crime if done with intent to defraud. Persons or companies injured by violations of the CFAA can sue in civil court for monetary damages.

What makes the CFAA so powerful is that when, for example, the data entry clerk takes a peek at his or her boss's personnel file using someone else's password, the CFAA is violated. Even high-level employees who have access to the entire computer system can be charged with a CFAA violation if, for example, they access information for an improper purpose, such as to sell it to a competitor.

Intentionally causing damage to a company's computer system by transmitting a program, information, code, or command is a violation of federal criminal law. *Denial-of-service attacks* or deletion of valuable data are good examples. So is theft of confidential electronic information.

Loyalty by Contract

An employer can gain protection beyond that provided by the common-law duty of loyalty, the *Uniform Trade Secrets Act*, and the *Computer Fraud and Abuse Act*. So long as the employer acts reasonably and for legitimate business reasons, employers in most states may require employees to sign binding contracts that go well beyond the limited protections provided by law. A typical contract might contain some or all of the following clauses:

- A *noncompetition clause* (sometimes called a *noncompete clause*, a *restrictive covenant*, or a *covenant not to compete*);
- A *nonsolicitation clause*;
- A *confidentiality clause*; and,
- A *work-for-hire clause*.

These clauses are discussed in the sections that follow.

Noncompetition

A contract that imposes restrictions on an employee's ability to compete with a former employer is enforceable in most (but not all) states if the restrictions are reasonable. The general rule is that an employee's agreement not to compete with an employer upon leaving the employment will be upheld if:

- It is supported by adequate consideration;
- The restraint is confined within limits that are no wider as to area and duration than are reasonably necessary for the protection of the employer's business;
- The restraint does not impose undue hardship on the employee; and,
- The restraint is not contrary to the interests of the public.

Noncompete agreements may be used to prevent unfair competition. They cannot be used to gain an unfair advantage. The general public also has an interest in free competition. If your employee really can provide a service that is better, cheaper, and more reliable than yours, the public would certainly want him or her free to do so.

Figure 19.2 lists circumstances in which a noncompete agreement might be used.

Figure 19.2: WHEN TO USE A NONCOMPETE AGREEMENT

- Sales positions, when the business is heavily dependent on the relationship between the salesperson and the customers and where the customers would likely follow the salesperson to a new employer;

- Professional practices, when the clients or patients tend to identify with particular professionals in the firm and not with the firm as a whole;

- Jobs for which the employer must make a substantial initial investment in the employee's education or training or when the employee is unproductive while awaiting a security clearance or a special license or certification;

- Jobs requiring unique skill sets;

- Jobs involving access to highly confidential trade secrets; and,

- High tech positions in which the employee is likely to generate or have access to intellectual property such as computer programs or patentable devices.

The restrictions imposed by a noncompete agreement must be *reasonable*. Traditionally, the courts have looked to three factors in determining reasonableness:

- The particular work that the employee is prohibited from doing;
- The geographic area in which the employee is barred from competing; and,
- The duration of the restriction.

A noncompete agreement that restricts an employee for six months from working within a radius of ten miles of the employer's place of business for companies that compete directly with the employer is likely to be held reasonable. A restriction of as much as two or even three years may be upheld as reasonable depending on the circumstances. But an agreement that prohibits an employee from working in any similar line of business, anywhere in the United States, for five years, is likely to be held an unreasonable restraint of trade. Unfortunately, drawing the line between reasonable and unreasonable is a case-by-case process, and it is difficult to predict in advance whether a particular restriction will be upheld by the courts.

The geographic restriction factor may be disappearing. As information technology assumes a greater role in the economy, and as the speed and ease of communications increase, it makes little difference whether a computer programmer works in the employer's office, in the employee's own mountain retreat, or in Bangalore, India. So merely prohibiting the programmer from competing within a ten-mile radius of the office will not be very effective.

Nonsolicitation

When an employee leaves with the intention of going into competition with a former employer, he or she will likely plan to contact former customers and invite them to become customers of the new business. Similarly, he or she will likely try to induce fellow employees to come work for the new business. A standard provision in noncompete and confidentiality agreements is a prohibition on soliciting customers and fellow employees.

A nonsolicitation provision may prohibit the departing employee from servicing all clients of the employer, not just the clients of the employer with whom the employee had contact or with whom he or she worked while employed.

A nonsolicitation provision may even be applied to customers that the employee brought to the employer, since relationships with those customers become part of the employer's goodwill. Thus, in defending a claim for breach of a nonsolicitation clause, it is no excuse that the customers for whom the employee did work after leaving the employer were also customers for whom he or she had done work before starting with the employer.

One other aspect of nonsolicitation clauses deserves mention. Companies that provide contract services to other businesses know only too well the risk of having their business customers cherry-pick their best employees by hiring them away and bringing the contract work in-house. While nonsolicitation and noncompete clauses should help prevent that practice, the company is in an even stronger position if its *business-to-business contracts* prohibit nonsolicitation as well.

Confidentiality

In a typical confidentiality clause, an employee acknowledges that all company information, trade secrets, customer lists, business plans, procedures, cost structures, profit margins, and so on belong to the company. The employee promises to maintain the confidentiality of that information throughout his or her employment and after the employment ends.

Confidentiality agreements supplement the Uniform Trade Secrets Act in important ways. Such agreements demonstrate that the employer is making reasonable efforts to keep information confidential, thus bringing the information within the definition of *trade secret*. Such agreements also impose a duty to maintain secrecy, so that breach of a confidentiality agreement may in certain circumstances be a violation of the statute as well.

Unlike noncompete agreements, confidentiality agreements may last for an indefinite period, or at least until the confidential information becomes known to the public generally.

Alert!

A broadly-worded confidentiality provision could be deemed to interfere with an employee's right to engage in concerted activities, in violation of federal labor law. (See Chapter 24 for more information.)

Work-for-Hire

In general, the right to patent an invention belongs to the inventor personally, and ownership of the copyright of a work belongs to the author personally. Federal patent law grants only limited rights to an employer whose employee is the inventor, even though the employee was being paid to create the invention.

QUICK TIP

Under the *shop rights doctrine*, an employer has the nonexclusive right to use an invention created by its employee on the employer's time and utilizing the employer's money, property, and labor. However, the employee owns the patent rights and can use the invention him- or herself, license it for use by others, or assign the patent to third parties.

While federal copyright law does provide that an employer is considered the author of a *work made for hire*—defined as a work prepared by an employee *within the scope of his or her employment*—a question can arise whether a particular work was prepared within or outside the scope of the employee's employment.

EXAMPLE: Suppose a salesperson's job is to sell complex, expensive medical equipment to hospitals and to train hospital personnel on the equipment. If the salesperson writes a lengthy manual on the maintenance and use of the equipment, who owns the rights to the manual—the salesperson or the employer? If the salesperson was instructed to write the manual and did so on the company's time and money, using a company word processor, then the manual is probably a work-for-hire, and therefore owned by the employer. But if the employee wrote the manual on his or her own time, at home, using a home computer, then probably the employee owns the manual, even though the employee acquired most of the information in the manual during the course of his or her work.

The salesperson's employer certainly cares about ownership of the manual because it likely contains valuable information not generally available to the public. The employer could also profit from the manual, either by selling it to customers or by giving it to them as part of a service package. Alternatively, the employer may want to keep the manual secret and out of the hands of competitors. The employer gains no benefit and actually stands to be harmed if the manual is not a work-for-hire.

In short, when an employer hires someone to work on a potentially patentable invention or a copyrightable work, the employer needs greater protection than federal law provides. The solution is to have the employee sign an agreement that all inventions and works created during employment and for some reasonable period after the employment ends are considered made for hire and belong to the employer. Such agreements usually contain an express assignment of all rights to the employer.

Consideration

As a matter of basic contract law, in order for a contractual promise to be enforceable, it must be supported by *consideration*.

In the case of a newly hired employee, the consideration for a noncompete agreement is the offer of employment itself. Even an offer of employment at will is generally sufficient consideration to support a noncompete agreement.

In the case of existing employees, continuing employment may provide the consideration. Employers should be aware, however, that not all states reach that conclusion. Some states require *fresh consideration* to support an existing employee's promise not to compete, in the form of a raise, a bonus payment, or some other benefit or item of value.

Departing employees are often asked to sign noncompete, nonsolicitation, and confidentiality agreements. In that case, the employer definitely will have to offer fresh consideration, such as a severance payment or salary continuation. The law will not enforce a noncompete from a departing employee absent fresh consideration. The departing employee is also unlikely to sign the agreement in the first place without some new consideration. For these reasons, it makes sense to get noncompetes at initial hire or at least at a time when employment is likely to continue for some substantial period.

Alert!

Threatening to withhold a departing employee's final paycheck until he or she signs a noncompete agreement will definitely not solve the consideration problem, since the employer has no right to withhold pay that is clearly due. (See Chapter 5 for more information regarding termination.)

Remedies for Breach of Contract

The typical remedy sought by an employer when a former employee breaches a noncompete, nonsolicitation, confidentiality, or work-for-hire agreement is an injunction. An *injunction* is a court order prohibiting specified conduct, violation of which could result in fines or jail time. The alternative remedy would be a suit against the employee for money damages, but the employer may have difficulty proving the dollar value of the injury suffered or proving that a decline in sales was caused by this particular employee's disloyalty and not by some other event.

QUICK TIP

A liquidated damages clause, specifying the amount of damages recoverable in case of breach, could overcome the problem of proving damages, so long as the amount specified is a reasonable estimate of actual damages and not merely punitive.

When an employer learns that a former employee is now working for the competition in violation of a noncompete agreement, the first step should be to write a cease and desist letter to the former employee. Whether the employer should also write to the new employer depends on how confident the employer is that the noncompete agreement is valid and enforceable.

A letter to the new employer, informing it about the agreement and insisting it not participate in the employee's breach of the agreement, can often be the simplest and cheapest means of enforcing the agreement. This works because the new employer, once on notice of the agreement, can be sued for *tortious interference with contract* if it ignores the agreement and continues to enjoy the benefits of the former employee's misconduct.

On the other hand, if the noncompete agreement has been poorly drafted so as not to apply in this particular circumstance or if it is unreasonably broad or otherwise unenforceable, the employer may have liability for interfering with the new employment relationship.

QUICK TIP

Arbitration agreements that require employment disputes to be resolved by binding arbitration instead of by lawsuits should contain an exception permitting the employer to go to court for an injunction against violation of restrictive covenants. (Arbitration agreements are discussed in Chapter 1.)

Employee Dishonesty

Employee theft is a recurring and, some say, growing problem. It covers a wide range of activities—from personal long-distance phone calls, to the misappropriation of goods held for sale, to embezzlement of hundreds of thousands of dollars—all of which are costly to the employer. Figure 19.3 identifies some safeguards that can be used to deter employee dishonesty.

If employee dishonesty is discovered, the employee involved will likely be terminated or at least be removed from the duties that enabled him or her to commit the dishonesty. If termination is appropriate, the exit interview procedures listed in Chapter 4 should be followed. The employer will also want to give prompt notice of any loss to its insurance carrier.

The decision whether to report employee theft to law enforcement is a delicate one. Some companies are reluctant to go public with internal problems for fear their clients or customers will lose confidence in them. On the other hand, the company's insurance carrier may require a police report as a condition to covering the loss. One thing the company cannot do is threaten the employee with criminal charges unless he or she repays the loss; doing so constitutes the crime of *blackmail.*

If the terminated employee applies for unemployment insurance benefits, the company's decision about going public may have to be made quite quickly. Misconduct usually disqualifies an employee from benefits, either permanently or for a specified period depending on the *degree of misconduct. Gross misconduct* also disqualifies a fired employee from COBRA benefits.

Figure 19.3: GUARDING AGAINST EMPLOYEE DISHONESTY

While no employer can be fully protected, these steps should help reduce the risk.

- Obtain background checks on prospective employees, particularly those who will have access to company finances.

- Consider instituting a drug testing program.

- Be sure company financial records are secure. Electronic records should be protected by passwords, and passwords should be changed frequently.

- Separate financial functions. For example, the employee who draws company checks should not be the same person who signs them. Bank and other financial institution statements should be reconciled by yet a third person.

- Assign someone not involved in company finances to open all mail and maintain a log of all payments received. The log should be reconciled periodically against bank deposits.

- Insist on seeing original vendor invoices before signing checks. Once a check is signed, the invoice should be marked paid and the date and check number should be written on the invoice.

- Compare invoices against a current list of vendors to guard against fictitious bills. Invoices should also be checked against contractual arrangements to prevent an over-billing or kickback scheme.

- Except in emergencies, limit check-signing responsibility to one person whose familiarity with billing cycles will help spot unusual invoices.

- Require a second signature for checks over a specified limit.

- Review payroll records periodically to weed out phantom employees.

- Cancel a departing employee's password and signature authority over bank accounts.

- Distribute company credit cards sparingly and have a supervisor who is familiar with specific employee assignments review each employee's monthly account statement.

- When a company event is being charged on a credit card, require that the card of the highest-ranking employee present be used, so that the charge record is reviewed by someone above him or her who did not participate in the event.

- Require employees with financial responsibilities to take periodic vacations so they are not able to continue a cover-up of improper activities.

- Adopt, publicize, and enforce a company code of ethics for all employees.

- Obtain employee dishonesty insurance coverage.

Chapter

Alternative Work Arrangements

- ▶ Telecommuting
- ▶ Flextime
- ▶ Contingent Workers

Employees, especially those in two-wage-earner households, are becoming less interested in money and more interested in lifestyle issues, such as time with their families and opportunities for leisure activities. In a tight labor market, employers have to recognize these trends to compete for quality employees.

Employers who are willing to be creative and to consider alternative working arrangements can reap huge rewards in terms of worker satisfaction, leading to greater productivity and less turnover. A number of options are suggested below.

Telecommuting

Telecommuting means working at a remote location that is connected with the office by high tech communications equipment. By some estimates, as many as 44 million employees now telecommute for at least some portion of the workweek. That number is likely to grow as our economy shifts from goods-based to service- and information-based. Figure 20.1 lists specific considerations for business owners who want to start a telecommuting program.

There is no technical reason why a computer programmer, for example, or a customer service representative, cannot work just as effectively at home in the suburbs as in a cubicle in the central business district. And establishing a virtual office for selected employees may well be in the employer's best interests. Consider the following.

- Many quality employees find the idea of telecommuting attractive. Implementing a telecommuting program should therefore help to attract and retain just such employees.
- So long as care is taken in selecting participants for a telecommuting program, productivity should not suffer. With fewer distractions, productivity may even increase.
- Telecommuting encourages employees to work independently and to problem-solve on their own (again, careful selection is critical).
- Office space (and rent) can be reduced.

Employers who are considering a telecommuting program often worry about trust. They are concerned whether an employee who spends most of his or her time out of the employer's presence will work as diligently as in the office. This concern is probably overstated, given that good candidates for telecommuting are the very employees who should be encouraged to work independently and whose productivity is not measured by hours logged. The programmer, for example, is evaluated less on the time put in, or even on the sheer volume of code produced, and more on the quality and timeliness of the product. If his or her programs work as required and are delivered by deadline, it makes little difference that he or she may have attended to personal matters during normal working hours.

Telecommuting is not risk-free. When considering a telecommuting program, the employer should keep in mind that any cost savings at the office may be outweighed by the added expense of installing and maintaining equipment and phone lines at remote sites. The employer also has less direct control over participating employees, over office supplies and equipment, and over confidentiality of business information.

Figure 20.1: STARTING A TELECOMMUTING PROGRAM

If you decide to try telecommuting, consider these suggestions.

- Start the program on an experimental basis. For example, limit the program to a particular department, start it on a one- or two-day per week basis, and set a trial period of no more than six months.

- Establish eligibility requirements for participation. For example, limit the program to particular job categories and to persons who have been with the company for some minimum period—two years, for example.

- Choose no more than half of those eligible as participants. That way a control group is retained in order to compare such things as productivity, turnover, and job satisfaction.

- Select participants carefully. Those who require close supervision and constant feedback, who do not enjoy working alone, or who do not have appropriate work space at home are not good candidates.

- Select only those who want to try telecommuting. And allow them to opt out if they find their work quality or job satisfaction deteriorating.

- Insist that telecommuters designate an appropriate space at home that is dedicated to work. (Some employers actually inspect the work area before allowing an employee to begin telecommuting.)

- Stress that telecommuting is not intended to resolve day care problems, nor is it a fringe benefit or perk. It is simply a different job assignment. (Some employers require evidence that the employee has made appropriate day care arrangements, although those inquiries can come dangerously close to gender discrimination.)

- Be sure that telecommuters understand they must be willing to come to the office for face-to-face meetings as needed.

- Remind participating employees that they, not the employer, are responsible for any tax consequences of maintaining a home office and for complying with zoning laws.

- Require nonexempt employees (those subject to minimum wage and overtime requirements) to maintain an accurate log of hours worked for FLSA purposes. An employee who was nonexempt before he or she began telecommuting continues to be nonexempt while telecommuting.

- Do not consider a switch to telecommuting as an opportunity to reclassify your employees as independent contractors.

- Do not consider a switch to telecommuting as an opportunity to reduce employee pay. This may give rise to equal pay violations and it will certainly hurt morale.

Telecommuting also raises additional legal issues.

FLSA

Under the *Fair Labor Standards Act*, nonexempt employees must be paid time and a half for overtime. As with other nonexempt employees, a nonexempt telecommuter must keep accurate time records so that wage-and-hour laws can be complied with. It may be more difficult to assure compliance for telecommuters.

OSHA

The *Occupational Safety and Health Administration* initially took the position that the federal safety and health law applies to all worksites, including home worksites. OSHA withdrew its ruling in the face of widespread objections, but the issue is sure to surface again. OSHA continues to take the position that the federal act does apply to hazardous or dangerous work assigned to telecommuters.

Workers' Compensation

An *accidental personal injury that arises out of and in the course of employment* is covered by workers' compensation. For traditional employees who work nine to five at the employer's regular worksite, an injury that occurs offsite and after normal working hours would generally not be covered. But with an injury to a telecommuter, chances are there were no witnesses so neither the employer nor the workers' compensation carrier can verify the employee's version of how the injury occurred. In other words, in the telecommuting situation, the employer is at the mercy of the employee in terms of coverage for injuries.

ADA

The *Americans with Disabilities Act* requires employers to make reasonable accommodations for persons with physical or mental disabilities. If a disabled worker requests telecommuting as an accommodation, the employer should at least consider such an arrangement.

Title VII

Discrimination laws apply to all employment policies and practices, including telecommuting. The opportunity to telecommute must be made available, without discrimination, to both genders.

Ownership of Work Product

Unless you have a contract with your employees as to ownership of *intellectual property* (see Chapter 19), employees may have a claim to any copyrightable works or patentable devices they create. Their claims may be particularly difficult to defeat if they are telecommuters and spend most of their time at home.

Flextime

Flextime is an arrangement by which an employee works a normal forty-hour week, but does not work the normal five eight-hour days. Instead, employee and employer agree on some alternative that yields forty hours. If, for example, an employee's long-term, trusted babysitter is only available Mondays through Thursdays, the employee could work four ten-hour days and take Fridays off. Another employee might have a much easier commute working ten-to-six rather than nine-to-five. If you can accommodate these needs without significant disruption or loss of productivity, then it may be to your benefit to do so. Figure 20.2 lists some suggestions that could make a flextime policy workable within your business environment.

Figure 20.2: FLEXTIME POLICY

These suggestions should help make a flextime policy work smoothly.

- *Flextime* means only that the employer is flexible in setting an alternative schedule. It does not mean that the employee can constantly reshuffle his or her workweek to suit the employee's day-by-day whim or convenience.

- As with all other employment decisions, the decision to permit or deny flextime must be made on a nondiscriminatory basis.

- Flextime may not work for all positions. Identify in advance which positions are likely candidates and which positions are not.

- Granting flextime may be a reasonable (and therefore a required) accommodation under the ADA where, for example, a disabled employee needs regularly scheduled medical treatment.

- Remember that whatever arrangements are made, the total number of hours a nonexempt employee can work in any given workweek without triggering overtime pay obligations is forty.

Contingent Workers

The term *contingent worker* is loosely defined as any worker who is outside the employer's core work force of full-time, long-term employees. As used here, the term refers to independent contractors, part-time employees, job-sharing employees, temporary employees, leased employees, and joint employees.

Independent Contractors

Classifying workers as *independent contractors* is fraught with peril. Nevertheless, in a few carefully designed situations, an independent contractor arrangement can be both safe and effective.

Suppose a key employee, with years of experience and a wealth of institutional knowledge, is approaching minimum retirement age. With the employee's stock options, retirement plan, and independent savings, the employee no longer needs to work and is looking forward to the free time retirement offers. Yet the employee is not quite ready for a clean break from the company.

A possible solution? A consultant agreement for a fixed time period, say two years, renewable year-by-year thereafter if both parties agree. The employee retires and then signs on to be available whenever needed to advise on strategic planning, special projects, and the like. Of course, with the employee's experience he or she may also be called upon occasionally to help solve the day-to-day problems routinely addressed as a full-time employee. In consideration for agreeing to hold him- or herself available, he or she is paid a monthly retainer by the company, perhaps in the neighborhood of one-half or two-thirds of the former salary. However, the employee is not expected to work any particular hours, no longer has his or her own office or support staff at the company, receives none of the fringe benefits provided regular employees, and is free to consult with other companies. The employee is, therefore, an independent contractor.

An independent contractor relationship also arises when a company contracts out certain functions without retaining control over who specifically performs those functions or how they are performed. Examples might include janitorial services, landscaping, operating a company cafeteria, and processing payroll. Legal and accounting services are examples of functions that could be performed by in-house employees or by outside independent contractors.

Part-time Employees

Say a valued employee or well-qualified candidate for employment is only available on a part-time basis. In the past, the company took an all-or-nothing approach—an employee worked either full-time or not at all. By abandoning this rigid approach, the company can benefit from the services of a valued worker, and the worker can remain productive without being tied to the daily nine-to-five or eight-to-six grind. Many companies report that their part-timers are so appreciative of the opportunity that their briefcases are always filled with homework and they end up working close to full time. If you are uncertain whether a part-time arrangement will work, try it on an experimental basis.

If you decide to try a part-time arrangement, be sure that you and the employee are clear about what benefits the employee will and will not qualify for. While it is theoretically permissible to provide the same benefits to part-timers as to full-timers—medical expense insurance or retirement, for example—your plan documents may limit eligibility to employees who work some minimum number or hours, such as 1,000 or 1,500 hours per year. Other benefits, such as vacation and sick leave, need to be considered as well.

Finally, keep in mind that discrimination laws apply to part-time as well as full-time employees. For example, the opportunity to go part-time should be made available without regard to sex, race, etc. Allowing a disabled employee or candidate to work part-time may also be a required reasonable accommodation under the ADA, so long as the employee can still perform the essential functions of his or her job.

Job Sharing

A variation on part-time employment is an arrangement by which two part-time employees share the same job, either long-term or for a temporary period. The difference is that, from an organizational viewpoint, the job is still considered a single position.

Frequently, although not always, a proposal to job-share will be initiated by the employee whose changed circumstances limit him or her to part-time work. Before making the proposal, the employee should first choose a compatible partner.

The employer and employees also need to think through issues such as those below.

- How will the time be shared? Will the employees work half days? Alternate days? Half weeks? Alternate weeks?
- How will the work be allocated? Will each employee perform all functions or only certain tasks?
- How will the employees communicate with each other to keep current?
- Will they overlap on a scheduled or as-needed basis?
- When travel is necessary, will they both go?
- Will the nonworking employee be available, if necessary, to provide continuity in resolving an ongoing problem or working on a long-term project?
- What impact will job-sharing have on the cost of employer-provided benefits?
- Will the employees be evaluated individually or as a team?
- What will the effect be on the remaining employee if one of the job sharers quits or is fired?

Note:

Job sharing can reduce an employer's overtime pay obligations. Even though the job is considered a single position for organizational purposes, if two part-time, nonexempt employees together work more than forty hours per week, but neither employee individually works more than forty hours, the employer will not have to pay time and a half for the excess hours.

Temporary Employees

The term *temporary employee* is used here to mean a full-time or part-time employee whose salary or wages are paid by the employer in the usual way, but whose job is expected to last for only a limited period of time. It does not refer here to a temp who is provided by an agency and who remains on the agency's payroll. When an employer hires a temporary employee, say to perform some specific, nonrecurring job, the employer will usually indicate that the employment is expected to terminate by a certain date. In doing so, the employer should also make clear that, despite the stated duration of the employment, the employee is still *at-will* and can be terminated at any time. The employer should also make clear what benefits will or will not be provided.

Alert!

If the temporary employee is kept on past the expected termination date, the employer should consider the need to enroll him or her in benefit plans provided to regular employees. Failure to enroll a so-called *perma-temp* in plans for which he or she is eligible could violate plan documents and cause loss of favorable tax treatment for the plan.

Leased Employees

Leasing arrangements may take several forms. In the familiar temp situation, a temp agency provides a worker for a short period of time, typically to fill in for an employee on leave or to help finish a large project. The employer describes the position to be filled but does not identify any particular employee to fill it. Although the temp is subject to the employer's control while actually at the employer's worksite, the agency hires, compensates, and fires the employee.

Another leasing arrangement involves shifting a company's existing employees from the company's payroll to a leasing agency's payroll, although the company, not the agency, continues to make all hiring and firing decisions. The purpose is simply to free the employer from payroll and related duties while retaining operational control over the employee.

Under leasing arrangements, the question arises of who the actual employer is for discrimination law purposes. The *Equal Employment Opportunity Commission* (EEOC) has issued guidelines addressing the question under various scenarios. For example, the true temp is generally considered the employee of the temp agency only, whereas the leased employee is generally considered an employee of both the leasing agency and the company that has retained operational control. In the final analysis, these distinctions do not really matter. The company that operates the worksite will be guilty of illegal discrimination if it discriminates against temps or leased employees at its worksite, if it encourages a temp agency to discriminate with regard to the selection and treatment of temps, or even if it simply knows that the temp agency discriminates.

Joint Employers

When a worksite employer enters into arrangements with a *professional employer organization* (PEO), its employees are considered to be jointly employed by both the worksite employer and the PEO. While the arrangement is similar to leasing, a PEO typically provides a wider range of employment-related services than just payroll. For example, a PEO might provide workers' compensation and unemployment insurance, and it might assist in hiring, evaluations, discipline, and firing (with the worksite company retaining ultimate control over those decisions). It might also provide qualified benefits (medical expense insurance, disability, pension, etc.), and it could handle discrimination and other employment-related claims. PEOs advertise themselves as being in the *business of employment*, enabling the PEO's client to focus on the *business of business*. Through economies of scale, PEOs may well be more cost-effective and efficient in providing employment-related services than some smaller, individual employers.

The relationship between a PEO and the worksite company is based on a lengthy written contract that spells out in detail the parties' responsibilities and their respective liabilities. Any employer considering the PEO option will want to review the contract with great care and arrive at a thorough understanding of just how the relationship works. The PEO should also be able to provide a comparative cost analysis showing whether the arrangement will, in fact, be a financial benefit. Finally, the employer should be satisfied as to the PEO's integrity, experience, and financial standing before signing on.

Chapter  21

Foreign Workers

Foreign workers have long played a significant role in our work force. Some claim that foreigners take positions from U.S. citizens. Others argue that they fill jobs U.S. workers either do not want or are not trained to do. Both perceptions are reflected in current law. On the one hand, employers face criminal penalties for knowingly hiring an undocumented alien. On the other hand, recent changes in visa policy make it easier for so-called high tech employees such as computer programmers to work in the U.S.

With terrorism now firmly planted in our collective consciousness, rules and restrictions affecting foreign workers are bound to play an increasing role in the workplace.

I-9 Requirements

It is illegal to knowingly hire, recruit, refer for a fee, or continue to employ persons who are not eligible to work in the United States. The *knowingly* qualification is not satisfied by staying ignorant. For these purposes, a don't-ask, don't-tell policy will not work.

Employers must check documents to establish the eligibility of *every* new employee (including U.S. citizens) to work in the U.S. It does not matter whether the employer knows to a moral certainty that the new employee is a U.S. citizen—the I-9 requirements must still be satisfied.

Form I-9 (Rev. 6/5/07) and accompanying instructions are available from the Bureau of Citizenship and Immigration Services (BCIS) of the Department of Homeland Security at: www.uscis. gov/portal/site/uscis.

BCIS also publishes a helpful guide called *Handbook for Employers* (Pub. M-274, revised 11/1/07), available at: www.uscis.gov/files/ nativedocuments/m-274.pdf.

Among other things, Form I-9 requires the employer to attest that it has reviewed documentation provided by the employee to establish his or her eligibility and that the documentation appears genuine. The employee must also attest to his or her eligibility to work here.

There is a variety of documents that can establish eligibility to work. However, in most cases it is up to the *employee* to choose which documents (among those listed on Form I-9) to show the employer; the employer cannot specify the documents it wishes to see. If the exhibited document or documents appear to be genuine, eligibility to work is established. Form I-9 should then be completed and kept on file for at least one year after the employee leaves, but not less than three years after the employment began.

If the employer receives a *no-match letter* from the Social Security Administration or a *notice of suspect documents letter* from Immigration and Customs Enforcement, the employer must attempt to resolve the discrepancy within specified time limits without relying on the nonmatching Social Security number or suspect document. (See Chapter 7 for more on no-match letters.)

QUICK TIP

It is good practice, though not required, to make a photocopy of any documents exhibited by the employee to establish his eligibility to work. Note, however, that attaching a photocopy of an exhibited document is not a substitute for filling out Form I-9 completely.

The verification process must be completed within three working days after the employee begins work. (For employees who are hired for three days or less, the entire verification process must be completed on the first day of employment.) For employees whose initial eligibility to work here is only temporary, the employer must either re-verify eligibility or terminate the employee upon expiration of the initial eligibility period.

In addition to criminal exposure, employers who fail to comply with I-9 requirements face civil liability. Several courts have ruled that an employer who uses illegal aliens can be sued by competitors of the employer under the federal Racketeer Influenced and Corrupt Organizations Act (RICO). Government contractors are also subject to debarment.

Work Visas Generally

The immigration laws authorize a number of categories of *non-immigrant* (temporary) work visas. These include:

- B-1, for foreigners here on business for the benefit of, and on the payroll of, their foreign employers;
- E-1 and E-2, for foreigners here on behalf of foreign firms seeking to trade with or invest in the U.S.;
- H-1B, for foreign professionals;
- H-2B, for foreign skilled and unskilled workers;
- L, for intracompany transferees; and,
- TN, for Canadian and Mexican professionals.

In addition to the above, there are a few other specialized categories, such as for students and trainees, persons participating in exchange programs, nurses, and seasonal workers in short supply. The H-1B, H-2B, and TN categories are the most significant for U.S. employers.

Immediate family members of persons here on work visas qualify for derivative visas. However, a family member may not perform any work while here on a derivative visa.

High Tech H-1B Visas

An H-1B visa allows a foreign *specialty worker* (a person whose profession requires at least a bachelor's degree or equivalent) to be employed in the U.S. for an initial three years, renewable for an additional three years. If the particular field of work also requires a license, then the worker must hold such a license as well. At the end of the renewal period, the worker must cease work and spend at least one year outside the U.S. before he or she is eligible for a new H-1B visa. H-1B visas are sometimes called *high tech visas* because they have enabled many computer programmers and other high tech workers to come here.

Obtaining an H-1B visa involves several steps, but they can usually be accomplished in a matter of several months or less. The downside is that, while Congress has raised the number of H-1B visas that can be granted each fiscal year, the quota is still reached long before the end of the year.

The employer, not the foreigner seeking to come here, is responsible for initiating the process and paying associated costs and fees. Employers can be fined for requiring reimbursement from the foreign worker. To initiate the process, the employer must obtain from his local employment office a *prevailing wage determination* for the position to be filled. The employer then files a *Labor Conditions Application* (LCA), Form ETA-9035CP, with the regional office of the Department of Labor, attesting that:

- For the position to be filled, the employer will pay at least the higher of the prevailing wage (as determined by his local employment office) or actual wages being paid to its comparable U.S. employees;
- The proposed employment will not adversely affect working conditions of workers similarly employed;
- There is no strike in progress involving the job to be filled; and,
- The employer posted a notice of filing the LCA in conspicuous locations at its workplace.

LCA and other Department of Labor forms are available online at: www.dol.gov/libraryforms/FormsByTitle.asp.

When the LCA has been approved, the employer then files a petition with the Bureau of Citizenship and Immigration Services (BCIS) of the Department of Homeland Security requesting issuance of an H-1B visa. If the petition is approved, the visa itself is issued to the alien by the appropriate U.S. consulate.

In addition to paying at least the prevailing wage to the foreign worker under an H-1B visa, the employer must also offer the same range of benefits as is available to its comparable U.S. employees. Even if the worker becomes unproductive ("benched") for some reason, he or she must still be paid. The employer must also pay for the worker's return trip home after the visa has expired.

H-1B visas are issued for employment in a specific position. If a foreign worker wants to change positions or employers once here, a new H-1B visa must be applied for. The foreign worker is not eligible for employment in the new position or by the new employer until the visa is issued.

Recent federal legislation has imposed additional certification burdens on employers who are *H-1B dependent*. An employer is H-1B dependent if it falls in one of the following categories: it has twenty-five or fewer full-time-equivalent (FTE) employees and more than seven of them work under H-1B visas; it has between twenty-six and fifty FTE employees and more than twelve of them work under H-1B visas; or it has more than fifty FTE employees and at least 15% of them work under H-1B visas.

H-2B Visas

H-2B visas are somewhat similar to H-1B visas, except that they apply to a far larger pool of prospective workers: the unskilled, and those whose skills fall below the professional level covered in the H-1B category. For that reason, the employer must satisfy the Secretary of Labor that it has been unable to find a sufficient number of U.S. workers who are able, willing, and qualified to fill the positions for which he seeks to import foreign workers.

H-2B visas are generally issued for one year and are renewable in one-year increments for a total of three years.

TN Visas under NAFTA

In addition to opening our northern and southern borders to trade, the *North American Free Trade Agreement* (NAFTA) made it easier for Canadians and Mexicans to come to the U.S. to engage in business at a professional level. A *professional* for NAFTA purposes is similar to an H-1B specialty worker—basically a person whose job requires at least a bachelor's degree. More information about TN visas, and a list of professionals who qualify, is available from the State Department's website at: http://travel.state.gov/tn_visas.html.

The procedure for Canadian nationals is simple. An employer desiring to hire a Canadian national writes a letter to the Canadian citizen, describing the job, agreeing to employ the worker, and setting out the terms of the arrangement (salary, etc.) and the dates the employment is to begin and end. The worker then appears at the U.S.-Canadian border and presents the letter, along with evidence of the foreign worker's professional qualifications, proof of Canadian citizenship, and a $50 fee. The worker is usually admitted to the U.S. on the spot under TN status without actually obtaining a TN visa.

Mexican nationals must obtain a TN visa to enter the U.S. According to the State Department, an interview at an embassy consular section is required for most visa applicants as part of the visa application process. Interviews are generally by appointment only. As part of the visa interview, an ink-free, digital fingerprint scan can generally be expected. The waiting time for an interview appointment for most applicants is a few weeks or less, but for some embassy consular sections it can be considerably longer. Mexicans must also submit specific documentation in support of their TN visa application, all of which is described at: http://travel.state.gov/visa/temp/types/types_1274.html#4.

Entry under a TN visa may be denied where the Secretary of Labor certifies that entry *may affect adversely the settlement of any labor dispute or the employment of any person who is involved in such dispute.* In other words, an employer cannot import Canadian or Mexican workers as strike breakers.

Persons in the U.S. under TN status may stay no longer than one year. While BCIS can grant repeated one-year extensions, TN status is not for permanent residence.

Workplace Protections

With passage of the law prohibiting employment of undocumented aliens, Congress had concerns that employers would discriminate against persons who are in fact eligible to work but who look or sound foreign. So at the same time, Congress made it illegal for employers having four or more employees to discriminate based on citizenship status or national origin. (Remember that although Title VII addresses national origin, it only applies to employers having fifteen or more employees. Title VII does not address citizenship status at all.) Under that law, it is illegal for an employer to adopt a *U.S. citizens only* policy.

However, it is not illegal for an employer to prefer a U.S. citizen over an eligible alien if the two are equally qualified. Nor do employers have an affirmative duty to sponsor foreign workers and they may refuse to sponsor a foreigner seeking employment here, whatever the reason for the refusal.

In addition to protecting foreign workers from discrimination on the basis of citizenship, U.S. laws generally cover foreign workers and workers employed in the U.S. by foreign employers to the same extent as U.S. citizens working here for U.S. companies. For example, Title VII, the ADA, the ADEA, wage-and-hour laws, and union antidiscrimination laws generally apply with full force to all persons working within the U.S., without regard to the worker's citizenship and without regard to the employer's foreign or domestic status.

There are several exceptions, however, discussed below.

FCN Treaties

One exception is based on treaties the U.S. has with many foreign countries. *Friendship, Commerce, and Navigation* (FCN) treaties permit foreign companies doing business in the U.S. to engage, at their choice, high-level personnel essential to the functioning of the enterprise. These treaty provisions have been held to permit foreign companies to discriminate in favor of their own nationals, even though doing so would otherwise constitute race or national origin discrimination.

Foreign Sovereign Immunities Act

Another exception is based on the *Foreign Sovereign Immunities Act* (FSIA). Under the FSIA, *foreign states* are immune from the jurisdiction of courts in the U.S. so long as they are engaged in governmental-type activities (as opposed to commercial activities).

CASE STUDY: EMPLOYER PROTECTED UNDER FSIA

Saudi Arabia hired a Virginia security firm to work with the Saudi military in providing protection for the Saudi royal family at a family residence in California. A female employee of the security firm quit after the security firm refused to assign her to a command post position for which she was fully qualified. The security firm based its refusal on instructions of the Saudi military that such an assignment would be unacceptable under Islamic law, since the female officer would have to spend long periods working with her Saudi male counterparts.

The female officer filed suit against her former employer claiming sex discrimination. The Fourth Circuit Court of Appeals ruled that providing security for members of the royal family is quintessentially an act peculiar to sovereigns and was therefore the type of government activity that fell within the FSIA's immunity protection. The court went on to hold that the security firm, even though it was a U.S. company, was entitled to derivative immunity when following the instructions of the foreign sovereign not to assign the female officer to the command post.

English Language Ability

Many employers require that their employees—particularly those who must deal with the public—be able to speak English. Even though such a policy might inadvertently exclude certain immigrant groups, it is usually a justifiable requirement. Employers cannot discriminate against those with accented English so long as the employee can communicate effectively.

Some employers go further and prohibit their bilingual employees from even *using* a language other than English while at work. It is difficult to see how that policy could be justified.

Remedies Available to Undocumented Workers

Suppose an employer discriminates against an undocumented worker by, say, refusing to promote him or her solely on the basis of nationality, or suppose an employer violates the Fair Labor Standards Act by refusing to pay overtime, or the employer violates federal labor law by firing him or her for protected union activity. May the undocumented worker go to court? And if so, what remedies does he or she have?

A pair of Supreme Court cases provides some guidance on these questions.

In 1984, in a case called *Sure-Tan*, the Court ruled that an employer committed an unfair labor practice by reporting his illegal aliens to the immigration authorities in retaliation for the employees' pro-union votes. The Court said if undocumented alien employees were excluded from participation in union activities and from protections against employer intimidation, there would be created a subclass of workers without a comparable stake in the collective goals of their legally resident coworkers, thereby eroding the unity of all employees and impeding effective collective bargaining.

In 2002, the Supreme Court decided *Hoffman Plastics*, which involved the question whether an illegal alien who was fired for union activity could be awarded back pay as a remedy for the employer's unfair labor practice. By a slim, 5-to-4 majority, the Court pointed out that Congress made combating the employment of illegal aliens central to the immigration laws. Under those laws it is impossible for an undocumented alien to obtain employment in the United States without some party directly contravening explicit Congressional policies. Awarding back pay in a case such as this, said the Court, not only trivializes the immigration laws, it also condones and encourages future violations.

The employer in *Hoffman Plastics*, although avoiding liability for a back pay award, was still subject to a cease and desist order and an order to post a notice setting forth employee rights under the federal labor law. Those orders are enforceable by contempt proceedings should the employer fail to comply.

Sure-Tan and *Hoffman Plastics* dealt with unfair labor practices in violation of the National Labor Relations Act. Do the same rules apply when it comes to employment discrimination against illegal aliens? Although the Supreme Court has not had occasion to answer the question as of this writing, there is every reason to think that the holdings in *Sure-Tan* and *Hoffman Plastics* will apply here as well. In other words, while discrimination against undocumented workers is illegal, the remedies available to them for illegal discrimination do not include reinstatement and back pay, since those remedies would contravene federal immigration policy.

Recognizing the likely impact of *Hoffman Plastics* on employment discrimination, the EEOC has amended its field manual, instructing its field offices to pursue all forms of relief without regard to an individual's immigration status *other than reinstatement and back pay.*

Yet another question involves violations of wage-and-hour laws. Suppose, for example, that, contrary to the Fair Labor Standards Act, an employer fails to pay an undocumented worker the minimum wage or overtime for work already performed. Most courts considering the question have concluded that payment should be ordered. They have reasoned that the *Hoffman Plastics* rule against back pay does not apply, since back pay involves compensation the employee failed to earn because he or she was improperly fired, not compensation that he or she actually earned.

Chapter

Government Contractors

- ◗ Statutory Framework
- ◗ Executive Orders
- ◗ Rehabilitation Act
- ◗ Veterans
- ◗ Drug-Free Workplace
- ◗ State and Local Government Contractors

Organizations that choose to do business with the federal government must comply with the same employment laws that apply to purely private-sector employers. In addition, there are a number of requirements uniquely applicable to government contractors. This chapter highlights some of the more important requirements.

Statutory Framework

The four basic statutes governing employer-employee relations of government contractors are the Walsh-Healey Public Contracts Act, Davis-Bacon Act, McNamara-O'Hara Service Contract Act, and Contract Work Hours and Safety Standards Act.

Walsh-Healey Public Contracts Act

The Walsh-Healey Public Contracts Act (PCA) requires contractors engaged in the manufacturing or furnishing of materials, supplies, articles, or equipment to the U.S. government to pay employees who produce, assemble, handle, or ship goods under contracts exceeding $10,000 the federal minimum wage for all hours worked and time and one half their regular rate of pay for all hours worked over forty in a workweek.

Davis-Bacon Act

The Davis-Bacon Act requires that all contractors and subcontractors performing on federal contracts in excess of $2,000 for the construction, alteration, or repair of public buildings or public works pay their laborers and mechanics not less than the prevailing wage rates and fringe benefits, as determined by the Secretary of Labor, for corresponding classes of laborers and mechanics employed on similar projects in the area.

McNamara-O'Hara Service Contract Act

The McNamara O'Hara Service Contract Act (SCA) applies to every contract entered into by the U.S. government, the principal purpose of which is to furnish services to the government. The SCA requires contractors and subcontractors performing services on covered federal contracts in excess of $2,500 to pay service employees in various classes no less than prevailing wage rates and fringe benefits found in the locality, or the rates (including prospective increases) contained in a predecessor contractor's collective bargaining agreement. Safety and health standards also apply to such contracts.

Contract Work Hours and Safety Standards Act

The Contract Work Hours and Safety Standards Act (CWHSSA) requires contractors and subcontractors on prime contracts in excess of $100,000 to pay their laborers and mechanics one and one half times their basic rates of pay for all hours over forty worked on covered contract work in a workweek.

While the CWHSSA's overtime requirement is similar to the Fair Labor Standards Act (discussed in Chapter 5), the exemptions are not identical. For example, the FLSA exempts drivers, drivers' helpers, loaders, and mechanics for motor carriers whose duties affect safe operation of commercial motor vehicles in interstate commerce and who are subject to regulation by the U.S. Department of Transportation, but the CWHSSA does not.

Executive Orders

In addition to statutory provisions, Executive Orders issued by the President, as head of the Executive Branch, impose a variety of requirements that must be included in procurement contracts between government contractors and Executive Branch departments. The more significant ones are described below.

Executive Order 11246

In 1965, President Lyndon Johnson issued EO 11246. As subsequently amended, EO 11246 requires all nonexempt government contracts to contain provisions pursuant to which the contractor agrees:

- Not to discriminate against any employee or applicant for employment because of race, color, religion, sex, or national origin;
- To take affirmative action to ensure that applicants are employed and that employees are treated during employment, without regard to their race, color, religion, sex, or national origin;
- To post notices of his obligations under EO 11246 in the workplace and to furnish notices to labor unions with which he has a collective bargaining agreement;

- To include an equal opportunity provision in all employment ads and postings;
- To furnish certain information and reports to the Secretary of Labor;
- That the contract may be canceled for noncompliance; and,
- To include all these same contract provisions in contracts with nonexempt subcontractors and vendors.

Within the Department of Labor, administration of EO 11246 is handled by the Office of Federal Contract Compliance Programs (OFCCP). Under authority of EO 11246, the OFCCP has exempted:

- From all EO 11246 requirements: contracts and subcontracts of $10,000 or less;
- From EO 11246 reporting requirements: prime contractors and first tier subcontractors who have less than fifty employees or whose contracts are for less than $50,000, and all second tier and lower subcontracts; and,
- From EO affirmative action requirements: contractors who have less than fifty employees or whose contracts are for less than $50,000.

Alert!

An exemption from EO 11246 requirements does not excuse an employer from complying with other, generally applicable nondiscrimination, record-keeping, and reporting laws.

Nonexempt government contractors are required to file an Employer Information Report, Form EEO-1, within thirty days after the award of a contract and annually by September 30 thereafter. Additional information may be required on a case-by-case basis.

Contractors who are not exempt from EO 11246's affirmative action requirements must develop a satisfactory affirmative action program, including specific steps to guarantee equal employment opportunity keyed to the problems and needs of members of minority groups. The program must be in writing, it must be signed by an executive officer of the contractor, and copies must be maintained at the worksite for inspection by the OFCCP. The contractor must also perform an annual evaluation of progress in achieving program goals.

Executive Order 12989

EO 12989, signed by President Clinton in 1996, provides for debarment of government contractors who fail to comply with the employment provisions of the Immigration and Nationality Act. Under the Order, whenever the Attorney General determines that a contractor is not in compliance, he is required to transmit that determination to the contracting agency. The agency is then required to consider possible debarment of the contractor.

Executive Order 13201

Under federal right-to-work laws, government contractors who are unionized cannot require their employees to be union members to keep their jobs. However, a collective bargaining agreement may require non-union employees to pay their share of costs relating to collective bargaining, contract administration, and grievance adjustment. (Right-to-work laws are discussed in Chapter 24.)

If an employer deducts dues from non-union employees and the dues are used for purposes in addition to collective bargaining, contract administration, and grievance adjustment, the employee is entitled to a refund to the extent of such other use. The employee may also be entitled to a future reduction in dues.

Most government contractors are required to post a notice—called a *Beck notice*—informing non-union employees of their right to opt out of dues payments.

Rehabilitation Act

The Rehabilitation Act of 1973 served as a model for the Americans with Disabilities Act, enacted in 1990. (See Chapter 17.) Both laws address, in similar terms, employment discrimination against persons with disabilities. While the ADA applies to all employers with fifteen or more employees, the Rehabilitation Act is limited to federal contractors and subcontractors whose contracts exceed $10,000.

In addition to prohibiting disability discrimination and requiring reasonable accommodation, the Rehabilitation Act requires inclusion of an equal opportunity clause in the contract itself. The Rehabilitation Act also requires contractors with fifty or more employees and contracts of $50,000 or more to have written affirmative action plans for employment of persons with disabilities.

OFCCP administers and enforces the Rehabilitation Act's federal contractor requirements.

Veterans

The Vietnam Era Veterans' Readjustment Assistance Act of 1974 (VEVRAA) applies to federal contractors and subcontractors whose contracts exceed $10,000. VEVRAA prohibits discrimination against "special disabled veterans" and "veterans of the Vietnam era." A special disabled veteran is defined generally as a veteran who has a 30% or greater disability rating or who was released from active duty because of a service-related disability. A Vietnam-era veteran is defined generally as a veteran (other than a veteran with a dishonorable discharge) who served in Vietnam or who served anywhere between August 1964 and May 1975.

In addition to prohibiting discrimination against disabled and Vietnam-era veterans, VEVRAA requires inclusion of an equal opportunity clause in the contract itself. VEVRAA also requires contractors with fifty or more employees and contracts of $50,000 or more to have written affirmative action plans for employment of disabled and Vietnam-era veterans. OFCCP administers and enforces VEVRAA's federal contractor requirements.

Drug-Free Workplace

The Drug-Free Workplace Act (DFWA) requires most federal contractors (and federal grant recipients) to:

- Adopt and publish a policy prohibiting the unlawful manufacture, distribution, dispensation, possession, or use of a controlled substance in the workplace and specifying the disciplinary action that will be taken for violations;
- Establish a drug-free awareness program to inform employees about the dangers of drug abuse and the availability of any drug counseling, rehabilitation, and employee assistance programs;

- Require employees to notify the employer within 5 days of any criminal convictions relating to drug violations in the work-place;
- Notify the federal granting or contracting agency within 10 days after receiving notice of the conviction; and,
- Either discharge the convicted employee or require him or her to participate satisfactorily in a drug abuse assistance or reha-bilitation program.

State and Local Government Contractors

State and local procurement regulations often have their own re-quirements. Typical are provisions requiring public works contracts to contain nondiscrimination clauses, requiring contractors to place similar clauses in all subcontracts, and requiring contractors to post notices informing employees of the nondiscrimination clauses.

Companies doing business with a state or local government may also be required to pay a prevailing wage or a specified living wage to employees doing work on the contract.

Chapter

23

Nonprofit Organizations

A typical business corporation is formed by shareholders who invest their capital in the business with the expectation of earning a profit in the form of dividends or on the later sale of their stock. Shareholders hold ultimate power over the corporation by electing directors and by deciding issues that are fundamental to the corporation's existence, such as whether to change the company's capital structure or to merge with another company. The directors, in turn, manage the company by appointing and overseeing corporate officers.

A nonprofit organization, on the other hand, is not formed to make a profit. Typically, it is a corporation organized under special provisions of state law which prohibit issuance of shares or the payment of dividends. Nonprofit organizations therefore have no shareholders and they do not distribute earnings to owners. (Nonprofit organizations may have members who elect directors or trustees, but the members do not *own* the organization. In fact, nobody owns a nonprofit.)

Although not organized to make a profit, nonprofit organizations are not required to operate at a loss. The point here is that any surplus of revenues over expenses must be retained or applied to nonprofit purposes and cannot be distributed to individual members.

Tax-Exempt Status

The term *nonprofit* is often used synonymously with tax-exempt. The two concepts, though related, are distinct. *Nonprofit* refers to the organization's purposes as expressed in its articles of incorporation and as governed by state law. *Tax-exempt* on the other hand means that the organization's net earnings are not subject to income tax. All tax-exempt organizations must be nonprofit, but just because an organization is nonprofit does not necessarily mean it qualifies for tax exemption.

Of course, the reason why an entity organizes as a nonprofit is usually to obtain tax-exempt status. For purposes of this chapter, the terms will be used interchangeably.

Section 501(c) of the Internal Revenue Code contains a long list of organizations that qualify for tax-exempt status, including:

- Corporations organized and operated exclusively for religious, charitable, scientific, testing for public safety, literary, or educational purposes, or for the prevention of cruelty to children or animals, no part of the net earnings of which inures to the benefit of any private shareholder or individual—so-called *501(c)(3)* organizations;
- Civic leagues organized and operated exclusively for the promotion of social welfare;
- Labor, agricultural, or horticultural organizations;
- Business leagues, chambers of commerce, real estate boards, and boards of trade; and,
- Recreational clubs.

To achieve tax-exempt status, a nonprofit organization must submit an application to the IRS. If the IRS is satisfied that the organization is organized and is being operated for one of the exempt purposes listed in the statute, it issues a determination letter to that effect. Exemption from state income taxes can usually be obtained on the basis of the IRS determination letter.

Another distinction that is often blurred has to do with the deductibility of contributions. While a tax-exempt organization pays no income tax, it does not necessarily follow that contributions to that organization qualify for a deduction. Deductibility of contributions to § 501(c)(3) organizations are governed by § 170 of the Internal Revenue Code. Payments to other types of nonprofit organizations, such as business leagues, may qualify as trade or business expenses under § 162 of the Internal Revenue Code.

Although tax-exempt nonprofits get special treatment for some purposes, with few exceptions federal and state employment laws apply to nonprofits to the same extent as they apply to for-profit businesses. For example, nonprofits must withhold taxes from employee salaries, they must provide workers' compensation, they cannot discriminate (except in limited circumstances involving religious organizations), and they must provide safe workplaces.

This chapter discusses the exceptions applicable to nonprofit organizations.

Employee Compensation and Withholding

The Internal Revenue Code allows for-profit corporations to deduct from gross income *a reasonable allowance for salaries or other compensation for personal services actually rendered.* As a result of this provision, every dollar a for-profit business corporation pays out in salaries or employee benefits reduces the corporation's federal and state tax liability by as much as 46 cents. In effect, the government pays almost half of a business corporation's employment-related costs.

Because of its tax-exempt status, the same is not true for a nonprofit organization. Salaries and benefits are borne 100% by the organization itself and reduce the amounts available for its nonprofit purposes on a dollar-for-dollar basis. (This may be one reason why compensation levels are typically somewhat lower in the nonprofit sphere.) The employees themselves pay tax on their incomes just like employees of for-profit companies, although special rules apply to clergy.

Ministers and members of religious orders are considered *self-employed* for Social Security purposes with respect to their ministerial duties. This means that the church or other ecclesiastical organization they work for does not withhold FICA from their compensation or make matching FICA contributions. (FICA is discussed in Chapter 7.) In addition, ministers and members of religious orders who have taken a vow of poverty are automatically exempt from FICA tax on self-employment income. Even if they have not taken a vow of poverty, they may obtain an exemption if they are opposed to Social Security on conscientious or religious grounds.

Ministers who are provided a parsonage or a payment specifically designated as a rental allowance do not need to include those items in gross income for income tax purposes.

Executive Compensation

Organizations such as charitable, religious, or educational organizations that are exempt under § 501(c)(3) of the Internal Revenue Code must be operated *exclusively* for the charitable, religious, or educational purposes for which they were organized. If they abuse their exempt status by engaging in nonexempt activities, the IRS has the power to revoke their tax exemption.

Revocation is a drastic remedy. It would often mean the end of the organization. So historically, minor abuses either went unpunished or they were punished in a disproportionately severe way. Now the IRS has a less deadly weapon—an excise tax to punish abusers.

A 1996 amendment to the tax code, coupled with more recently issued IRS regulations, prohibit *disqualified persons* from receiving excess benefits from a tax-exempt organization. A *disqualified person* includes any person who is in a position to exercise substantial influence over the affairs of the organization. This would cover high-level employees, board members, and officers. Family members of those persons are also covered. An *excess benefit* is any economic benefit provided to a disqualified person in excess of the consideration received by the organization. For example, the board of a charitable organization cannot vote itself exorbitant directors' fees, nor can senior managers pull down salaries far above the norm for comparable positions.

A disqualified person who receives an excess benefit is subject to an initial 25% excise tax on the amount of the excess. The management of the organization is also subject to a 10% tax. If the excess benefit transaction is not promptly corrected, then the disqualified person is subject to an additional *200 percent* excise tax.

Benefit Plans

With limited exceptions, the same array of benefit plans that are available to for-profit companies are also available to tax-exempt organizations. (Deferred compensation plans and other types of employee benefit plans are discussed in Chapters 8 and 9.) Tax-exempt organizations may even have a profit-sharing plan, although they don't have profits in the normal sense.

403(b) Plans

In addition to the usual array of plans, organizations that are exempt under § 501(c)(3) of the Internal Revenue Code—educational organizations, churches, public and private schools, etc.— may adopt a special type of pension plan available only to them, called a *tax-sheltered annuity* or *403(b) annuity*. Although called annuity plans, the funding vehicle for these plans is not limited to annuity contracts issued by insurance companies. Other vehicles, such as bank custodial accounts, are also available.

Prior to 1958, employees of tax-exempt organizations could divert any or all of their compensation to an annuity on a tax-sheltered basis. In 1958, Congress imposed a ceiling on the amounts that could be diverted. Subsequent amendments to the Internal Revenue Code have made tax-sheltered annuities conform in many respects to other types of pension plans. Nevertheless, tax-sheltered annuities retain some attractive features. One feature is their portability. When the funding vehicle is an individual annuity contract owned by the employee, the employee can leave one tax-exempt organization, go to work for another, and simply have his new employer make contributions to his existing plan.

Church Plans

A *church plan* is a plan established and maintained for employees of a tax-exempt church or a convention or association of churches. Unless a church plan voluntarily elects to be subject to the Employee Retirement Income Security Act, it is exempt from most of ERISA's requirements, including requirements relating to coverage, vesting, benefit accrual, and funding. (ERISA is discussed in Chapter 9.)

QUICK TIP

While being exempt from ERISA is generally considered beneficial from the employer's viewpoint, one downside is that ERISA's preemption provision does not apply. This makes nonelecting church plans subject to state laws, rather than uniform federal law. As a result, church plans and their sponsors can be sued in state court, can be subjected to jury trials, and can have compensatory and punitive damages awarded against them if permitted under state law.

Since nonelecting church plans are generally exempt from ERISA, they do not have to provide health insurance continuation benefits under the amendment to ERISA known as COBRA. On the other hand, HIPAA does apply to church plans. (COBRA and HIPAA are covered in Chapter 10.)

Unemployment Insurance

Some states allow tax-exempt organizations described in § 501(c)(3) of the Internal Revenue Code the option of either contributing state unemployment tax just like other employers or reimbursing the state dollar-for-dollar for actual claims charged to their accounts. Electing to reimburse may improve a charity's current cash flow, but it could prove expensive in the event several employees are terminated at the same time.

Religious Organizations

The First Amendment to the Constitution provides that *Congress shall make no law respecting an establishment of religion, or prohibiting the free exercise thereof.* Countless federal statutes have the potential for interfering with religious practices, but they either contain express exemptions, or they have been held inapplicable or unconstitutional when applied to religious organizations.

Ministerial Exception

One such federal statute is Title VII of the federal Civil Rights Act, which prohibits discrimination in employment based on race, color, religion, sex, or national origin. (Title VII is discussed in Chapter 14.) Under a literal reading of Title VII, a Catholic church, for example, could be forced to ordain women priests, contrary to Catholic religious doctrine. But most federal courts that have considered the question recognize a so-called *ministerial exception* that prevents such a controversial result.

A case in the D.C. Circuit Court of Appeals, for example, involved a nun who held a doctorate in canon law from Catholic University and was an associate professor in that school's canon law department. When the nun's application for tenure was rejected, she sued claiming sex discrimination. The Court characterized the case as "a collision between two interests of the highest order: the Government's interest in eradicating discrimination and the constitutional right of a church to manage its own affairs free from governmental interference." The Court resolved these colliding interests by dismissing the suit under the ministerial exception, saying that religious institutions are exempt from civil suits in connection with the selection and employment of clergy.

The ministerial exception is not limited just to members of the clergy. It also covers lay employees of religious institutions whose primary duties consist of teaching, spreading the faith, church governance, supervision of a religious order, or participation in religious ritual and worship.

Discrimination Based on Religion

Even for employees who are not covered by the ministerial exception, religious organizations may discriminate on *religious* grounds. Title VII, by its express terms, does not apply to religious organizations *with respect to the employment of individuals of a particular religion* to perform work connected with the organization's activities.

Federal labor law offers another good example of potential interference with First Amendment rights to religious freedom. By statute, an employee in a union shop who is a member of a bona fide religion that forbids union membership or union financial support may pay his dues to charity instead of to the union. And a 1979 Supreme Court decision, known as *Catholic Bishop*, held that religious organizations themselves are exempt from National Labor Relations Board jurisdiction.

Tenure

From the Latin *tenere* (to hold), the word *tenure* is usually associated with job security for faculty members at academic institutions. Basically, by granting tenure to a member of its faculty, the employer institution agrees that the faculty member is no longer an employee at will and can only be discharged for specified reasons and after following specified procedures. In simple terms, a tenure arrangement is a contract of employment. (Employment at will and employment contracts are discussed in Chapter 1.)

Alert!

Faculty members at *public* institutions are government employees and therefore enjoy certain due process rights not applicable in the private sector. (See Chapter 4.)

Tenure is sometimes a controversial subject. Those in support argue that it is essential to protect teachers from arbitrary decisions, to promote institutional self-governance, and to preserve academic freedom. Critics contend that tenure encourages neglect of teaching responsibilities, removes any checks on the growth of irresponsible opinions, and generally fosters laziness and lack of productivity. Tenure lets professors *think (or idle) in ill-paid peace, accountable to nobody.* Regardless, in adopting a tenure policy, the employing institution retains ultimate control over how and when tenure is granted and how and when a tenured teacher can be removed.

Nearly all colleges and universities have a tenure system, according to the U.S. Department of Education. The specifics of the system are usually contained in the institution's bylaws or other governing documents or in a faculty handbook. Typically, the system provides for tenure-track professors to be considered for tenure after a probationary period lasting a specified number of years. (Non-tenure tracks exist for part-timers, temporary appointees, and in some cases even regular, full-time teachers.) The system identifies the criteria to be considered in granting tenure, which normally includes an evaluation by faculty colleagues.

QUICK TIP

Except for religious schools, academic institutions are no different from other employers when it comes to discrimination. The granting or withholding of tenure based on race, gender, age, or other prohibited grounds violates federal and local fair employment laws.

Once a professor is granted tenure, the employing institution is restricted in its ability to terminate him or her. Termination usually requires cause, based on such factors as neglect of duty, incompetence, or professional or personal misconduct. (See Chapter 4 for a discussion of for-cause terminations.) Termination is also typically permitted if the institution abolishes the professor's program or department, or if the institution faces serious financial problems.

Since tenure policies amount to employment contracts, an institution that fails to follow its policies can be sued for breach of contract. Courts are generally reluctant to inject themselves directly in the academic process by requiring, for example, that an institution grant tenure or rehire a professor who was wrongfully terminated. But courts will award money damages where tenure policies have not been followed.

CASE STUDY: DAMAGES AWARDED FOR VIOLATION OF TENURE POLICY

George Washington University in Washington, D.C., had a tenure policy that required it to give a year's advance notice to any tenure-track professor who would not be getting tenure at the expiration of his or her probationary period. The policy went on to say that any faculty member who is not so notified shall acquire tenure at the end of the term.

When the University violated its own policy by terminating a particular professor without giving him the requisite notice, the professor sued, asking the court to order that he be granted tenure. The court refused to order tenure, reasoning that it would not serve the University's academic interests to have a body of professors whose tenure resulted from administrative neglect or oversight. The court did, however, require payment of money damages equal to one year's salary.

Chapter 24

Unions and Labor Relations

An in-depth exposition on labor relations law would go well beyond the scope of this book. Employers need experienced labor law counsel when faced with union organizing activity, when engaged in collective bargaining, or when responding to a strike threat. What follows is a discussion of the basic principles arising under the National Labor Relations Act (NLRA).

According to the NLRA, inequality of bargaining power between employees and employers prevents the stabilization of competitive wage rates and working conditions. To remedy this inequality, the NLRA:

- Protects concerted activities by employees;
- Provides a mechanism for union representation elections;
- Promotes collective bargaining between employers and unions; and,
- Prohibits unfair labor practices by employers and unions.

The principal enforcer of the NLRA is the National Labor Relations Board. The Board has primary jurisdiction over labor disputes and union elections. And when it is not clear whether an activity is governed by the NLRA, the Board itself—not the state or federal courts—gets to decide in the first instance whether the NLRA applies.

Despite having primary jurisdiction, however, the Board will often defer to arbitration procedures in a collective bargaining agreement for resolving grievances, even where the grievance involves an unfair labor practice.

NLRA Coverage

The NLRA, and hence the Board's enforcement power, extends to any employer whose activities affect interstate commerce—virtually any employer. However, the Board has chosen not to exercise its jurisdiction over employers in a variety of industries that fall below specified revenue levels.

In general, the Board will not exercise jurisdiction over nonretail establishments whose gross cash flow across state lines is less than $50,000. As to retail establishments, at least $500,000 in revenue is required for the Board to exercise its jurisdiction. Separate revenue tests also apply to office buildings, hotels and motels, private colleges and universities, symphony orchestras, and certain health care institutions, among others.

The NLRA protects employee rights. But typical of federal labor laws, the term *employee* is defined in an unhelpful, circular way. (See Chapter 14, discussing the term for federal antidiscrimination law purposes.) The NLRA does, however, exclude from the definition various specific groups, including independent contractors and supervisors.

Independent Contractors

Historically, the Board drew the employee/independent contractor distinction based on whether the employer exercised, or had the right to exercise, control over the means and manner by which the worker did his job. Recently, the Board adopted a new test for independent contractors, which the D.C. Circuit Court of Appeals has approved.

The case involved Corporate Express Delivery Systems, of Oklahoma City. Corporate Express engaged two types of drivers to deliver its packages—those who drove company vehicles and those who operated their own vehicles. The employer considered the first type as employees, but it treated owner-operators as independent contractors.

When several of the owner-operators began holding meetings to discuss forming a union, the company spied on them, threatened to close its Oklahoma City branch, and fired three of the union organizers. The company's actions would clearly be illegal under federal labor law if the owner-operators were employees for labor law purposes, but if they were only independent contractors, there would be no violation.

In concluding that the owner-operators should be classified as employees, the Board and the Court of Appeals considered whether the worker has a significant entrepreneurial opportunity for gain or loss. Stated another way: Who takes the economic risk connected with the worker's job—the company or the worker? If the risk is with the company, then the worker should be classified as an employee. But if the worker bears the risk, then he or she is an independent contractor. Applying this new test to Corporate Express's owner-operators, the Court observed that the company prohibited them from employing others to do the company's work and it also prohibited them from using their vehicles to deliver packages for other companies. This, said the Court, made them employees, not entrepreneurs.

Supervisors

The NLRA defines *supervisor* generally as any individual having authority to hire, transfer, suspend, lay off, recall, promote, discharge, assign, reward, or discipline other employees, or responsibly to direct them, or to adjust their grievances, or effectively to recommend such action. By statute, supervisors have no right to organize or to require employers to bargain with them, although employers may, if they wish, agree to treat supervisors as employees for bargaining purposes. Absent employer consent, however, the inclusion of supervisors in a bargaining unit is not permitted and employers cannot be forced to bargain with such a unit.

Professionals

In contrast to the exclusion of supervisors from NLRA protection, professional employees are entitled to unionize. (Professionals can't be forced into a bargaining unit with nonprofessionals unless a majority of the professionals approve the arrangement.) While professionals necessarily exercise independent judgment in the course of supervising others, they still don't qualify as supervisors if their supervisory duties are merely routine or clerical and not independent.

Concerted Activities

Employers are prohibited from interfering with employees' concerted activities—efforts to better wages, hours, and working conditions. This includes, among other things, the right to self-organize by forming or joining a union.

Soliciting

Union organizing efforts have engendered bitter disputes and a multitude of decided cases. One recurring issue is the extent to which employees and outside organizers may solicit at the workplace and may distribute pro-union literature. As the Supreme Court has said, the right to unionize necessarily encompasses the right effectively to communicate with one another regarding self-organization at the jobsite. Employee rights at the jobsite are not unlimited, however, since those rights can conflict with the employer's own property rights and managerial interests. In short, some balance must be struck between the competing interests of employers and employees.

In general, an employer may ban solicitation by employees of other employees during working time and it may ban distribution by employees during working hours and in working areas. Conversely, an employer generally may not restrict employee solicitation during nonworking time, and it may not ban employee distribution during nonworking time and in nonworking areas, such as employee lounges, parking lots, etc. The only exception is if the employer can show special circumstances which would make a ban necessary to maintain production or discipline.

Outside Organizers

When it comes to outside organizers, the employer has greater rights. So long as the employer acts in a nondiscriminatory fashion, he may impose a blanket ban on solicitation and distribution by nonemployees on employer property, unless the union can demonstrate that employees are not otherwise accessible to union organizers.

QUICK TIP

Restrictions on soliciting and distribution—even those that are consistent with the rules stated here—should have a reasonable business justification other than anti-union animus. Employers who base restrictions on safety concerns can usually expect to have them upheld.

Selective (discriminatory) enforcement of nonsolicitation and nondistribution rules can be an unfair labor practice. By way of example, suppose a company completely bans employee use of the company's bulletin board—a perfectly legal rule under the NLRA if the employer is not unionized or if the rule is the result of good-faith bargaining. But then the company allows employees to post personal notices, such as items for sale, church raffle notices, cartoons, etc. Under these circumstances, the company's attempt to enforce its ban against pro-union material will amount to an unfair labor practice.

In another example, a nurse at a Florida hospital programmed her computer to display a screen saver saying, "Look for the U," meaning "Look for the Union." When she was disciplined for doing so, she filed an unfair labor practice charge. Finding that a wide variety of other personal screen saver messages were allowed, such as "Go Buccaneers" and "Have a nice day," the Board upheld the nurse's charge.

Non-Union Shops

Although the right to engage in concerted activities covers *self-organization*, it also protects employees who are not unionized and it protects activities that have nothing to do with the formation of a union. Examples of protected concerted activity, whether in a union or non-union context, include the following.

- *Discussing wages and working conditions.* Since the right of employees to self-organize and bargain collectively necessarily encompasses the right to communicate with one another, an employer cannot adopt a rule prohibiting employees from discussing wages or other working conditions among themselves.
- *Discussing employee sexual harassment complaints.* The Board has ruled that a company confidentiality requirement prohibiting discussion of a pending sexual harassment investigation is an unfair labor practice.
- *Inquiring about benefits.* Employees can be persistent in pursuing benefit claims so long as their conduct is not so flagrant or egregious as to interfere with company business practices.
- *Complaining about working conditions.* An employee cannot be disciplined for complaining to management about matters of common concern to all employees. Although the employee may initially be acting alone, his actions will be considered concerted so long as they are intended to initiate or induce group action. The intent to initiate or induce group action will be assumed if, for example, the complaint is voiced at a group meeting called to discuss working conditions.

• *Wearing pro-union buttons and insignia.* Wearing buttons and insignia is protected activity unless there are special considerations relating to employee efficiency and plant discipline.

QUICK TIP

Concerted activity by union members or groups of employees to better wages and working conditions is exempt from antitrust laws, even though the activity may amount to a restraint of trade.

Alert!

The National Labor Relations Board and the courts have ruled that a confidentiality provision in an employee handbook could infringe on the employee's right to engage in concerted activity. Figure 24.1 contains a suggested employee handbook provision addressing this issue.

Figure 24.1: HANDBOOK PROVISION ON CONFIDENTIALITY

Nothing in this Handbook is intended to interfere with or restrain any employee's rights under the federal labor laws, including the right to engage in concerted activity and the right to discuss with others the terms and conditions of employment.

Representation Elections

The Board has adopted detailed rules for initiating and conducting representation elections. The process usually starts with a union organizer obtaining signatures on union cards authorizing a particular labor organization to represent the employees. When a substantial number of employees (at least 30%) have signed such cards, the labor organization then files a petition with the Board requesting recognition as the exclusive bargaining representative. The cards themselves also get filed with the Board to demonstrate that there is in fact substantial union support. The Board, through one of its field offices, then conducts an investigation to determine:

- Whether the employer's operations affect commerce within the meaning of the NLRA;
- The appropriateness of the bargaining unit;
- Whether the election would further the policies of the NLRA and reflect the free choice of employees in the bargaining unit; and,
- Whether there is a sufficient probability, based on the evidence of representation, that the employees have selected the union to represent them.

If the Board is satisfied on these points, it orders a representation election to take place by secret ballot and supervises the actual conduct of the election. If a majority of employees in the bargaining unit vote in favor of the union, the union is then certified as the bargaining representative of all employees in the unit.

Ordinarily, the Board uses a simple formula to determine who is eligible to vote in a representation election: workers are eligible if they are employed on the date of the election itself and if they also were employed during the payroll period preceding the Board's order that the election take place. However, in determining who has sufficient continuity and regularity of employment to be included in the bargaining unit, the Board sometimes has to tailor its usual formula to fit varying employment situations.

The Board also determines the appropriateness of the bargaining unit. As an example, the Board has included temporary employees along with the employer's permanent employees in a unit for bargaining purposes. There are limits, however, on how far the Board can go. As noted above, supervisors cannot be included without the employer's consent. Nor can the Board fashion a multi-employer unit without the consent of the affected employers. The Board is also prohibited from designating a unit that includes both professionals and nonprofessionals unless a majority of the professionals vote for inclusion.

An employer is free, if it wishes, to recognize the union without an election if more than 50% of the employees in the bargaining unit have signed cards indicating they want to be represented by the union. Alternatively, the employer can insist on an NLRB-supervised election. An employer is prohibited by law from recognizing a union without an election where fewer than 50% of the employees have signed authorization cards.

Laboratory Conditions

The elections themselves must be conducted in *laboratory conditions*, free from threats, coercion, promises, or other misconduct that might reasonably tend to interfere with the voters' free choice. An election can be set aside even if the misconduct does not arise to the level of an unfair labor practice.

Management need not, of course, muzzle itself during an organizing campaign. Management is free, for example, to express the company's views, arguments, and opinions about unionization. But management cannot *threaten* employees with retaliation for voting pro-union, *make promises* conditioned on rejection of the union, *interrogate* employees about their organizing activity, or *conduct surveillance* to determine who is supporting the union.

Union conduct, too, can destroy laboratory conditions and warrant setting aside an election. When union organizers at a clay mine in North Carolina made threats that employees could be "squeezed out of" their jobs if they didn't support the union and told anti-union employees, "You won't be able to work here when the union comes in," the Fourth Circuit Court of Appeals ruled that the resultant pro-union vote was invalid.

CASE STUDY: COMPANY BAN ON ABUSIVE LANGUAGE UPHELD

A company that refurbishes rail cars for the Bay Area Rapid Transit System in California had an employee handbook that classified use of abusive or threatening language on Company premises as serious misconduct warranting suspension for a first offense and possible termination for subsequent offenses. Since the Company was not unionized, the Machinists and Aerospace Workers union (part of the AFL-CIO) began organizing efforts in 1998. In December of that year an election was held, which the union lost. The union then filed unfair labor practice charges citing, among other things, the Company's abusive and threatening language rule. The union argued that vulgar expletives and racial epithets are part and parcel of a vigorous exchange that often accompanies labor relations. Incredibly, the National Labor Relations Board agreed and voided the election.

The D.C. Circuit Court of Appeals reversed, strongly criticizing the Board in the process. The Court ruled that unions were perfectly capable of acting civilly while conducting organizing campaigns. The Court also pointed out that an employer may be exposed to claims if it fails to maintain a minimal level of civility in the workplace and allows racial, gender, or similar forms of harassment.

Duty to Bargain

Federal labor law makes it an unfair labor practice for a unionized employer to refuse to bargain collectively with its unions. The term *bargain collectively* is defined as the performance of the mutual obligation of the employer and the representative of the employees to meet at reasonable times and confer in good faith with respect to wages, hours, and other terms and conditions of employment.

Closely connected with an employer's duty to bargain is its duty to provide the union with all requested information relevant to the union's duties as representative of union members. The courts apply a broad definition of *relevant* in this context, so that there need only be a probability that the information will be useful to the union.

Normally, an employer's duty to bargain with a union does not arise until after the Board has conducted a union representation election, the union has been successful, and the Board has certified the election results. This has been called the preferred and most satisfactory method for a union to obtain representative status. However, the duty to bargain can arise based entirely on union authorization cards signed by a majority of the employees in the proposed bargaining unit, if the cards unambiguously state that the signing employees want the union to represent them. (Cards that just indicate a desire for a representation election are insufficient.)

When faced with a demand to bargain based solely on union authorization cards, the employer is entitled to investigate to determine whether the cards truly represent the sentiment of a majority of employees. The employer is also allowed to file its own petition for a formal election.

Alert!

Under the Employee Free Choice Act, pending in Congress as of this writing, a *card check* system could replace representation elections and secret ballots. If the Act is passed, an employer would be required to recognize a union as the exclusive bargaining agent based simply on a majority of employees signing authorization cards.

The duty to bargain can even apply to a union that has lost a representation election. Suppose an employer, motivated by anti-union animus, so poisons the atmosphere with unfair labor practices that a would-be union loses the election. Traditionally, the Board will order a new election. But if the employer's actions make it impossible to conduct a fair and reliable new election, the Board may simply treat the union as the employees' legitimate representative.

Project Labor Agreements

Special provisions of the NLRA apply to employers in the building and construction industry. An employer in that industry is allowed to enter into a *project labor agreement* (PLA) with a union, even though the union has not yet been established as the representative of a majority of the employees to be covered by the PLA. Typically, a PLA requires all contractors and subcontractors who will work on a project to agree in advance to a master collective bargaining agreement under which wages, hours, and other conditions of employment are standardized for all employees at the project. The PLA requirement is incorporated into bid specifications, so any company that is awarded a contract is bound to join in the PLA.

Mandatory vs. Permissive Bargaining

Bargaining over some subjects is *mandatory*, because those subjects involve wages, hours, and other terms and conditions of employment. Other subjects are *permissive*, in that employers and unions are free to bargain over them if they wish, but neither side can insist, to the point of impasse, on inclusion of a mere permissive subject in a collective bargaining agreement.

What are the mandatory subjects over which employers *must* bargain if requested to do so by their unions? According to the Supreme Court, they are subjects that are *directly germane to the working environment*. However, a company has a right to run its business without interference. So a company need not bargain over managerial decisions which lie at the core of entrepreneurial control, such as decisions concerning the commitment of investment capital and the basic scope and direction of the enterprise.

In addition to wages, hours, and benefits, examples of mandatory bargaining subjects include:

- Company decisions that directly affect job security, such as a decision to contract out work previously done by union employees (but decisions that only indirectly affect job security, such as a decision to discontinue a particular product line, are not subject to mandatory bargaining);
- Changes in working conditions;
- Union security clauses, where such clauses are not forbidden under state right-to-work laws (discussed later in this chapter);
- Seniority rights;
- Management rights clauses reserving, for example, the company's right to sell its business free of liabilities under the collective bargaining agreement, to discontinue operations, to determine the number of hours per day and per week that operations should be carried on, and to suspend, discharge, or otherwise discipline employees;

- Prices and availability of services at in-plant cafeterias and vending machines;
- Hiring practices;
- Tardiness policies;
- Use of company bulletin board;
- Drug and alcohol testing; and,
- Installation of security cameras to deter employee theft.

This last item is drawn from a recent case before the D.C. Circuit Court of Appeals affirming a decision by the Board. The case involved a company's practice over many years of installing hidden surveillance cameras to investigate specific cases of employee theft or other wrongdoing. Faced with unauthorized use of a manager's telephone for long-distance calls, the company placed a camera in the manager's file cabinet. The camera caught an employee (who happened to be a union member) using the phone, and the company promptly fired him.

The union filed a grievance over the firing and, at a subsequent hearing, discovered for the first time the company's practice of using hidden surveillance cameras. The union then asked the company for detailed information about the cameras, indicating that it wanted to bargain with the company over the practice. The company refused to provide the information and it refused to bargain.

The Board ruled that the company was wrong on both counts. It said use of surveillance cameras is a subject of mandatory bargaining, just like physical examinations, drug and alcohol testing, and other investigatory tools and methods used by employers to discover employee misconduct. Further, the company was required to provide pertinent information to the union—or at least bargain over what information would be provided. While the company may have a legitimate concern over keeping confidential such information as the location of the cameras, the company still had a duty to seek an accommodation that would meet the needs of both the union and the company.

Conflicts with Other Laws

Sometimes an employer's duty to bargain will conflict with, or appear to conflict with, other legal duties imposed on the employer.

Take, for example, a disabled employee who requests reassignment to a vacant position as an accommodation for his disability. (The duty of reasonable accommodation under the Americans with Disabilities Act is discussed in Chapter 17.) While ADA principles might well require the reassignment, doing so may at the same time violate established seniority practices. In that circumstance, the Supreme Court has ruled that in the run of cases seniority will trump ADA requirements. Of course, if the employer's seniority practice is one in name only, then the employer will have a difficult time defending his refusal to accommodate based on seniority.

In another Supreme Court case, a truck driver for a mining company twice tested positive for marijuana. The mining company attempted to terminate the employee, but the union filed a grievance and insisted on arbitration. The arbitrator ruled that, in light of certain mitigating circumstances, there was no just cause for termination (*just cause* being the standard prescribed by the collective bargaining agreement) and ordered the employee reinstated. The mining company then went to court, arguing that, notwithstanding its collective bargaining agreement and the arbitrator's order, public policy justified refusal to reinstate the employee. This was especially so, said the mining company, because the employee was engaged in safety-sensitive tasks requiring random drug testing under Department of Transportation regulations.

The Supreme Court rejected the company's argument and upheld the reinstatement order, finding no overriding public policy that would justify refusal to comply with the order.

Or take the case of a union employee who was accused of sexual harassment. The employee in the case had a long history of offensive, sexually-charged conduct directed at female coworkers. Finally, the employer's equal opportunity employment officer recommended that the employee be fired, but that recommendation had to be approved by the employer's labor relations manager, who was on vacation. By the time the labor relations manager returned, more than 30 days had expired. Since the employer's collective bargaining agreement required that discipline be imposed within 30 days of the misconduct, no further action was then taken. Eventually, after additional incidents, the employee was fired. In the meantime, however, the victims of his conduct filed sex discrimination charges.

The employer defended against the discrimination charges by claiming that under its collective bargaining agreement it could not fire the employee without following the procedures specified in the agreement. The Seventh Circuit Court of Appeals ruled, however, that a collective bargaining agreement is not *imposed* on an employer. Rather, it is an agreement every provision of which has been consented to by the employer. In this case, for example, the employer could have negotiated for special rules applicable to harassment, but it did not. Since the employer cannot by agreement limit its obligations under federal antidiscrimination laws, the employer alone must bear the consequences of its labor-relations decisions.

This decision illustrates an important point. Just because a subject of negotiation falls in the mandatory category, employers should still remember that their only duty is to *discuss* the subject in good faith. The duty to bargain does not mean that the employer is obligated to *agree* with the union's position.

The employer's duty to bargain ends if a majority of employees in the bargaining unit no longer support the union. For the first three years while a collective bargaining agreement (CBA) is in place, a conclusive presumption exists that the union enjoys majority support. However, after three years or when a CBA expires, the presumption of majority support is no longer conclusive. The employer may then attempt to rebut the presumption by showing that, in fact, the union no longer represents a majority of workers.

Other Unfair Labor Practices

Unfair labor practices (ULPs) come in many flavors. A number of them have been discussed above, such as refusal to bargain, selective enforcement of no-solicitation rules, adoption of workplace policies that interfere with concerted activities, etc. The NLRA itself lists the following as employer unfair labor practices:

- Interfering with, restraining, or coercing employees in the exercise of the rights guaranteed by the NLRA;
- Dominating or interfering with the formation or administration of a labor organization or contributing financial or other support to it;

- Discriminating in regard to hiring or tenure of employment or any term or condition of employment to encourage or discourage membership in any labor organization;
- Discharging or otherwise discriminating against an employee because he or she has filed charges or given testimony under the NLRA; and,
- Refusing to bargain collectively with the employees' representative.

A few of these merit further discussion.

Company-Dominated Employee Committee

Historically, a favorite way for employers to keep out, or at least keep control of, unions was to form an organization for its employees which appeared to, but in reality did not, give employees a voice in their conditions of employment. By making it illegal for an employer to dominate or interfere with a *labor organization* (defined as any organization of employees that exists to deal with the employer concerning grievances, wages, hours, or working conditions), the law effectively stops this practice.

Not all employee committees are illegal, however, as a recent Board decision shows. A non-union manufacturer in Texas uses a management system in which it delegates substantial operational authority to its employees. It accomplishes this through numerous committees in which employees and management participate. These committees make decisions by consensus on a wide variety of workplace issues such as production, quality, training, attendance, safety, maintenance, and even discipline short of suspension or discharge. Although senior management retains ultimate authority, it routinely approves all committee recommendations.

The Board ruled that these committees are not labor organizations because they do not exist to deal with management. Instead, the committees themselves perform management functions, exercising authority that, in the traditional plant setting, would be considered supervisory. So when a committee interacts with company officials, the interaction is really between two management bodies. In effect, these committees do not deal with management, they *are* management.

Discrimination against Salts

In an attempt to unionize a non-union shop, a union may *salt* the shop by sending union organizers as applicants for job openings. When an employer refuses to hire, or even consider, such applicants and the employer is motivated, at least in part, by anti-union animus, the employer commits an unfair labor practice. (Some say that the purpose of salting is not in fact to organize a union but to precipitate an unfair labor practice.) The Seventh Circuit Court of Appeals has even held that a salt can lie on his job application, so long as the lie concerns his status as a salt and not his qualifications for the job. In the Seventh Circuit case, for example, the salt said he was "laid off" from his previous job, at $11 an hour, when applying for an $8.50 an hour job. Had he told the truth—that he in fact took a voluntary leave of absence— the new employer might well have guessed his status as a salt.

Collusion with Union

In a recent case before the Fourth Circuit Court of Appeals, an employee of a Rochester, New York, freight company ran for union office against an incumbent Teamsters official. Despite a hard-fought campaign, the employee failed to defeat the incumbent. During later re-negotiations of the labor contract between the Teamsters and the freight company, the union offered to concede on a point important to the company if the company would fire the employee. The company eventually did so. The Court ordered reinstatement, saying that the NLRA prohibits the discharge of an employee for engaging in protected activity such as running for a union election. The Court went on to say that unions themselves cannot cause an employee to be fired for engaging in protected activity, nor can unions act in a manner contrary to the interests of their members, as the Teamsters did here by putting the personal gain of incumbent union officers ahead of the interests of union members.

Union Security and the Right to Work

Union security clauses are designed to protect union membership, or at least union revenue. For example, under a *union shop* arrangement, all eligible employees must join the union on being hired and must maintain membership as a condition of continued employment. In an agency shop, employees need not be union members but they must pay the same union dues that members pay.

Federal labor law permits union shop and agency shop agreements between employers and unions. However, since 1947 when the National Labor Relations Act was amended by the Taft-Hartley Act, federal labor law has also permitted individual states to enact so-called *right-to-work laws* making union security agreements illegal in those states. Some twenty-three states have done exactly that. At this writing, the following states have right-to-work provisions in their state constitutions or statutes:

- Alabama
- Arizona
- Arkansas
- Florida
- Georgia
- Idaho
- Indiana (only applicable to school employees)
- Iowa
- Kansas
- Louisiana
- Mississippi
- Nebraska
- Nevada
- North Carolina
- North Dakota
- Oklahoma
- South Carolina
- South Dakota
- Tennessee
- Texas
- Utah
- Virginia
- Wyoming

For a current listing, go to: www.dol.gov/esa/programs/whd/state/righttowork.htm.

Suppose an employee in a union or agency shop holds religious or moral convictions against union participation? Federal law provides a limited escape clause. It says that any employee who is a member of a bona fide religion which has historically held conscientious objections to joining or financially supporting labor organizations may, instead of paying union dues, pay an equal amount to a designated charity.

Special rules apply to government contractors. In February 2001, President Bush signed Executive Order 13201, requiring all federal government contracts to contain a provision that the contractor will post a notice—the so-called Beck notice—informing employees of their rights not to join a union and to limit their dues payments only to specified union functions.

Strikes and Lockouts

The NLRA says that except as otherwise expressly stated in the Act, nothing in the Act shall be construed so as either to interfere with or impede or diminish in any way the right to strike. The courts have characterized the right to strike as a legitimate economic tool which implements and supports the principles of the collective bargaining system and which labor unions may use as they see fit.

The right to strike includes the right to picket. In general, picketing must relate to a primary dispute (a labor dispute between the picketing workers and the employer who is being picketed). Secondary pickets, like secondary strikes, are not protected by the NLRA. The right to strike also includes the right to refuse to cross a picket line in connection with a primary dispute. The right to strike *does not* include slowdowns, unannounced walkouts, sit-in strikes, violence or threats of violence, or defamation of the employer's goods.

While the NLRA preserves the right to strike, it does not guarantee unions the right to choose the timing of a strike. Once the employer has exhausted its duty to bargain in good faith and reached an impasse, it is free to use the economic weapons at its disposal, just as the workers are free to strike. As the Supreme Court said in 1965, an employer's use of a *lockout* in support of a legitimate bargaining position is not in any way inconsistent with the right to bargain collectively or with the right to strike.

When workers are out on strike, they remain employees, since the statutory definition of *employee* includes any individual whose work has ceased as a consequence of, or in connection with, any current labor dispute or because of any unfair labor practice, and who has not obtained any other regular and substantially equivalent employment. This means that an employer cannot retaliate against strikers for their union activity.

An employer's right to hire permanent replacements for striking workers depends on the nature of the strike. If the strike is economically motivated (to improve wages, hours, or other terms and conditions of employment), the employer may hire permanent replacements. However, if the strike is to protest an unfair labor practice, the strikers are entitled to reinstatement with back pay upon making an unconditional offer to return to work.

An employer cannot hire foreign workers on H-1B visas as replacements for economic strikers, since the employer must certify in its H-1B application that there is no strike in progress involving the job to be filled. Similarly, a TN visa may be denied if the Secretary of Labor certifies that issuance of the visa may adversely affect settlement of a labor dispute. (See Chapter 21 for more on work-related visas.)

Even for economic strikes, the employer faces certain limitations. For example, it cannot pick and choose who will be replaced based on the extent of involvement in union activities. The employer also cannot offer super seniority to replacements. In one case the employer did just that, arguing that it needed to offer super seniority as an inducement to the replacement workers. The Supreme Court held that doing so was an unfair labor practice because it discriminated between strikers and nonstrikers, both during and after the strike.

QUICK TIP

A worker who is out on strike is generally ineligible for unemployment insurance benefits. However, a nonstriking, unemployed worker will not become ineligible for benefits by turning down a job offer which would involve replacing a striking worker.

An employee's good faith refusal to work under abnormally dangerous conditions is not a strike under the NLRA. So unlike workers who are on strike for economic reasons, employees who are absent for safety reasons cannot be permanently replaced.

Although the NLRA preserves workers' right to strike, the right is subject to a number of limitations, discussed below.

Duty to Bargain

Perhaps the most import exception to the right to strike arises from the union's duty to bargain in good faith over matters that are considered mandatory subjects of bargaining. Until the employer and the union have bargained to impasse, the union may not strike and the employer may not lock out.

No-Strike Clause

Employees can bargain away their right to strike by agreeing to a no-strike clause in their collective bargaining agreement.

Secondary Strikes

The NLRA expressly prohibits labor unions from engaging in strikes or boycotts for the purpose of forcing a different employer to recognize or bargain with a labor union.

Taft-Hartley Injunctions

When a strike or lockout affects an entire industry (or a substantial part of an entire industry) and, if permitted to occur or continue, would *imperil the national health or safety*, the President of the United States may appoint a board of inquiry to investigate the issues in dispute and make a report to the President. With the board of inquiry's report in hand, the President may direct the Attorney General to go to court and request an 80-day injunction against the strike or lockout.

Health Care Institutions

The NLRA requires labor organizations whose employees work at health care institutions to give at least ten days' prior notice, both to the institution itself and the Federal Mediation and Conciliation Service, of its intent to strike, picket, or engage in some other concerted refusal to work. If the Service believes a strike would *substantially interrupt the delivery of health care in the locality concerned*, the Service may appoint a board of inquiry. Pending the board's report and for fifteen days thereafter, the pre-impasse status quo must be *maintained*.

Conclusion

This book has accomplished much if it has provided you with a broad understanding of the employment relationship and alerted you to the hazards you face as an employer. The next time you hear a racial epithet on the factory floor or see a sexist cartoon on the company bulletin board, you will know that trouble lurks. And when rumors start flying that a handful of employees have been talking about a union, you will consult competent labor counsel instead of firing the troublemakers.

Equipped with this new knowledge, and no longer bewildered by the complexities of the employment relationship, you are now free to devote your energies where they belong—making your business a success!

Appendix

Federal Statutory Thresholds

Many, although not all, federal statutes require that the employer have a specified minimum number of employees before the statute applies. Listed below are some of the more significant federal statutes affecting employment, along with the statute's applicable threshold, if any. Employers who fall below any particular threshold should keep in mind that parallel state and local laws may nevertheless apply to them. In addition, the thresholds in most cases are *not jurisdictional*, meaning that unless the employer affirmatively raises a defense that it falls below the applicable threshold, a court or administrative agency may proceed to hear a complaint brought under the statute.

Americans with Disabilities Act (ADA): 15 or more employees

Age Discrimination in Employment Act (ADEA): 20 or more employees

Drug-Free Workplace Act (DFWA): Federal contractors and grant recipients

Electronic Communications Privacy Act (ECPA): All employers

Electronic Privacy Protection Act (EPPA): All employers

Employee Retirement Income Security Act (ERISA): All employers with employee benefit plans

Fair Credit Reporting Act (FCRA): All employers

Fair Labor Standards Act (FLSA): Most employers with annual sales volumes of $250,000 or more, and construction companies, laundries, cleaners, tailors, hospitals, nursing homes, schools, and other institutions regardless of sales volume

Family and Medical Leave Act (FMLA): 50 or more employees

Health insurance continuation provisions of COBRA: 20 or more employees

Health Insurance Portability and Accountability Act (HIPAA): All employers

Immigration Reform and Control Act (IRCA): All employers as to eligibility to work and I-9 requirements; four or more employees as to nondiscrimination provisions

Occupational Safety and Health Act (OSHA): All employers as to compliance with health and safety standards; eleven or more employees as to record-keeping, posting, and reporting requirements

Sec. 1981, Title 29, U.S. Code: All employers

Title VII: 15 or more employees

Worker Adjustment and Retraining Notification (WARN) Act: 100 or more employees

Appendix B

Internet Resources

The Internet has become a ubiquitous source of information—some useful, some not. The U.S. government has been a leader in providing information, opening to the world its vast collection of laws, regulations, forms, policies, and guidelines. For those readers who want more information on an employment issue, who have a question not explicitly answered in this book, or who need primary source material, this appendix lists the websites of most of the federal agencies whose activities touch upon the employment relationship.

Administrative Office of U.S. Courts

www.uscourts.gov

www.pacer.psc.uscourts.gov (PACER homepage)

Education, Dept. of

www.ed.gov

Equal Employment Opportunity Commission

www.eeoc.gov

www.eeoc.gov/eeo1survey/index.html (EEO-1 information)

www.eeoc.gov/employers/smallbusinesses.html (information for small businesses)

Federal Judicial Center

www.fjc.gov

Federal Trade Commission

www.ftc.gov

www.ftc.gov/os/statutes/fcrajump.shtm (Fair Credit Reporting Act)

www.ftc.gov/opa/2004/11/facta.shtm (Fair & Accurate Credit Transactions Act)

General Services Administration

www.gsa.gov

www.usa.gov/Business/Business_Gateway.shtml (information for businesses)

www.fedforms.gov (federal forms)

www.firstgov.gov (links to government agencies)

Government Accountability Office

www.gao.gov

Government Printing Office

www.access.gpo.gov

www.access.gpo.gov/su_docs/gils_whatgils.html (GILS)

www.gpoaccess.gov/uscode/index.html (U.S. Code)

www.access.gpo.gov/nara/cfr/cfr-table-search.html (Code of Federal Regulations)

Health & Human Services, Dept. of

www.hhs.gov

http://151.196.108.21/ocse (new hire reports for multistate employers)

Homeland Security, Dept. of

www.dhs.gov

www.uscis.gov (Citizenship & Immigration Services)

www.ice.gov (Immigration & Customs Enforcement)

House of Representatives

www.house.gov

Internal Revenue Service

www.irs.gov

www.irs.gov/formspubs/index.html?portlet=3 (forms & publications)

Justice, Dept. of

www.usdoj.gov

www.usdoj.gov/crt/ada/publicat.htm (ADA technical assistance)

Labor, Dept. of

www.dol.gov

www.dol.gov/asp/programs/guide (employment law guide)

www.dol.gov/esa (Employment Standards Administration)

www.dol.gov/esa/whd (Wage & Hour Division)

www.dol.gov/osbp (Office of Small Business Programs)

www.dol.gov/ebsa (Employee Benefits Security Administration)

www.dol.gov/eta (Employment & Training Administration)

www.dol.gov/vets (Veterans Employment & Training Service)

www.dol.gov/wb (Women's Bureau)

www.osha.gov (Occupational Safety & Health Administration)

www.bls.gov (Bureau of Labor Statistics)

Library of Congress

www.loc.gov

www.copyright.gov (copyright information & forms)

http://thomas.loc.gov (legislation)

National Archives

www.archives.gov

www.archives.gov/federal_register/index.html (Executive Orders)

National Labor Relations Board

www.nlrb.gov

www.nlrb.gov/publications/rules_and_regulations.aspx (rules &
   regulations)

www.nlrb.gov/research/decisions/index.aspx (decisions)

www.nlrb.gov/publications/manuals/index.aspx (manuals)

Patent & Trademark Office

www.uspto.gov

Pension Benefit Guaranty Corporation

www.pbgc.gov

Postal Service

www.usps.gov

Securities & Exchange Commission

www.sec.gov

www.sec.gov/edgar.shtml (filings & forms, EDGAR)

Senate

www.senate.gov

Small Business Administration

www.sba.gov

Social Security Administration

www.ssa.gov

www.ssa.gov/employer/bsohbnew.htm (business services online)

www.ssa.gov/employer/hiring.htm (hiring foreign workers)

www.ssa.gov/employer/ssnv.htm (verifying Social Security
   numbers)

State, Dept. of

www.state.gov

www.unitedstatesvisas.gov (general visa information)

http://travel.state.gov/visa/temp/types/types_1271.html
   (temporary work visas)

http://travel.state.gov/visa/temp/types/types_1274.html (TN
   visa information)

Supreme Court

www.supremecourtus.gov

www.supremecourtus.gov/opinions/opinions.html (opinions)

Tax Court

  www.ustaxcourt.gov

  www.ustaxcourt.gov/UstcInOp/asp/HistoricOpinions.asp
    (opinions)

Transportation, Dept. of

  www.dot.gov

  www.dot.gov/ost/dapc (drug & alcohol policy)

Treasury, Dept. of

  www.treas.gov

  www.treas.gov/sba (Office of Small & Disadvantaged Business
    Utilization)

White House

  www.whitehouse.gov

Glossary

360-degree evaluation. An evaluation system under which employees are rated not only by supervisors, but also by peers, direct reports, and sometimes clients and customers.

401(k) plan. A type of qualified retirement plan authorized by Section 401(k) of the Internal Revenue Code.

A

abusive discharge. Sometimes called *wrongful discharge*, the termination of an at-will employee that has the effect of contravening some important public policy.

affirmative action. Action required of most government contractors, subcontractors, and federal grant recipients to assure equal employment of minorities, women, persons with disabilities, and certain veterans.

Age Discrimination in Employment Act (ADEA). The ADEA prohibits discrimination because of age against persons forty or more years old.

agency shop. A type of union security arrangement where union membership is optional. However, as a condition of continued employment, non-union members pay to the union amounts equal to initiation fees and periodic dues paid by union members.

agent. A person who acts on behalf of another (called the *principal*) and has the power to bind the other person in contract. Employees and independent contractors can each be, but are not necessarily, agents of their employers.

alternate payee. An employee's spouse, child, or other dependent who, pursuant to a *Qualified Domestic Relations Order* (QDRO), is awarded an interest in the employee's pension plan. Also, an employee's child who, pursuant to a *Qualified Medical Child Support Order* (QMCSO), becomes entitled to health insurance coverage under the plan in which the employee participates.

alternative dispute resolution (ADR). A procedure for resolving disputes other than by a lawsuit. Arbitration and mediation are forms of ADR.

Americans with Disabilities Act (ADA). The ADA prohibits discrimination against a qualified person with a disability and requires reasonable accommodation of disabled applicants and employees.

arbitration. One of several forms of dispute resolution that are alternatives to litigation in court.

attributed tip income program (ATIP). A voluntary, three-year pilot program for reporting tips in the food and beverage industry.

at-will employment. Employment that is not for any fixed or definite term. In an at-will employment relationship, the employee can quit at any time and the employer can fire the employee at any time with or without cause.

B

back pay. Pay awarded to an employee or applicant for employment that, but for discrimination, an unfair labor practice, or other wrongful conduct by the employer, would have been earned between the time of the wrongful conduct and the time the award is made.

base period. For unemployment insurance purposes, the most recent four out of five completed calendar quarters (quarters in which the employee worked) preceding the filing of a benefit claim.

base period employer. Any employer for whom an unemployment insurance claimant worked during his or her base period.

Beck notice. A notice posted by U.S. government contractors pursuant to Executive Order 13201, informing employees of their right to opt out of paying union dues.

belo plan. An exception to the *Fair Labor Standards Act*'s general overtime rules that allows an employer to pay a fixed salary to non-exempt employees, such as emergency workers, who work an irregular number of hours from week to week because of the nature of the job.

blacklisting. The practice of circulating the names of former employees who should not be hired because of their history of union organizing efforts or other protected activity.

bona fide occupational qualification (BFOQ). BFOQs are exceptions to certain forms of discrimination.

borrowed servant. An employee who is transferred from his or her regular employer to another employer on a temporary basis.

Bureau of Citizenship and Immigration Services (BCIS). Part of the U.S. Department of Homeland Security. The BCIS is the successor agency to the Immigration and Naturalization Service of the Department of Justice.

C

cafeteria plan. *See Section 125 plan.*

cash balance plan. A pension plan that has characteristics of both a defined contribution plan and a defined benefit plan. In a cash balance plan, the ultimate benefit is the amount resulting from periodic contributions to a separate hypothetical account for each employee and an assumed interest rate earned on those contributions.

cash or deferral arrangement (CODA). A feature of some deferred compensation plans under which the employee can elect to take taxable cash or a nontaxable contribution to the plan.

casual employee. An employee who is not covered by workers' compensation because he or she works irregularly, for a brief period only, and does work not normally performed by employees of the employer.

cause. A reason that is legally sufficient to discharge an employee who has an employment contract.

Chapter 13. A provision of the U.S. Bankruptcy Code that allows an individual with a regular income to spread out repayment of his or her debts for up to three years.

child labor. Labor by a person under 18 years of age. *See oppressive child labor.*

Circular E. An IRS publication for employers, also known as Publication 15, containing instructions and tables for federal income tax withholding and payroll tax obligations.

Civil Rights Act of 1866. A Reconstruction-era federal statute that extends to all citizens the same right to make and enforce contracts as was previously enjoyed by the white citizens.

Civil Rights Act of 1964. The principal federal statute prohibiting discrimination in employment and public accommodations. The Act was substantially amended in 1991.

closed shop. A type of union security agreement under which employees must be union members in order to be hired.

collective bargaining agreement (CBA). An agreement between an employer and a union dealing with employee pay, benefits, discipline, grievance procedures, and other conditions of employment.

commerce clause. A clause in Article I of the U.S. Constitution empowering Congress to regulate commerce with foreign nations, among the several states, and with Indian tribes.

common-law. The body of legal principles developed by court decisions in England and the United States that are not based on legislative enactments.

compensatory time (comp time). Leave taken in lieu of overtime pay. Use of comp time to compensate a nonexempt employee who works more than forty hours in one workweek generally violates wage-and-hour laws.

concerted activity. Union organizing activity or other activity by employees for the purpose of bettering wages, hours, or working conditions. Concerted activity is protected by the *National Labor Relations Act.*

consideration. In contract law, the inducements, rights, or things of value that the parties to a contract agree to exchange.

Consolidated Omnibus Budget Reconciliation Act (COBRA). COBRA requires continuation of group health insurance coverage under certain circumstances when coverage would otherwise end.

constructive discharge. A termination where the employee is effectively forced to quit as a result of intolerable working conditions.

constructive receipt. In tax law, the doctrine that treats compensation as having been received by and taxable to an employee when the compensation is credited to the employee's account or is otherwise made available to the employee.

consumer report. A credit report and/or an investigative report about a person. The obtaining and use of consumer reports by employers are regulated by the *Fair Credit Reporting Act* and by some state laws.

consumer reporting agency (CRA). A person or entity which, for a fee, regularly assembles or evaluates credit information or other information on consumers for the purpose of furnishing consumer reports to third parties. The obtaining and use of consumer reports from a CRA is regulated by the *Fair Credit Reporting Act* and by some state laws.

contingent worker. A worker who is outside an employer's core work force of full-time, long-term employees. Contingent workers include independent contractors, part-time employees, job sharers, temporary employees, and leased employees.

D

defamation. A false statement that injures a person's reputation. False written statements may be libelous and false spoken statements may be slanderous.

deferred compensation. Compensation set aside for an employee, but not currently taxable to the employee because the employee's receipt and enjoyment of the compensation is deferred.

defined benefit plan. A type of retirement plan in which the benefit amount is fixed by a pre-determined formula including such factors as years of service and pre-retirement compensation. Employer contributions to the plan are calculated so that the plan will have sufficient funds to pay the promised benefit.

defined contribution plan. A type of retirement plan in which the amount contributed to the plan is fixed by a pre-determined formula and the benefit amount depends on the value of each participant's separate account within the plan.

dilution. Reduction in the value of a company's outstanding stock caused by issuance of additional stock for less than the value or market price of the stock.

direct liability. Liability for an employer's own negligence in hiring, retaining, or failing to supervise an employee who presents an unreasonable risk of injury or damage to the public.

directors and officers (D & O) insurance. Coverage that protects company officials from personal liability for good faith actions taken in the course of their employment.

direct threat defense. A provision of the *Americans with Disabilities Act* that allows employers to exclude disabled employees from certain jobs in which the disabled person would pose a direct threat to his or her own health or safety or to the health or safety of others in the workplace.

disability. For *Americans with Disabilities Act* purposes, a physical or mental impairment that substantially limits one or more major life activities.

discovery. The formal process by which parties to court proceedings obtain information and documents from opposing parties and question opposing parties and nonparty witnesses under oath.

discrimination. Adversity suffered by an applicant, an employee, or a group of applicants or employees for a reason that is prohibited by law, such as race, color, religion, gender, national origin, age, disability, etc.

disparate impact. In discrimination law, the effect of workplace rules or requirements that appear neutral on their face but that have an adverse impact on a particular race, age group, etc.

disparate treatment. In discrimination law, intentional adverse treatment of an applicant or employee because of his or her race, religion, gender, and so on.

domestic partners. Persons other than spouses and relatives who live together and have a voluntary, committed relationship with each other.

due process clause. A clause in the Fifth Amendment to the U.S. Constitution which provides that no person shall be deprived of life, liberty, or property without due process of law. The Fourteenth Amendment also prohibits states from depriving any person of life, liberty, or property without due process of law.

E

earned rate. For unemployment insurance purposes, the rate used to compute an employer's contribution obligation based upon the employer's actual claims experience.

Electronic Communications Privacy Act (ECPA). The federal law that regulates the interception of wire, electronic, and oral communications.

Electronic Federal Tax Payment System (EFTPS). The system for paying employment taxes and other federal taxes electronically.

emergency action plan. A plan required by *OSHA* for responding to workplace emergencies that affect employee safety or health.

employee. A person whose manner of work the employer has a right to control.

employee assistance plan (EAP). A fringe benefit some employers offer that may include short-term counseling, alcohol or drug abuse treatment, and similar services.

employee handbook. A handbook of rules, policies, procedures, and so on, issued by the employer for the guidance and information of employees.

Employee Polygraph Protection Act (EPPA). The EPPA prohibits employers from using lie detectors except in extremely limited circumstances.

Employee Retirement Income Security Act (ERISA). The principal federal law regulating retirement plans and other employee benefit plans.

employee stock ownership plan (ESOP). A form of benefit plan in which the retirement fund holds stock of the employer company.

employee stock purchase plan. A plan for granting stock options to an employer's general work force in proportion to their compensation.

Employer Identification Number (EIN). The number employers obtain from the IRS to use in filing tax returns and reports.

Employer Information Report (EEO-1). The form filed annually with the *Equal Employment Opportunity Commission* by employers who have one hundred or more employees, and by certain government contractors and federal grant recipients, to provide the EEOC with a breakdown of the work force by sex, race, and national origin.

employment contract. An agreement that employment will last for a specific term and/or that the employment will only be terminated for cause or in accordance with specified procedures.

employment practices liability (EPL) insurance. A form of coverage that protects employers from employment-related claims.

Equal Employment Opportunity Commission (EEOC). The principal enforcer of Title VII of the federal *Civil Rights Act of 1964*, the *Age Discrimination in Employment Act*, and the employment provisions of the *Americans with Disabilities Act*.

Equal Pay Act. *See Fair Labor Standards Act.*

ergonomics. The science that studies the relationship between workers and their work environment.

excess benefit plan. An unfunded plan maintained by an employer solely to avoid the contribution and benefit limitations imposed on qualified plans by Section 415 of the Internal Revenue Code. Excess benefit plans are exempt from most provisions of the *Employee Retirement Income Security Act*.

exempt employee. An employee who is not covered by minimum wage and overtime requirements of the federal *Fair Labor Standards Act* (and the parallel provisions of state law) because he or she is employed in an executive, administrative, or professional capacity or falls within some other statutory exemption.

Executive Order 11246. An executive order issued by President Lyndon Johnson in 1965, which, as amended, prohibits employment discrimination and requires affirmative action plans by most federal contractors and subcontractors.

exit interview. A meeting between an employee and management in connection with termination of the employee's employment.

F

Fair and Accurate Credit Transactions Act (FACTA). FTC regulations under FACTA govern the disposal of consumer information.

Fair Credit Reporting Act (FCRA). The FCRA regulates the obtaining and use of *consumer reports*.

fair employment practice agency (FEPA). FEPAs, also known as deferral agencies, are state or local agencies that enforce equal employment laws comparable to federal law.

Fair Labor Standards Act (FLSA). The FLSA establishes minimum wages and overtime requirements and prohibits oppressive child labor. As amended by the *Equal Pay Act*, the FLSA also prohibits employers from paying different wages to males and females who do the same work.

False Claims Act. A federal law that permits a whistleblower to file suit in the name of the U.S. government against companies that have allegedly committed fraud.

Family and Medical Leave Act (FMLA). The FMLA requires employers who have fifty or more employees to grant extended leave to employees with serious medical conditions, for the birth or adoption of a child, and when a family member has a serious medical condition.

Federal Arbitration Act (FAA). The FAA provides for enforcement of arbitration agreements.

Federal Insurance Contribution Act (FICA). FICA imposes a tax on employers and an identical tax on employees to fund the social security system.

federal per diem rates method. A method for reimbursing employees for business travel based on daily rates established by the federal government. The rates are divided into two groups, known as CONUS (continental U.S.) and OCONUS (outside continental U.S.).

Federal Unemployment Tax Act (FUTA). The FUTA imposes a tax on employers to help finance the unemployment insurance program.

fiduciary. A person who holds a special position of trust with respect to another person, such as the trustee of a pension plan. Fiduciaries are required to act solely in the best interests of the persons for whom they hold the special trust position and not in their own self-interest.

flexible spending arrangement or flexible spending account (FSA). An employer-sponsored arrangement under which an employee can contribute pretax dollars to a special trust account and obtain reimbursement out of the account for uninsured medical expenses and/or dependent care expenses.

flextime. An arrangement under which employees may choose a work schedule different from the employer's normal work schedule, so long as the total hours worked per week meet the employer's minimum requirement.

Foreign Sovereign Immunities Act (FSIA). Under the FSIA, foreign states are immune from the jurisdiction of courts in the U.S. so long as they are engaged in governmental-type activities.

fresh consideration. Something of value, such as a bonus or pay raise, offered to an existing employee in exchange for the employee's signing a *noncompete agreement*.

Friendship, Commerce, and Navigation (FCN) Treaties. FCN treaties permit foreign companies doing business in the U.S. to engage, at their choice, high-level personnel essential to the functioning of the enterprise, effectively permitting them to discriminate in favor of their own nationals.

front pay. Pay awarded to an employee or applicant for employment that, but for discrimination, an unfair labor practice, or other wrongful conduct by the employer, would have been earned after the time the award is made. Front pay is awarded when it would be impractical to require the employer to offer continuing or future employment.

full faith and credit clause. A provision in Article IV of the U.S. Constitution that requires each state to recognize the laws of every other state.

G

garnishment. A wage attachment. A court order requiring the employer to pay a percentage of the wages of an employee (the garnishee) to someone (the *garnisher*) who has obtained a money judgment against the employee.

General Duty Clause. The *Occupational Safety and Health Act* requirement that every employer furnish its employees with employment and a place of employment free from recognized hazards that cause or are likely to cause death or serious physical harm.

general employer. An employer who transfers an employee to another employer (called the *special employer*) for a limited period of time. While the transfer is in effect, the special employer has temporary responsibility and control over the employee's work.

glass ceiling. The invisible barrier to advancement sometimes faced by women and minorities.

golden parachute. Payments promised to key personnel in the event of a change in ownership or control of a company.

H

half-time plan. Sometimes called a fluctuating workweek plan, an exception to the *Fair Labor Standards Act*'s general overtime rules that allows an employer to pay only half-time, instead of time and a half, for overtime worked by nonexempt employees. The exception only applies where the employee's workweek fluctuates and where the employer has entered into an agreement to pay a fixed salary to cover the straight time component of all time worked in a workweek.

harassment. A form of discrimination involving conduct that has the purpose or effect of unreasonably interfering with a person's work performance or that creates an intimidating, hostile, or offensive work environment.

Health Insurance Portability and Accountability Act (HIPAA). HIPAA imposes requirements on group health plans to make it easier for employees who change jobs to be eligible for full coverage under their new employer's plan.

health reimbursement arrangement (HRA). An employer-funded health insurance plan, often paired with a high-deductible group health insurance policy, to reimburse employees for uninsured medical expenses.

health savings account (HSA). An account established by an individual employee in conjunction with a high deductible health plan and funded by the employer, employee, or both, to pay the employee's current and future medical expenses.

hostile environment. A work environment made offensive by *harassment.*

I

I-9. The form employers must complete and maintain for each employee as a record that the employee is eligible to work in the U.S.

Immigration and Customs Enforcement (ICE). Part of the U.S. Department of Homeland Security, ICE enforces U.S. immigration and customs laws.

Immigration Reform and Control Act of 1986 (IRCA). An amendment to the Immigration and Nationality Act, IRCA prohibits employers from hiring aliens who are ineligible to work in the U.S. IRCA also prohibits discrimination against noncitizens.

indemnity plan. A type of health insurance plan in which the plan participant chooses his or her own health care provider, and the insurer pays the provider directly or reimburses the participant according to a formula or schedule specified in the plan.

independent contractor. A person whose work methods the employer does not have a right to control.

inevitable disclosure. A legal doctrine, adopted in a few states, permitting a court to enjoin a former employee from working for a competitor when the former employee has confidential information, and when the old and new jobs are so similar that disclosure of the confidential information is considered inevitable.

inside buildup. The accumulation of tax-exempt income within a deferred compensation plan.

insider trading. Buying or selling publicly-traded securities using information that is generally not available to the public. Insider trading is illegal under federal and state laws.

International Labour Organization (ILO). An agency of the United Nations that promotes rights at work, encourages decent employment opportunities, enhances social protection, and strengthens dialogue in handling work-related issues.

involuntary servitude. Slavery or other forms of compulsory work, prohibited by the Thirteenth Amendment to the Constitution and federal law.

L

last chance contract. An agreement between an employer and an employee that gives the employee a final opportunity to conform to company requirements or else be fired.

libel. See *defamation.*

liquidated damages. In contract law, an amount specified by the parties in advance that a party would be entitled to receive if the other party breaches the contract. Also, damages awarded for minimum wage and overtime violations of the *Fair Labor Standards Act* in addition to the wages due.

living wage. A wage rate higher than the federal minimum wage that some local jurisdictions require government contractors to pay their employees.

litigation hold. An employer policy of preserving documents and data that may be relevant to a pending or threatened claim.

love contract. A contract required by some employers that sets out certain ground rules for an office romance, especially one between a supervisor and a lower-level employee.

M

managed care plan. A type of health insurance plan in which the participant is limited in his or her choice of health insurance providers but pays either nothing or only a small amount for services.

managers-only manual. A manual of workplace policies and procedures distributed only to management-level employees.

mass layoff. Under the *Worker Adjustment and Retraining Notification (WARN) Act*, a layoff of at least fifty employees at a single site that amounts to at least 33% of the work force at that site.

master-servant relationship. An outdated reference to an employer-employee relationship.

Material Safety Data Sheet (MSDS). An *Occupational Safety and Health Administration* form used to communicate information about hazardous chemicals.

minimum wage. The minimum hourly amount that employers must pay employees pursuant to the *Fair Labor Standards Act* and similar provisions of state law.

ministerial exception. An exception, available to religious organizations, to discrimination laws. Under the ministerial exception, religious organizations may discriminate in the selection of their clergy.

N

negligent employment. *See direct liability.*

nepotism. The practice of hiring relatives or favoring them in workplace decisions.

no-match letter. A letter issued by the Social Security Administration to an employer stating that an employee's name and Social Security number as reported on a W-2 form do not match the Administration's records.

noncompete agreement. An agreement that an employee will not compete with his former employer for a specified period after the employment terminates.

nonexempt employee. An employee who is covered by minimum wage and overtime requirements of the *Fair Labor Standards Act* and similar provisions of state law.

nonqualified deferred compensation plan. Any arrangement other than a *qualified plan* under which a worker receives a legally binding right to compensation in one year but is not in actual or constructive receipt of that compensation until a later year. Unless such plans satisfy detailed Internal Revenue Code requirements, the compensation may be immediately taxable to the worker.

North American Industry Classification System (NAICS). A system of six-digit numbers used to classify industries. The NAICS is replacing the *Standard Industrial Classification* system.

O

Occupational Safety and Health Act (OSHA). An act that requires employers to comply with a variety of safety and health standards for the protection of their employees.

Office of Federal Contract Compliance Programs (OFCCP). An office within the U.S. Department of Labor's Employment Standards Administration that administers government contractors' compliance with various employment-related statutes and Executive Orders.

Older Workers Benefit Protection Act (OWBPA). An amendment to the *Age Discrimination in Employment Act*, OWBPA imposes special requirements for releases of ADEA claims in connection with exit incentive programs offered to groups of employees.

open shop. A workplace that employs both union and non-union employees.

oppressive child labor. With certain exceptions, employment of any child who is under the age of 16, regardless of the occupation, and employment of a child who is between the ages of 16 and 18 in mining, manufacturing, or other hazardous industries.

P

paid time off (PTO). PTO plans replace various forms of leave traditionally offered to employees.

peonage. A system, no longer permitted in the U.S., by which debtors are bound in servitude to their creditors until their debts are paid.

perma-temp. Slang for a worker who, despite long tenure on the job, is still classified as temporary for benefit or other purposes.

personal protective equipment (PPE). Equipment required by various *Occupational Safety and Health Administration* standards to be worn to reduce excessive exposure to workplace conditions that could cause personal injury. Employers are required to cover the cost of most PPE.

personnel manual. See *employee handbook.*

polygraph. A lie detector. Polygraph testing in connection with employment is prohibited in most circumstances.

predatory hiring. A campaign to hire workers away from a particular company in order to harm that company's ability to compete. Predatory hiring may violate antitrust laws.

Pregnancy Discrimination Act (PDA). An amendment to *Title VII* of the federal *Civil Rights Act of 1964* that defines sex discrimination to include discrimination because of pregnancy, childbirth, or related medical conditions.

prevailing wage. The usual wage paid for a particular job category in a particular locale. An employer must obtain a prevailing wage determination as part of the process of applying for an H-1B visa. Some government contracts contain provisions requiring contractors to pay prevailing wages.

principal. The person on whose behalf an agent acts.

professional employment organization (PEO). An organization that, for a fee, jointly employs a company's employees in order to provide HR-related functions, such as benefit plan administration, payroll services, and workers' compensation coverage.

progressive discipline. A policy of imposing increasingly severe discipline for repetitive workplace misconduct.

project labor agreement (PLA). A multi-employer pre-hire agreement used on construction projects, that requires all contractors and subcontractors who will work on the project to agree in advance to a master collective bargaining agreement.

protected health information (PHI). Information about employees and others that is subject to privacy regulations of the *Health Insurance Portability and Accountability Act.*

Q

Qualified Domestic Relations Order (QDRO). An order entered by a domestic relations court in compliance with the *Employee Retirement Income Security Act* that awards an interest in a pension plan to an *alternate payee* such as a spouse.

Qualified Medical Child Support Order (QMCSO). An order entered by a domestic relations court requiring an employer with a group health insurance plan to enroll an employee's child (the *alternate payee*) if the employer's plan includes family coverage.

qualified plan. An employee benefit plan that qualifies for favorable tax treatment under the Internal Revenue Code.

qualifying event. An event that triggers an opportunity to elect COBRA coverage.

quid pro quo. A type of sex discrimination involving sexual favors in exchange for tangible job benefits.

R

rabbi trust. A *deferred compensation* arrangement for select management or highly compensated employees. Employer contributions to a rabbi trust are not currently deductible by the employer and may not be includible in the employer's income if the trust assets remain subject to claims by creditors of the employer.

Racketeer Influenced and Corrupt Organizations Act (RICO). A 1970 federal statute, primarily aimed at organized crime, that has been applied to employers who repeatedly violate immigration or other laws.

reasonable accommodation. A requirement under the *Americans with Disabilities Act* to protect persons with disabilities. A requirement under *Title VII* of the federal *Civil Rights Act* to allow for employee religious practices.

Rehabilitation Act. Federal law that prohibits most federal contractors and subcontractors from discriminating against persons with disabilities and requires affirmative action to ensure equal employment opportunity.

respondeat superior. The legal doctrine that imposes vicarious liability on an employer for the negligence of its employees.

restrictive covenant. An agreement that restricts an employee from competing with his or her employer or using confidential employer information.

retaliation. Taking adverse action against a current or former employee for exercising rights protected by law.

reverse discrimination. Discrimination against members of a historically advantaged group, which results from treating members of a historically disadvantaged group more favorably. Quota systems and some affirmative action plans can amount to reverse discrimination.

right-to-work law. A state law that prohibits collective bargaining agreements from containing *union security clauses.*

S

salt. A person who applies for a job in order to unionize the workplace once hired.

second injury fund. A special fund established under state workers' compensation laws. Second (or *subsequent*) injury funds share responsibility for benefits due employees who have preexisting, nondisabling conditions and who become disabled through the combined effects of the preexisting condition and a subsequent injury.

Section 125 plan. A benefit plan that offers cash, or a variety of benefits in lieu of cash from which the employee may choose. Cash payments are taxable to the employee, but qualified benefits are not.

Section 1981. See *Civil Rights Act of 1866.*

seniority system. A system followed by management, either by custom or pursuant to a *collective bargaining agreement* with a union, under which an employee with greater longevity will be favored for promotion or reassignment over otherwise equally qualified candidates.

shop rights. In patent law, an employer's right to use an invention created by an employee on the employer's time and utilizing the employer's money, property, and labor. A shop right is nonexclusive, meaning that the employer cannot prevent the employee or others from using the invention.

slander. See *defamation.*

special employer. An employer who has borrowed an employee from another employer (called the *general employer*) for a limited time period and has temporary responsibility and control over the employee's work.

spoliation. The destruction or alteration of documents or data that may be relevant to a pending or threatened claim.

Standard Industrial Classification system (SIC). A system of four-digit numbers used to classify industries. The SIC system is being replaced by the *North American Industry Classification System.*

statute of frauds. A provision in state law requiring certain contracts to be in writing to be enforceable in court.

statute of limitations. A provision in law that bars lawsuits that are not filed within a specified time period.

statutory employee. A person who, by law, is classified as an employee for income tax, workers' compensation, or other purposes, even though he or she might otherwise qualify as an independent contractor.

statutory nonemployee. A person who, by law, is classified as an independent contractor, even though he or she might otherwise qualify as an employee.

subrogation. The right of a person who pays a claim to seek reimbursement from the wrongdoer. When an employee is injured on the job by the negligence of a third party and receives workers' compensation benefits from his or her employer, the employer or its insurance carrier is subrogated to the employee's rights and may sue the third party.

Summary Plan Description (SPD). A written description, required by the *Employee Retirement Income Security Act,* of the provisions of a benefit plan provided by the employer.

supremacy clause. The provision in Article VI of the U.S. Constitution stating that the Constitution, the laws of the United States, and treaties "shall be the supreme Law of the Land," binding in every state.

T

tax deferral. A feature of some employee benefit plans, such as qualified pension plans, that permits the employee to exclude plan contributions from gross income for income tax purposes until a later time, such as retirement.

telecommuting. Working at home or at a facility other than the employer's office that is connected with the office by high tech communications equipment.

teleworking. The *Equal Employment Opportunity Commission*'s name for telecommuting.

tester. A person who applies for a job for the sole purpose of testing the employer's hiring practices for discrimination.

third party administrator (TPA). A company that administers a health insurance plan but does not provide any insurance against the risk involved.

time off plan. An exception to the *Fair Labor Standards Act*'s general overtime rules that allows an employer under certain narrow circumstances to award compensatory time to nonexempt employees in lieu of time and one half for overtime.

Tip Rate Alternative Commitment (TRAC). An agreement between the IRS and an employer in the food and beverage industry under which the employer agrees to establish an educational program and reporting procedures designed to promote accurate tip reporting by employees, and the IRS agrees to assess payroll taxes based on tips as reported by employees.

Tip Rate Determination Agreement (TRDA). An agreement between the IRS and an employer under which the IRS and the employer determine and agree in advance on the rate of tips to be reported by employees.

Title VII. The sections of the *Civil Rights Act of 1964* that prohibit discrimination in employment.

top hat plan. See *excess benefit plan*.

trade secret. Business information, such as a customer list, formula, or process that has value because it is not widely known and its confidentiality is protected.

U

unemployment insurance. A federal/state system funded by employers, under which employees who have involuntarily lost their jobs receive temporary benefits.

unfair labor practice (ULP). Conduct by an employer or a union that violates the *National Labor Relations Act*.

Uniformed Services Employment and Reemployment Rights Act (USERRA). USERRA requires service members on military leave to continue to be carried as employees for certain benefit and seniority purposes and to be reemployed when they return from military leave.

union security clause. A provision in a *collective bargaining agreement* that protects union membership or revenue. A union security clause may require that employees be union members in order to be hired (*closed shop*), that they join a union after being hired (*union shop*), or that, in the case of non-union employees, they pay dues as if they were members (*agency shop*).

union shop. A type of union security arrangement under which employees are required to join a union within a specified time after hire.

V

variable pay. Pay, such as bonuses or commissions, that may vary in amount depending on productivity, company profitability, or other factors.

vested. Nonforfeitable. When pension plan benefits are vested, they belong to the employee, even if employment ends or the plan is terminated.

vicarious liability. Liability imposed on an employer for the negligence of an employee that occurs in the course and scope of employment.

Vietnam Era Veterans' Readjustment Assistance Act (VEVRAA). VEVRAA prohibits most federal contractors from discriminating against Vietnam-era and disabled veterans and requires affirmative action to ensure equal employment opportunity.

W

W-2. The federal tax form employers issue to employees and also send to the IRS to report wages.

weekly benefit amount (WBA). For unemployment insurance purposes, the amount a claimant is entitled to (but for any disqualification) as determined from his or her base period wages.

whistleblower. An employee who discloses fraud or other wrongdoing by an employer.

white collar exemptions. Exemptions from the *Fair Labor Standards Act*'s overtime requirements for persons employed in bona fide executive, administrative, or professional capacities or as outside salespersons.

withholding order. A court order in a domestic relations case, similar to a *garnishment*, requiring an employer to withhold and turn over a portion of an employee's earnings to cover the employee's family support obligations.

Worker Adjustment and Retraining Notification (WARN) Act. A federal law that requires employers with one hundred or more employees to give sixty days' advance notice of a *mass layoff* or plant closing.

workers' compensation. A state statutory arrangement funded by employers, under which employees who suffer work-related injuries or occupational illnesses receive benefits while out of work or while limited in their ability to work. Death benefits are provided to dependents of employees who are killed. The statutes also typically provide for payment of medical expenses, funeral benefits, and vocational rehabilitation.

work-for-hire. A product created or invented by an employee for his or her employer, the copyright or patent rights of which belong to the employer.

work-sharing agreement. An agreement between the *Equal Employment Opportunity Commission* and a state or local *Fair Employment Practice Agency* that allocates responsibility for processing charges of employment discrimination. Work-sharing agreements usually provide that a filing with one agency constitutes a filing with the other agency as well.

Work Opportunity Tax Credit (WOTC). A federal tax credit allowed to employers who hire persons in targeted groups of hard-to-employ individuals.

workweek. A 168-hour period used in determining an employer's obligation to pay overtime.

wrongful discharge. See *abusive discharge.*

Index

About the Author

Charles H. Fleischer has an undergraduate degree in political science from the University of Rochester in Rochester, New York, and a law degree (with honors) from the George Washington University in Washington, D.C. He is admitted to practice law in Maryland and the District of Columbia. He is a member of the law firm of Oppenheimer, Fleischer & Quiggle, P.C., of Bethesda, Maryland. The firm's website is www.OFQLaw.com.

Fleischer was a principal author of the employer's briefs in *Meritor Savings Bank v. Vinson*, the first Supreme Court case dealing with sexual harassment. He has advised numerous businesses and associations on employment law issues and he writes and speaks extensively on the topic.